Stories from a Sacred Landscape

Stories from a Sacred Landscape

Croghan Hill to Clonmacnoise

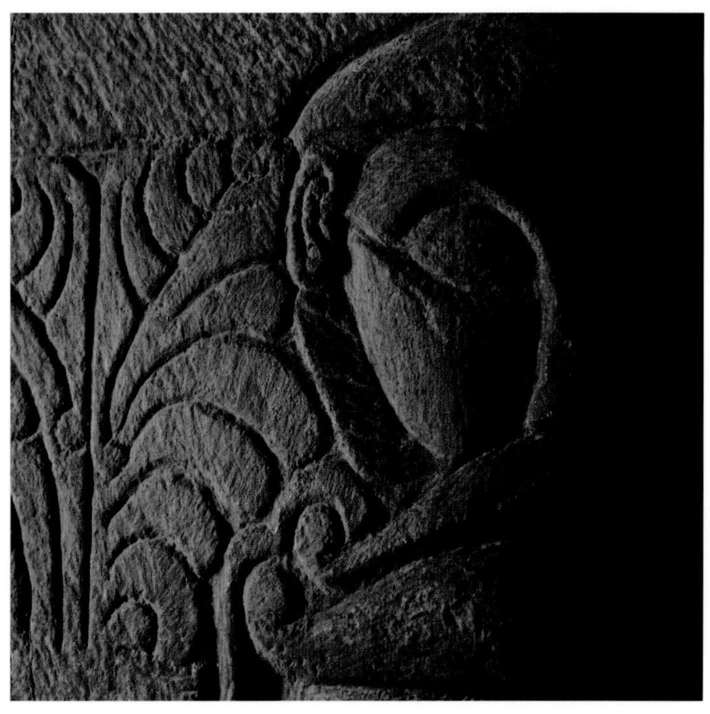

BY CAIMIN O'BRIEN

FEATURING SELECTED PHOTOGRAPHS BY JAMES FRAHER

EDITED BY MARY ANN WILLIAMS

DESIGNED BY CONNIE SCANLON, BOGFIRE INC.

CONCEIVED AND DIRECTED BY KEVIN O'DWYER

CONCEIVED AND PRODUCED BY AMANDA PEDLOW

Published by Offaly County Council

Distributed by

Stories from a Sacred Landscape:

Croghan Hill to Clonmacnoise

is dedicated to the people of Offaly.

Caimin O'Brien is an archaeologist with the Archaeological Survey of Ireland, a section of the National Monuments Service of the Department of the Environment, Heritage and Local Government. His publications include *The Archaeological Inventory of County Offaly, The Medieval Churches of County Offaly* and *The Archaeological Inventory of County Tipperary, North Riding.*

For reprint permission contact:
Offaly Heritage Officer
Offaly County Council
Áras an Chontae
Charleville Road
Tullamore, County Offaly
(05793) 46800 www.offaly.ie/offalyheritage

Mercier ISBN 1 85635 489 X
Trade enquiries to: Columba Mercier Distribution
55a, Spruce Avenue, Stillorgan Industrial Park
Blackrock, Dublin
www.mercierpress.ie

BRITISH LIBRARY CATALOGUING-IN-PUBLICATION DATA.
A catalogue record for this book is available from the British Library.

Project manager: Kevin O'Dwyer, Silver River Studios, Tullamore, County Offaly
www.millennium2000silver.com

Graphic design by Connie Scanlon and James Fraher, Bogfire Inc. www.bogfire.com

Edited by Mary Ann Williams, mawlula@eircom.net

Typeset in Minion, Papyrus and ATDelphian Open
Printed in Hong Kong by Regal Printing

Supported by the Heritage Council

Le cuidiú an Chomhairle Oidhreachta

Contents

Acknowledgements

The creation of *Stories from a Sacred Landscape: Croghan Hill to Clonmacnoise* required considerable time and financial resources.

Without the enthusiasm and support of Offaly County Council, this book would never have been possible. I would like to thank the Council for commissioning this book and also for the range of its other projects to conserve and promote Offaly's early Christian Monastic sites.

This project began when Atlantic Corridor Ireland/Offaly Regeneration Ltd. approached Offaly County Council with the idea for this specific book. Atlantic Corridor Ireland/Offaly Regeneration Ltd., Shannon Development and the Heritage Council are the major sponsors of its production.

For their encouragement and advice throughout the development of this project, I would like to thank Anne Coughlan of the County Library Service in Offaly County Council and Mary Feehan of Mercier Press.

For the provision of and permission to use illustrations thanks go to Martine O'Byrne of Trinity College, Dublin; Petra Schnabel of the Royal Irish Academy; Rose Desmond of Cambridge University; Frank Cruise and Aoife McBride of the National Museum of Ireland; Tony Roche of the Department of the Environment, Heritage and Local Government; Patricia Buckingham of the Bodleian Library, University of Oxford; Margaret Hogan, Rev. Irene Morrow and Teresa Ryan Feehan of Birr and the staff of the Brosna Press, Ferbane.

Many people offered information and provided access to sites during the photography and research stage of this project. With gratitude, I would like to acknowledge the help of Father Sean Burke of Boher; Michael Byrne, Stephen McNeill and the members of the Offaly Historical and Archaeological Society; Father Kieran Cantwell of Clareen; Seamus Corcoran, Sean Corcoran, Sean Halligan and Pat Kilmartin of Lemanaghan; Mary Darmody of the North Tipperary County Council Library Service, Anna Dolan of the OPW, John Flanagan of Tullamore, Rev. Gerard Field and the Vestry of Tullamore and Rahan, Sean Grennan and Susan Thomas of Rahan, Charles McDonald of Gallen, Ken and Janet Mathews of Killeigh, Matti Mooney of Lynally, Father Moorhead of Drumcullen, Tom Moore of Clonmacnoise, Iris Peavoy of Kinnitty, the Rahan and Island Development Group, the Jobs Initiative Team with Offaly County Council, Father Murray of Ferbane and, finally, Lord Rosse, Rev. Wayne Carney and Canon Shalloe of Birr. Special thanks for reviewing the book go to Pat Wallace, Director of the National Museum of Ireland, Dr. Peter Harbison, Honorary Academic Editor at the Royal Irish Academy, and former Chief Archaeologist of Ireland, David Sweetman.

We were very fortunate with the team who came together on this project. In their determination to make this a great book they worked extraordinarily long hours. Project manager Kevin O'Dwyer brought the team together and oversaw the delivery of the book. Caimin O'Brien provided so much interesting information that this book had to be written. Mary Ann Williams worked with Caimin to shape the text. Catherine Martin created and illustrated maps. Emma Philbin Bowman helped with proofreading. And finally, photographer James Fraher and designer Connie Scanlon really pushed out the boat while creating the visual presentation.

—Amanda Pedlow
Offaly County Heritage Officer

FOREWORD

This book sets out to tell the story of twenty-three of Offaly's early Christian monastic sites. While many of the churches are now ruins, each chapter explores aspects of the history of the site in the context of the wider monastic settlement. This includes the stories of the founding saints, associated folklore and their importance in the greater monastic Ireland and Europe. The book gives the reader an opportunity to visualise the full richness of each monastic settlement and encourages further exploration.

This generation of Offaly people have inherited a remarkable living landscape. A predominately rural county, Offaly's landscape had largely remained unchanged from the end of the first millennium until recent times. Over the last half century, the structure of society and work patterns have altered significantly. The accelerated rate of growth requires us to be ever sensitive to the rich legacy imprinted on our landscape, while supporting and nurturing economic and social development. Achieving this very delicate and sensitive balance is extremely challenging.

Monastic Offaly is a key element of the distinctiveness of this landscape. Not only is this evidenced physically by the large enclosures, high crosses, holy wells, grave slabs and church ruins but also by the pride communities take in the associated history and folklore. For over a thousand years, worship has continued at many of these monastic settlements and we continue to cherish our rich tradition.

We welcome the role of Atlantic Corridor Ireland /Offaly Regeneration Ltd., a local development agency, in promoting the concept and supporting this special publication on Offaly. Offaly County Council is delighted to work in partnership with them.

The county has benefitted from the appointment of Amanda Pedlow, Offaly's Heritage Officer, who established a team of professionals to bring the publication to fruition. We also acknowledge Kevin O'Dwyer, project manager, whose vision for the book was ambitious but realisable, with the support of a professional and talented team. The author, Caimin O'Brien, has long associations with the archaeological heritage of the county. *The Medieval Churches of Offaly*, 1998, which he co-authored with Elizabeth Fitzpatrick, is a landmark publication. The renowned international photographer, James Fraher tells the story through the photographer's eyes. He focuses on unique visual aspects of the sites and allows us to see a new perspective. The quality of the photography and design combine to produce an exciting visual publication. The engaging design work was completed by Connie Scanlon and the text was expertly edited by Mary Ann Williams.

Offaly County Council takes great pride in publishing *Stories from a Sacred Landscape: Croghan Hill to Clonmacnoise*, another chapter in the unfolding of the legacy of our early Christian monastic heritage.

—Peter Ormond,
Cathaoirleach, Offaly County Council

—Niall Sweeney
Offaly County Manager

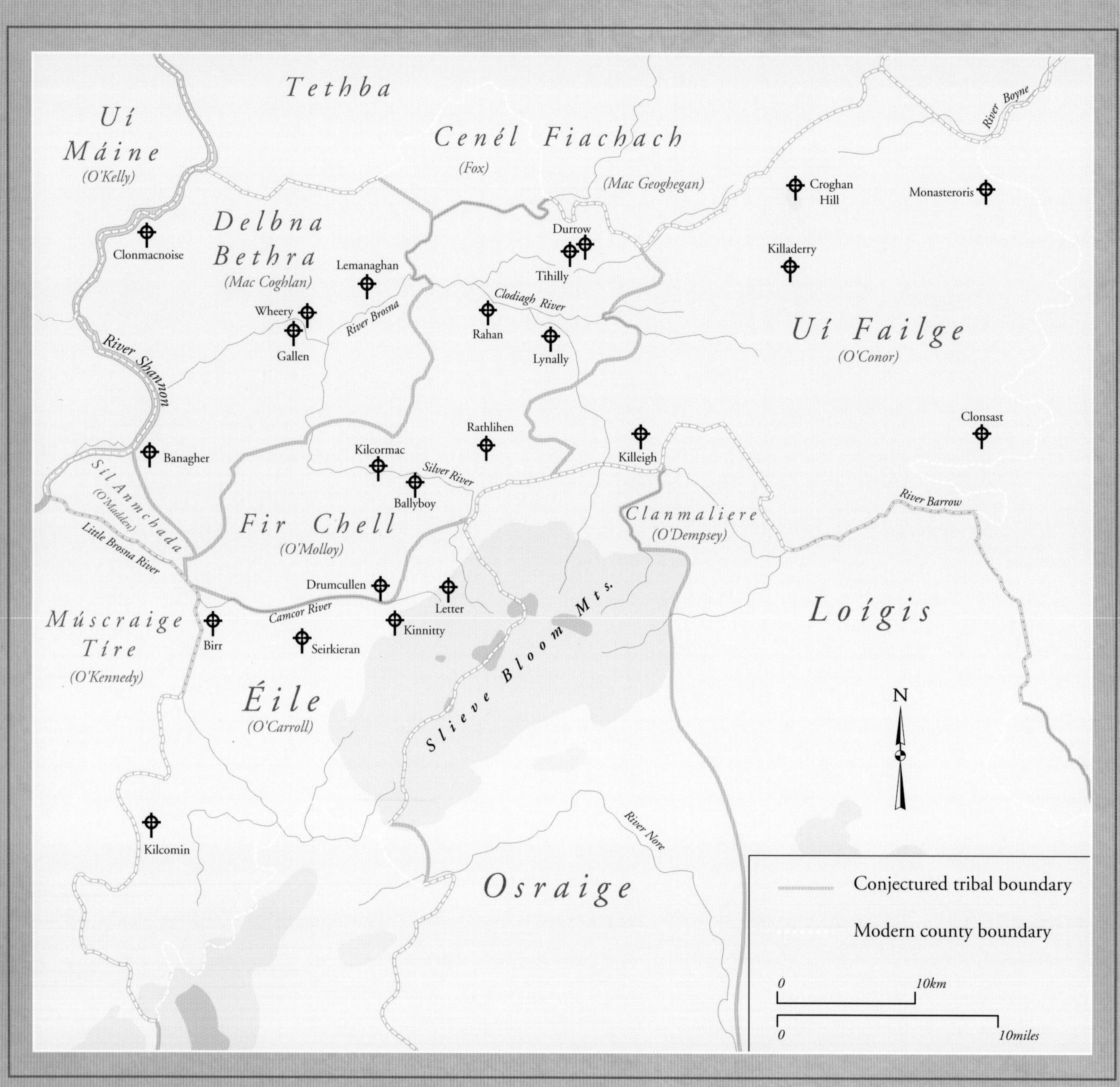

Tribal territories and ruling families circa AD 900

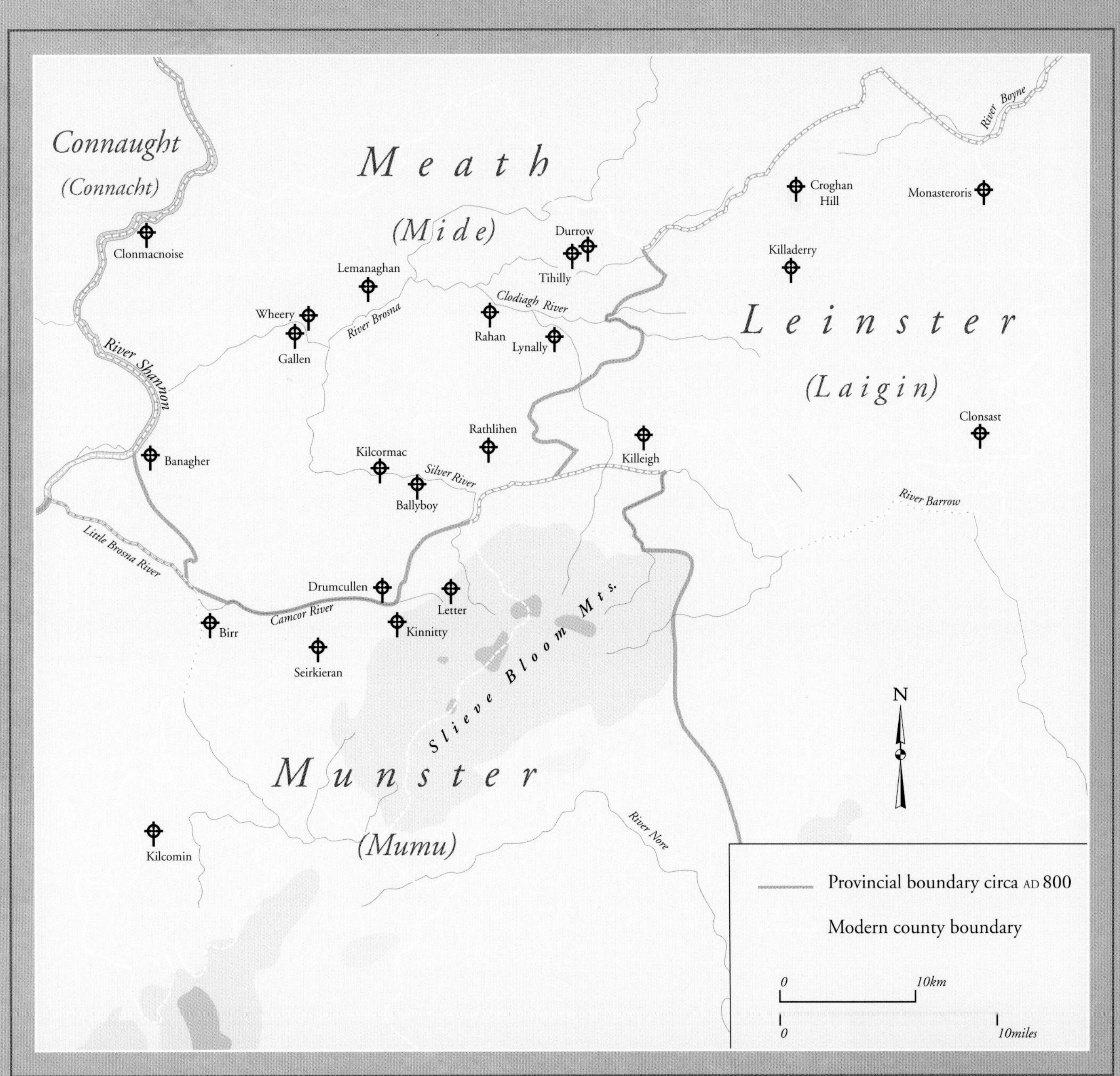

Provincial boundaries in Offaly circa AD 800

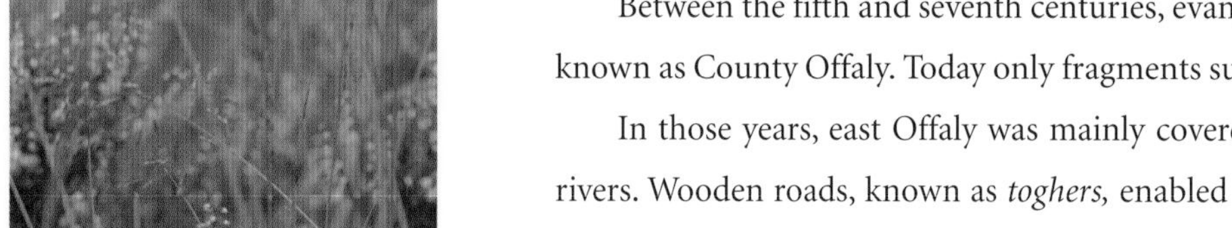

Introduction

Offaly—'A flowering garden of monasteries'

Between the fifth and seventh centuries, evangelist monks arrived in the territory now known as County Offaly. Today only fragments survive of the landscape they encountered.

In those years, east Offaly was mainly covered in uncultivated bog, crossed by a few rivers. Wooden roads, known as *toghers,* enabled people to transport goods and information across the otherwise impassable bogs. Then as now, Croghan Hill, an extinct volcano, rose above this plain, offering magnificent views of the surrounding region.

This landscape was vividly captured in a seventeenth-century description of the barony of Coolestown in east Offaly:

> *It is soe interlaced and invironed with great boggs and low moorish grounds and rivers, that there is no passage from one part thereof to another; nor out of it to any other barony or county but through the straights of foords, causeways or passes, whereof the passes of the most note is the passe of Edenderry over the river of Boyne to the county of Kildare on the east, the pass of Eskerbegg on the west and the passe of Togherga and through the woods of Moyleigh on the south.*[1]

The slow river currents of east Offaly were unsuitable for mills or weirs (dams). Also the rivers, which contained few fish, were unable to sustain large settlements of people.[2] Because of the overall conditions, only a few early Christians established monasteries in this area, among them St Broghan, who founded the island monastery of Clonsast.

A similar landscape existed in the northwest of the county, with one major difference. Through it flowed the River Shannon, capable of providing sustenance to large monastic communities. This impressive river also acted as a natural communication route through heavily wooded parts of the Midlands. The monks created small clearances or meadows in this wooded landscape; eventually some grew into large monastic towns. Places like Lemanaghan grew up on natural islands of dry land surrounded by extensive tracts of bog.

The south of the county contains the Slieve Bloom Mountains—the only mountain range in Offaly. It is in this region that the landscape changes. Stretching up from the toe of the county is a tract of dry land, part of which was once covered in great oak forests, known as the Great Wood of Fercall (Fir Chell).

Several glacial ridges, known as eskers, run through this part of the county. People of the region travelled along these ridges, which became the foundations for some of Ireland's first roads. It is no surprise that the early monks were drawn to these important routeways. Near the Slighe Mór ('Great Road') Colum Cille founded his monastery at Durrow. At the point where the great ridge called the Eiscir Riada met the River Shannon, Ciarán founded Clonmacnoise.

Superimposed on this natural landscape was a political landscape that was equally complex. Offaly was the place where the boundaries of four of the five ancient provinces of Ireland came together. Because of this, monasteries founded here expanded into some of the largest foundations in Ireland.

Central location and proximity to the provinces made the monasteries of the Midlands ideal for church synods and assemblies between rival Irish kings. Their border position also gave them an important strategic role in supporting territorial claims of the local rulers. In return for their support, the nobility of Ireland gave the monasteries land, cattle and material goods. This patronage turned Clonmacnoise into one of the wealthiest towns in Ireland. In fact, the proliferation of large religious foundations in this part of the Midlands has led historians to describe this region as 'a flowering garden of monasteries.'[3]

But how did the monks go about establishing their religion amongst the Gaelic kings? By converting the rulers of the region, the monks would ensure the future of their religion, as the subjects of each king would be obligated to accept the new religion. However, beliefs that had been held for millennia were not given up easily.

Conversion to Christianity offered several advantages to Irish rulers. In pre-Christian Ireland the responsibility of the king was to be the source of well-being for his people. A good and powerful king ensured the fertility of the soil, which resulted in healthy livestock and an abundance of crops, which in turn maintained the health and wealth of his subjects. If crops failed or livestock died and the subjects suffered, it was in the king's interest to remedy the situation by whatever means possible.

If a king failed to rectify the situation, his rule— and very possibly his life— would come to an end.

Christianity may have offered kings a means to reduce their liability for the weather and other factors that affected the crops and the livestock, and hence the health, of their people. The adoption of one all-powerful God relieved the king of direct responsibility for the fertility of the soil.

In times of famine or war, a Christian ruler was able to ask the monasteries to approach God on his behalf. If his people still starved or were defeated in battle, it was no longer solely the fault of the ruler, but could be attributed to the will of God.

The monasteries also promoted the importance of cereal cultivation in the cattle-driven economy of the Irish. This may have resulted in a more efficient and productive society in which food shortages were less frequent and consequently, subjects were more content.

When it came to conversion, the early saints had a few advantages on their side. In order to convince pagan kings of the value of Christianity, monks had to win over the poets who were the harbingers of tradition. It is not surprising therefore that early saints, such as Manchan and Colum Cille, were both clerics and poets.

The preaching skills of the early saints would have impressed a society that highly valued the powers of speech and boasting. Also, their education in the Christian world, or by people with strong ties to the churches of Britain, Gaul and Rome, meant that the saints probably had a level of medical knowledge that enabled them to treat diseases that had been immune to the powers of the pagan gods. And finally, the highly educated monks introduced more efficient methods of farming. For local people, this was another confirmation that the one Christian God was more powerful than the multitude of pagan gods.

The evangelists were also adept at taking local belief systems and making them their own. The presence of prehistoric standing stones at both Durrow and Rahan may suggest that these were pre-Christian ritual centres converted by the early saints.

As well as Christianising sacred places, the evangelists also converted existing rituals. They substituted Christian saints for the 'old Gods' worshiped in festivals. At Drumcullen, the important agricultural festival of Midsummer's Eve became St John's Eve. The Feastday of St Brigid, 1 February, took the place of Imbolc, the pre-Christian festival associated with Spring, the arrival of the growing season and the fertility of the soil.

Acceptance of Christianity by these rulers and their tribes changed the landscape of the county. Before Christianity came to Ireland, it had no towns. Settlement consisted of dispersed, small-scale isolated clusters in the countryside. Some people lived in ringforts; others in unenclosed settlements.

By the year 600, the county had been Christianised and the monasteries that would become the first towns of the Midlands were established. These places brought technological change to farming practices and provided work for artisans, such as skilled metal-workers.

In the Roman world, Christianity had been a religion of the cities. In its urban form, it was suited to a diocesan system with centralised rule by the papacy. In contrast, in Ireland there developed a system of independent monasteries scattered throughout independent tribal kingdoms. Free from a centralised authority, the monasteries—which were a mirror image of Irish secular society—flourished.

Some of these foundations were noted as places of learning throughout the Christian world. From these centres of learning, Irish monks journeyed throughout Europe bringing Christianity back to the people after its practice had been devastated as a consequence of the fall of the Roman Empire.

Contacts with the wider world ensured that monasteries were well aware of events throughout the known world. Finds of pottery and, in particular, wine jars, from excavations on the southwest coast of Ireland support the idea that during the first half of the seventh century Ireland was in contact with the eastern Mediterranean. It is likely that shipping routes touched upon the coasts of North Africa, Spain and southwest France, allowing for the interchange of ideas, books, texts, motifs, symbols and material goods.[4]

In time the very success of the church came to threaten its spiritual mission. As early as the eighth century, some clerics believed that the burgeoning wealth of the church had caused it to lose touch with its spiritual role. They founded the Céili Dé movement, which emphasised the spiritual aspect of monastic life.

Over the coming centuries the church would try to reform itself several more times. The conflict between the material life of the church and its spiritual life would be central to the story of the monasteries in County Offaly, as well as to the history of the church in Ireland.

A major effort to reform the Irish church was driven by Malachy of Armagh and the Kings of Munster during the twelfth century. Their main aims were to remove secular noblemen from the affairs of the church, to establish celibacy among clerics and to stop the system in which a priest would leave his position to his sons. Finally, they hoped to introduce some centralised form of government over the independent monasteries.

Until this time monasteries had functioned as small independent political institutions whose power extended beyond tribal—and in some instances, national—boundaries. A diocesan system set up by the reformers resulted in the first parish churches of Ireland. Also, to appease the church reformers, most monasteries adopted the Rule of St Augustine, which emphasised personal poverty, celibacy and obedience to the church hierarchy.

Arrival of the Anglo-Normans around 1169 gave this reform movement a new lease of life. As keen supporters of the reformed church, these French lords patronised existing parish churches and established new ones. They also introduced continental monastic orders, including the Cistercians, Franciscans and the Dominicans. This period marked the beginning of the decline of the old monastic order in Ireland.

There was a brief surge in the fortunes of Irish monasteries during the fifteenth century, when they benefited from the patronage of the Gaelic aristocracy.

These chieftains accumulated wealth through successful raids on their rival kings. In that feuding society, aristocratic families in Offaly did not invest large sums of money in building large-scale monuments as symbols of their power. Constructing such buildings in a turbulent society proved difficult, and their long-term survival could not be guaranteed. Instead, as an expression of their social obligations, Gaelic chieftains hosted lavish feasts and gatherings. They also commissioned works of literature and music so that their names and deeds would become immortal.[5] The *Annals* and the Irish bardic poems are a testament to aristocratic patronage by individuals, such as Margaret O'Conor, while the stone buildings in which they dwelled and worshipped have long since fallen into ruins.

During this period, the Gaelic chieftains became directly involved in the parochial churches within their territories. Clergymen were selected because of their ancestry, rather than their education or vocation, and very often were used by local rulers as political pawns. As a result, the Irish regional church strayed from the ideals of the centralised papal church. Inevitably, this led to conflict between the Irish church and the official church in Rome.

In 1536 the Irish Parliament declared Henry VIII to be 'the only supreme head in earth of the whole church of Ireland.' This marked the start of the 'reform' of the Irish church, which included the suppression of the monasteries.

For most of the monasteries in Offaly, this would be the final blow. Penal Laws enacted in the following century made it difficult for Catholic people to practice their faith, even in parish churches. As a counter movement, there was a growing devotion to saints at holy wells, many of which were located on the grounds of or near abandoned monasteries.

During the same period, a new community whose faith centred around the ideals of the reformed church took up worship at some of the old monasteries. At places like Rahan and Killeigh, the community of the Church of Ireland continues a tradition of worship in one place that extends, unbroken, for more than 1500 years. This has ensured the preservation of several important churches in the county.

No historical source is without bias. The authors of the various Irish *Annals,* the *Calendar of Papal Letters* and other sources used in writing this book seldom described everyday life or the peaceful events of Irish society. However, these sources do contain insights into Irish life that would otherwise have been lost. As long as we are aware of the bias in these sources, we can use them to illustrate the more colourful aspects of our past.

Today Offaly is a sacred landscape, enriched by the folklore, history, poetry, art and architecture of our Christian past. This landscape tells a story not only of our county, but of our nation. How we care for this priceless resource will be our legacy to future generations.

—Caimin O'Brien

THE HOLY MOUNTAIN

Croghan Hill—Cruachán Brí Éile—Mound or Hill of Brí Éile

The plains of Offaly stretch southwards to the foot of the Slieve Bloom Mountain and to the Sugar Loaf Hills at Killowen in the Queen's County, and eastwards to the Hill of Allen.

Lord of Offaly of the cattle abounding land
A fact not unknown to poets
Is O'Conor, hero of the plain
Of the green, smooth Hill of Croghan.[1]

Croghan Hill was an important burial place in prehistoric times. By the fifth century, the O'Conors, lords of the Uí Failge tribe in the ancient kingdom of Laigin (now known as Leinster) had claimed this mountain as their own. It is fitting that one of the most important symbols of the Uí Failge tribe, for whom Offaly is named, was also one of the first places within the county to be Christianised.

Atop this extinct volcano, a large, flat-topped burial mound offers panoramic views over the surrounding countryside. An ancient poem called 'Laoidh na Leacht' ('Poem of the Monuments') describes this burial mound as the 'Monument of Congal on the Hill of Brí Éile.'[2] The land below Croghan Hill was once known as Móin Éile ('Bog of Éile'); that name was anglicised into the Bog of Allen.

According to local legend, Brí Éile was the daughter of Eochaid Feidleach, the King of Tara. Her sister was Queen Maeve of Connacht, and her husband was Fergal Mac Magach. Local people say that she is buried inside the mound, along with her chariot.[3]

Whether or not Brí Éile is actually buried there, one thing is for certain: Croghan Hill was always an important place. The Irish term *cruachán* ('mound/hill'), from which the hill takes its name, suggests that Croghan Hill may have been a holy mountain, similar to Croagh Patrick in County Mayo.

A mountain such as this one was considered to be a 'place of revelation, a source of life, a pathway to heaven, an abode for the dead and a place where mortals can communicate with Gods.'[4]

Because Croagh Patrick was a sacred mountain for local people, St Patrick chose it to establish the supremacy of his Christian God over their old gods. It is very possible that a Christian church was placed on Croghan Hill for similar reasons.

In the 1830s, John O'Donovan, a historian and antiquarian, captured the setting of the hill and its surroundings:

> *The plains of Offaly stretch southwards to the foot of the Slieve Bloom Mountain and to the Sugar Loaf Hills at Killowen in the Queen's County, and eastwards to the Hill of Allen.*[5]

The landscape is also remembered in an ancient poem recorded in the *Ordnance Survey Letters:*

> *Over the Leinster Carbury of plains*
> *Is O'Kiery of red-bladed swords*
> *The twig of Allen*
> *By whom battles were kindled around Croghan.*[6]

Hill of Tara

Legends offer insight into just how important hilltops, such as the one at Croghan Hill, were to pre-Christian people. The *Annals of the Four Masters* contains such a legend about how Tea (wife of Érimón, son of Míl of Spain)[15]—the queen for whom the Hill of Tara was named—went about selecting this site for her burial place. This sacred hill went on to become an important ritual centre and the seat of the Kings of Tara.

> *Tea . . . requested of Eremhon a choice hill, as her dower, in whatever place she should select it, that she might be interred therein, and that her mound and her gravestone might be thereon raised, and where every prince ever to be born of her race should dwell. The guarantees who undertook to execute this for her were Amhergin Gluingeal and Emhear Finn. The hill she selected was Druim Caein, i.e. Teamhair [the Hill of Tara]. It is from her it was called, and in it was she interred.*

In the middle of the fifth century, Bishop Mac Caille (Mac Hale) set up a church on the side of the hill just below the summit, but within view of the burial mound.

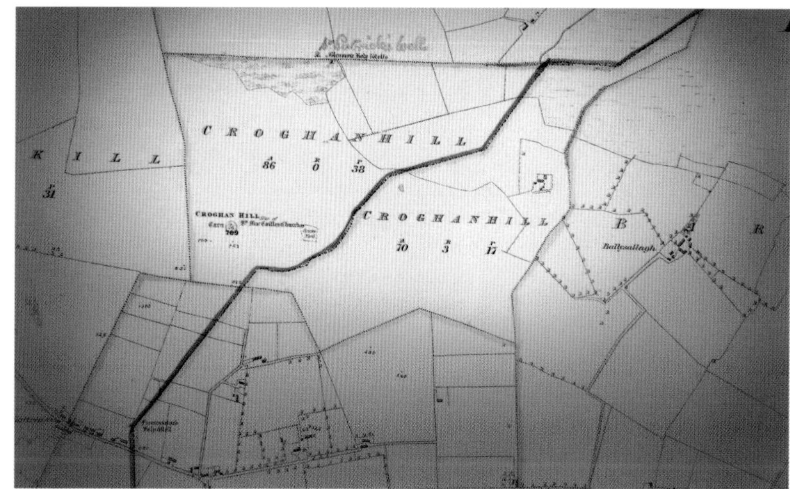

Who was Bishop Mac Caille? And why did he choose to establish his church in this place?

The *Martyrology of Donegal* lists the bishop's feastday as 25 April and says that his mother was Darerca, sister of St Patrick. According to Dr. Lanigan's *Ecclesiastical History of Ireland,* Mac Caille, who died in 489, was:

> *Maceleus, the same in all probability as Macaleus, whose name has become memorable in consequence of his having been the Bishop from whom Saint Brigid received the veil, about, as some writers have calculated, A.D. 467. His Church; that is, as now usually expressed, his See, was at Cruachan Bri Eile* [Croghan Hill] *in Hy Falgia, a place somewhere in the King's Country* [County Offaly], *but his jurisdiction seems to have extended over a considerable tract of country.*[7]

The choice hill that Tea sought could be seen as a holy mountain. As her legend shows, in these places the rulers of a region not only were interred, but their descendants continued to dwell.

The combination of the living and the dead in one location appears to have been extremely important to the people who gave us this legend. Hilltops, bearing burial mounds, may have functioned as portals to the Otherworld. They might have allowed the living to keep in contact with their deceased ancestors, and vice versa. Another possibility is that the holiness of these hilltop burial places was part of a tradition of ancestor worship.

Cogitosus's *Life of Saint Brigit* tells us that Brigit, seeking to become a servant of God, received her veil from Bishop MacCaille in his church on Croghan Hill:

> *. . . when her parents wanted to betroth her to a man according to the custom of the world, Brigit, inspired from above and wanting to devote herself as a chaste virgin to God, went to the most holy bishop Mac Caille of blessed memory. Seeing her heavenly desire and modesty and seeing so great a love of chastity in this remarkable maiden, he placed his white veil and white garment over her venerable head.*
>
> *Kneeling humbly before God and the bishop as well as before the altar and offering her virginal crown to almighty God, she touched with her hand the wooden base on which the altar rested. And to commemorate her unsullied virtue, this wood flourishes fresh and green to the present day as if it had not been cut down and stripped of its bark but was attached to its roots. And to this day it rids all the faithful of afflictions and diseases.*[8]

Saint Brigit: Abbess of Ireland

Of all the Irish saints, St Brigit is second in holiness only to St Patrick. According to accounts of her life, she went to Croghan Hill on her quest to become a servant of God.

One version of her consecration abounds with miracles. According to this tale, Brigit journeyed, along with seven virgins, to Croghan Hill. There she met Mac Caille—the same person believed to have founded the church on the hill. In this version of the story, he is described as a youth and pupil of another evangelist, Bishop Mel.

Brigit asked Mac Caille to lead her to Bishop Mel, but he replied: 'The way is trackless, with marshes, deserts, bogs and pools.' Undaunted, Brigit appealed to God and a 'straight bridge' appeared over the marshy terrain. This may be a reference to the Togher of Croghan (Tochar Cruachán Brí Éile), a straight and ancient roadway that still crosses the base of Croghan Hill.

When they reached Bishop Mel, angels raised the veil from Mac Caille's hand and placed it on Brigit's head. The consecration was so charged with holiness that Bishop Mel ordained Brigit to a higher office than he had intended:

> *The bishop being intoxicated with the grace of God there did not recognise what he was reciting from his book, for he consecrated Brigit with the orders of a bishop. 'This virgin alone in Ireland,' said Mel, 'will hold the Episcopal ordination.' While she was being consecrated a fiery column ascended from her head.*

Certainly, Brigit and the monastery she founded in the fifth century had great power and prestige. In Cogitosus's *Life of Saint Brigit,* written in the seventh century, Brigit is described as: 'the head of almost all the Irish churches with supremacy over all the monasteries of the Irish and its paruchia extends over the whole land of Ireland, reaching from sea to sea.'[16]

Nothing remains of Bishop Mac Caille's church today, although the 1838 Ordnance Survey map marks the site of a church inside the graveyard on the side of Croghan Hill.

Was Croghan Hill a pagan holy mountain taken over by the early evangelists? The conversion of places, as well as people, appears to have been one of the strategies practised by early Christian leaders in Ireland. This policy is explained in advice Pope Gregory issued to the early missionaries of England. He advised Mellitus, one of his missionaries:

> *. . . I have decided after long deliberation . . . that the idol temples of that race should by no means be destroyed, but only the idols in them. Take holy water and sprinkle it in these shrines, build altars and place relics in them. For if the shrines are well built, it is essential that they should be changed from the worship of devils to the service of the true God. When this people see their shrines are not destroyed they will be able to banish error from their hearts and be more ready to come to the places they are familiar with, but now recognizing and worshipping the true God.*[9]

It seems very possible that before Christianity came to the region now known as Offaly, Croghan Hill was the centre of pagan worship. By placing their church on Croghan Hill, evangelists would have created a physical symbol of how the new religion replaced old beliefs.

As the hill was already a place of religious importance, the construction of a church on the side leading to the summit would have been a shrewd move. It allowed for the continuation of worship in the same place, just to a different God.

The fact that there was no economic reason to establish a church on this site further emphasises its spiritual importance. Unlike the monasteries of the lowlands, the church on Croghan Hill was a parochial church ruled by a bishop. Even in its heyday, it remained a parish church devoted to bringing Christianity to the people of Croghan.

Edmund Spenser, who wrote the *Faerie Queene* in the late sixteenth century, captured the essence of the church on Croghan Hill:

> *Thence forward by that painfull way they pas,*
> *Forth to an hill, that was both steepe and hy;*
> *On top whereof a sacred chappell was,*
> *And eke a litle Hermitage thereby,*
> *Wherein an aged holy man did lye,*
> *That day and night said his devotion,*
> *Ne other worldly busines did apply;*
> *His name was heavenly Contemplation;*
> *Of God and goodnesse was his meditation.*

Holy Wells

On the lower slopes of Croghan Hill there are several holy wells. One in Glenmore ('the Great Valley') is dedicated to St Patrick, and a pattern is still held there every St Patrick's Day. Local legend has it that Glenmore Well was dedicated to St Patrick after his horse, bearing the saint, leapt from the summit of the hill and landed on a flagstone near the well. The well sprung up where the horse's hooves struck the ground. When the horse knelt to drink the water, the impression of its knees were left in the flagstone beside the well.

The water in this well is believed to cure anyone suffering from a toothache.[17]

A second well on Croghan Hill has the intriguing name of Finurenashark, derived from the Irish Fionnabhair Na Searc, meaning 'the Well of the Lovers.' Stations were performed at this well as late as the nineteenth century,[18] but the well no longer attracts pilgrims.

At Cannakill a well known locally as St Brigid's Well was once visited by people seeking cures. As they prayed for an end to their ailments, they often gave the following recitation:

Dear St Brigid of the kine [cows]
Bless these little fields of mine,
The pastures and the shady trees,
Bless the butter and the cheese,
Bless the cows with coats of silk
And the brimming pails of milk,
Bless the hedgerows, and I pray
Bless the seed beneath the clay,
Bless the hay and bless the grass,
Bless the seasons as they pass,
And heaven's blessings will prevail,
Brigid— Mary of the Gael.[19]

As well as being a sacred place, the burial mound on the summit may also have been re-used as the site where the O'Conors were inaugurated as Kings of Uí Failge. By placing their church in association with the inauguration place of the ruling kings, early Christian leaders would have created a powerful link between the secular rulers and the new church. This alliance would have been crucial in establishing a strong and prosperous religion.

Certainly hilltops such as Croghan Hill were used by the Irish as centres of assembly. Writing in 1596, Edmund Spenser offered the following description:

> *There is a greate use amonge the Irishe, to make greate assemblies togeather upon a Rath or hill, there to parlie (as they saye) about matters and wronges betwene Towneship and Towneship, or one private person and another. But well I wott, that knowe, yt hath bene oftentymes approved, that in these meetinges many mischiefes have benn both practized and wrought: for to them doe commonly resorte all the scumme of loose people, where they may freelie meete and conferre of what they list, which ells theye could not doe without suspicon or knowledge of others.*
>
> *Besides, at these parlies I have divers tymes knowen that many Englishmen, and other good Irishe subjectes, have benn villanouslie murdered, by movinge one quarrell or another amongest them. For the Irishe never come to those Rathes but armed, whether on horsebacke or on foote, which the English nothinge suspectinge, are then commonly taken at advantagge like sheepe in the pynfolde.*[10]

Spenser goes on to comment that burial mounds on hill summits had many functions. He explains why they were built and the effects of Christianity upon them:

> *But besides these twoe sortes of hilles, there were auncientlie divers others; for some were raysed, where there had bene a greate battayle, as a memorye or trophes thereof; others, as monuments of buryalls of the carcasses of all those that were slaine in any fyghte, upon whome they did throwe up such rounde mounts, as memorialls for them, and sometimes did cast up great heapes of stones, as you may read the like in many places of the Scripture, and other whiles they did throw up many round heapes of earth in a circle, like a garland, or pitch many long stones on ende in compasse, every one of which they say, betokened some worthie person of note there slayne and buried; for this was theire auncyent custome, before Christianitie came in amongest them that church-yardes were inclosed.*[11]

St. Patrick and his Assassin

According to a legend in the *Tripartite Life of St. Patrick,* when Patrick entered the lands of the Uí Failge (present-day Offaly), two powerful men governed the O'Conors. The first, Failge Ros, treated the saint with 'affection and honour.' However, the other leader, Failge Berraide, hated Patrick from the day that he destroyed the chief idol of Ireland, called the Crom Cruach ('crooked hill'). Failge Berraide had worshipped that idol 'as if were a god'; its destruction left him enraged.

Hearing that Failge Berraide had sworn to kill Patrick, his supporters became concerned for his life. As they passed through the lands ruled by Failge Berraide, Odranus, who was Patrick's charioteer, tricked the saint. Saying that he had grown weary, Odranus asked Patrick to let him sit in the saint's usual place in the main part of the chariot. Minutes later, Failge Berraide approached the chariot and, thinking that Odranus was Patrick, drove a lance through his body.

Infuriated, Patrick began to curse Failge Berraide. But as Patrick thundered the words: 'May a curse descend . . .' Odranus arose from his death throes. In an act of Christian charity, he begged the saint not to curse his killer but rather to let the curse fall on a certain large tree that stood on Croghan Hill.

Patrick agreed to the dying wish of Odranus. Though uncursed, Failge Berraide died on the spot, 'a just punishment of the sacrilege he had committed.' However, Patrick blessed the children of Failge Ros 'who to this very day hold the government of that region.'

While not an account of actual events, this legend does offer insight into how people made sense of what happened at Croghan Hill— and in the rest of Ireland— as sacred pagan sites became Christianised.

A man named Failge Berraide was one of the leaders of the O'Conors in the fifth century, the same period in which Christianity came to that region. In the legend, Crom Cruach, the idol worshipped by Failge Berraide, may have been a standing stone that had ritual significance, either as an object of worship, or as part of the inauguration process of local rulers, or both. Also in ancient times, sacred trees were often found on inauguration sites. Such a tree would be considered the symbol of the tribe. By cursing the tree, one was placing a curse of the highest order on the tribe it represented.[20]

Whether or not the actual Failge Berraide tried to murder Patrick, his mythical counterpart would understandably have been enraged by a threat to an idol that he worshipped and/or which gave him authority.

In this legend, Christianity triumphs over pagan beliefs four times: when Patrick destroys the idol Crom Cruach, when the dying Odranus begs for mercy for his killer, when Patrick curses the tree and finally, when the leaders of the O'Conors who support Patrick are blessed and survive to govern the region.

Throughout history, Croghan Hill was a site of conflict. The King of Tara defeated the Laigin tribe in a battle at Croghan Hill in 475.[12] This was one of several battles at Croghan Hill between the Laigin and the King of Tara in the late fifth century. According to *The Book of Leinster,* after the battle of Drum Derge in about 516, a dividing line between the provinces of Leinster and Meath was drawn across the hill of Croghan.[13] For years afterward, the hill was a feature of the frontier zone between those two provinces.

At the base of the hill, an ancient roadway known as the Togher of Croghan (Tochar Cruachán Brí Éile) crossed the Bog of Allen. A map of Offaly from 1563 shows the roadway running from the base of Croghan Hill towards Kilclonfert, onwards to Durrow and eventually to Clonmacnoise. During the late medieval period (1350-1650), a castle guarded this roadway, which witnessed several important battles between the English and the O'Conors.

The *Annals of the Four Masters* record in 1385 that:

> *Morogh O'Conor, Lord of Ui Failgia and the Kinel-Fiacha [the Mageoghegans] defeated the English of Meath at the Tochar of Cruachan Bri Eile; Nugent of Meath, Chambers and his son and a countless number of the nobles and plebeians of the English were slain.*

Nothing remains of the castle that guarded the Tochar of Cruachán Brí Éile. However, at the foot of Croghan Hill are ruins of the castle where the O'Conors lived during the late medieval period (1350-1650). Nearby are the remains of a medieval church, graveyard and village. It may be that this forgotten church and graveyard were the ones that replaced Bishop Mac Caille's first buildings in the parish.

In 1546 Croghan Hill was the site of one of the last battles between the O'Conors and the English. The *Annals* state:

> *The plain of Cairbre and Castle-Carbury were plundered and burned by the aforenamed insurgents, and by Donough, the son of O'Conor Faly. O'Conor himself (Brian) and O'More (Gilla-Patrick) afterwards rose up, to join in this insurrection. When the Lord Justice, Anthony St. Leger, had heard of this, he came into Offaly, and plundered and burned the country as far as the Togher of Cruachan; and he remained there two nights, but he returned without receiving battle or submission. O'More and the son of O'Conor (Rury) attacked the town of Ath-Ai, and burned the town and monastery, and destroyed many persons, both English and Irish, both by burning and slaying, on this occasion.*

Soon afterwards, in 1549, the O'Conors submitted to the forces of the English government[14] and their lands were confiscated. So ended Gaelic rule of the Uí Failge territory. Croghan Hill—a mountain revered by pagans, Christians and kings—became better known as an important geographical feature in the landscape of North Offaly.

Writing around the ninth century, Oengus the Culdee, an early Christian monk, described the places sacred to pagans as 'great hills of evil.' He gloated: 'Paganism has been destroyed though it was splendid and far flung. The great hills of evil have been cut down with spearpoints.'[21]

BURYING PLACE OF THE KINGS OF OSSORY

Seirkieran—Saighir Chiaráin—The Fountain of Ciarán

The monastery Ciarán founded became one of the most impressive religious communities in all of Ireland.

Sometime before the end of the fifth century,[1] a monk named Ciarán founded a monastery at a place called Saighir in a gently sloping valley beside the Fuarawn River.

Dates for Ciarán's life — and the foundation of his monastery — vary wildly. In some sources, he pre-dates St Patrick and founds his monastery in 402.[2] In others, he is described as a contemporary of Patrick.

Whatever the truth, the monastery Ciarán founded became one of the most impressive religious communities in all of Ireland. Local rulers granted it large amounts of land and supported its production of chalices, crosses, bells and manuscripts. Seirkieran became the final resting place of many kings.

According to legend, Ciarán's father, Lugna, was a member of the Ossory (Osraige) tribe, which occupied lands that today belong to County Kilkenny and southeast Laois. During Ciarán's time, it was common for rulers to send their children to be fostered in another location, and that is probably why the boy was raised in present-day Cape Clear, County Cork.

It is not known when Ciarán — or the members of his family — adopted Christianity. However, his mother, Liadáin, of the Corcu Loigde tribe in what today is southwest Cork, established a nunnery at nearby Killyon (Cill Liadáin), which is named after her. In that townland, a small plantation of trees known as the 'nunnery grove' may preserve the site of her religious community.

Ciarán went to Rome, where he spent 30 years studying the scriptures. He received his episcopal orders. Then, carrying some relics of St Peter and of St Paul, he returned to Ireland to spread the Word of God.

At first, Ciarán did not know where to establish his monastery. According to the *Life of Old Ciarán of Saighir,* St Patrick told him to found his community in the middle of Ireland beside a little cold spring known as the Úarán, in the Éile region of Munster.

Perplexed, Ciarán said to Patrick, 'I do not know the way to it, for I know not this Úarán at which I should abide, from any other.'

Patrick replied: 'Thou shalt take my bell, and it will be dumb till it reaches the Úarán, and it will ring when it reaches it, and Bardán Ciaráin will be the name of it [the bell] till doom, and mighty deeds and miracles will be done by you together and Saighir ['the fountain'] will be the name of the place.'[3]

That Patrick, the foremost saint in Ireland, revealed the location for Ciarán's monastery suggests that it was a holy place. It is possible that the saints believed that such a place, chosen by God and revealed through Patrick, was a portal through which they could access heaven.[4] In the legend the bell would not ring at any other location, indicating that this was the chosen site.

Cooleeshill, the Satellite Monastery

In the 1930s, James Shanahan of Killanure recorded local folklore that traces the route that Ciarán took on his approach to Bell Hill:

St Kieran on his way to this place passed through Coolisheal [Cooleeshill]. He came along the road that now leads from Roscrea to Boheraphuca chapel and over Aghagurty Bridge, then on to Loftus's Bridge, then over a road and on to the top of Bellhill.[21]

Interestingly enough, archaeological remains in the landscape also link Cooleeshill, a townland near Roscrea, with Seirkieran. Cooleeshill contains the remains of a large enclosure known as St Kieran's Church Yard. At its centre is a spring well known as St Kieran's Well.

It is possible that this enclosure was a satellite monastery of Seirkieran. If so, monks would have been able to leave behind the bustling monastic town of Seirkieran for a peaceful hermitage at Cooleeshill, where they could meditate in their cells on the Word of God.

In *The Life of St Ciarán of Saigir,* the bell that signalled his arrival was made by Germanus, a servant bishop of Patrick. It was kept in the monastery, where it was an object of great veneration throughout the diocese. The chiefs of the territory swore oaths upon this bell. It was also used throughout the region for the defence of the poor and for the collection of dues owed to the monastery.[5]

Place-names near Seirkieran reflect the legend of the bell. From the site of the monastery it is possible to see Bell Hill. According to local folklore, this is the place where the bell, given by St Patrick, rang out. In one version of the story, '. . . a hawthorn bush (bellbush) marks the spot where the bell rang. The bush is small and never grows any bigger.'[6] Today, there is a small white thorn bush, known locally as 'Bellbush,' on Bell Hill.

When he arrived at Bellhill, the bell, which St Patrick had given him, rang out. A hawthorn bush (bellbush) marks the spot where the bell rang. The bush is small and never grows any bigger.

Along the bottom fields of the monastery runs the Fuarawn River. Its name is anglicised from the Irish 'Fuarán,' possibly the same as the River Úarán identified by Patrick as the proper location for Ciarán's monastery.

As well as being the water source for the monastery, this river probably also served a spiritual role. It is likely that Ciarán baptised converts in this river. Also, *The Life of Ciarán* describes how the monks used the river in the penitential acts they performed to demonstrate their devotion to God. In one tale Germanus joined Ciarán in the middle of the river. As the icy water rushed around them, the two men performed their devotions. Germanus was in agony from the cold of the water. Noticing his pain, Ciarán used his pastoral staff to make the sign of the cross. At once, the icy water seemed warm to Germanus, and he was able to continue.

The monastery that Ciarán founded at Seirkieran was a cenobitic or communal monastery, which participated in the material world and interacted with the lay people of the region. It was also a royal monastery that enjoyed the patronage of the Kings of Ossory and served as their final burial place.[7]

As evidence of its former glory, Seirkieran contains one of the largest and most imposing enclosures in the county— if not Ireland. Today it is possible to see the impressive remains of two earthen banks, which form a D-shaped enclosure measuring 320 metres in diameter. The banks run down to the Fuarawn River, which completes the enclosure. The total enclosed area measures over 20 acres, which may reflect the large population of this monastery in early Christian times.

The impressive enclosure at Seirkieran may be evidence of its strong ties to the rulers of this region. A seventeenth-century narrative, written by Dubhaltach MacFirbisigh, attributes construction of the enclosure of Seirkieran to Sadhbh (Sabia), the wife of Donnchad (Donagh), who was King of Meath (879-916). In the account, Sadhbh demands that the monastery be enclosed before she will consider it fit to be the burial place for her father, the King of Ossory.

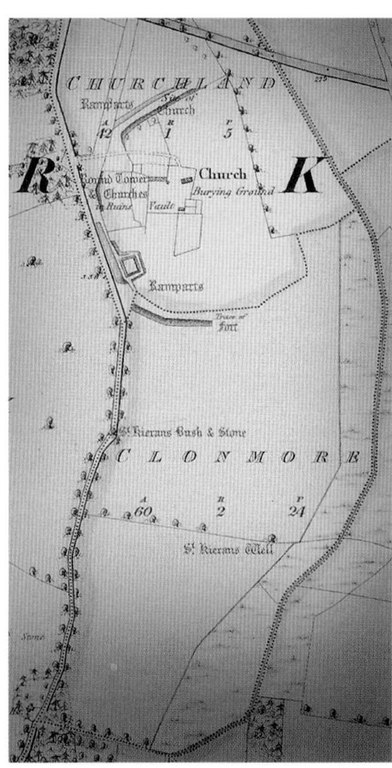

> *Donagh leads an army to erect a wall and sink a trench round the church of Saighir Chiaráin, at the behest of his wife Sabia (Sadhbh) . . . It created great envy in her mind that every one of the distinguished churches of Ireland was enclosed with a wall and ditch, while her own family church of Saighir was without wall or ditch.*[8]

Today one can trace a possible roadway from the centre of the graveyard to a gap in the banks. This gap probably marks the location of the gateway, or gatehouse, that protected the entrance to the monastic town. Within the enclosure, the low grass-covered walls of several houses and plots are the remains of burgess plots, which date from the twelfth and thirteenth centuries when the monastery was a thriving community.

Burial place of the Kings of Ossory

When the King of Ossory died, his daughter, Sadhbh, demanded that the church that she attended, Saighir Chiarain (Seirkieran), be enclosed with a great wall before she would consider it worthy to be the burial place of her father.

Her husband, the King of Meath, sent his men to build a large enclosure around the church. Once the fence was complete, the body of Donnchadh, King of Ossory, was buried in the ground.

But as soon as night fell, 'nine hairy jet-black crosans [poets/keeners] came upon the grave and set to choir-chanting . . . their eyes and their teeth were whiter than snow, and all their other limbs blacker than blacksmith's coal.' The crosans chanted a lay (poem) from nightfall until morning. According to the legend, all who saw them 'grew sick a day and a night at the sight.'

Knowing that the dead king had been a pious Christian and friend to the poor, the clergy and people of the church were bewildered by the presence of these 'demons.'

The priests fasted and prayed to learn why 'demons should be openly attending the body of that most virtuous king.' After three days, one of the priests had a vision in which an angel appeared. The angel complemented the priests on keeping their fast, and then explained: 'These are nine of the company of Uí Coingheoidh, and this is the third time they have come to Ireland from hell; and since they could not find an occasion against this king during his life, they are causing a disturbance over his body after his death.'

'Do ye have Mass said and water blessed to-morrow,' continued the angel, 'and let it be sprinkled on the grave and throughout all the churchyard, and all the demons will go away.'

When the priests followed the angel's instructions, the company of Uí Coingheoidh took the form of jet black birds in the air above the church because they were unable to light on churchyard ground, which had been blessed. The birds told the clergy to continue fasting and blessing the king's grave '. . . for we would be after his body on earth since we have not power over his soul in heaven.' And with that, they disappeared and were never seen again.[22]

CERBALL

The graveyard at Seirkieran contains a replica of an early Christian grave slab, inscribed with a beautiful cross. Its inscription reads: 'OR DO CHERBALL' ('Pray for Cerball, King of Ossory') who died in 885.[23]

Cerball macDúnlainge, Lord of Ossory, was a cunning and successful king. He fought in many battles both with and against Vikings and rival Irish kings. Before entering any conflict, Cerball would weigh up the options and decide which alliance would be best for his kingship.

In 845 Cerball triumphed over the foreigners of Ath Cliath (Vikings of Dublin) in a great battle at Carn Brammit. He was again victorious in 856, this time in alliance with the Norsemen against the Cinél Fiachach, his Ossory neighbours to the north. The same year he plundered Leinster for a second time and 'took their hostages.'

Records tell of a counter-attack by the men of Leinster on 'the fort of Chearball,' which is probably the large triple-banked ringfort, known locally as 'Lisnaskeagh,' that overlooks the monastery of Seirkieran. Eventually Cerball's warriors forced the men of Leinster to retreat.

Cerball formed an alliance with Máelsechnaill (Maelseachlainn), King of Meath, and submitted to his authority. This was a great aid to Máelsechnaill as he battled against his neighbours, the Kings of Munster. One factor that strengthened this alliance was the marriage of Cerball's son to a daughter of Máelsechnaill.

By the time Máelsechnaill died in 862, Cerball's shrewd political manoeuverings and marriage alliances had made him the second most powerful king in Ireland.[24]

By giving some of his daughters in marriage to Norsemen, Cerball also formed alliances with the Vikings. Because of these marriages, in Iceland Cerball was known as Kjarvalr Irakonungr (Kjarvall the Irish King) and his daughters became important figures in Icelandic sagas.[25] Evidence suggests that after 873, Cerball became a protector of Viking Dublin.

On top of a pile of stones in the centre of the graveyard are the impressive remains of the base of a ninth-century high cross. The socket on top of this base is so wide and deep that it would have supported one of the largest crosses in Ireland. Unfortunately, the shaft and the head of this enormous cross have never been discovered.

Biblical scenes are carved on the two faces of this base. The carvings depict the Temptation of Adam and Eve and David's Confrontation with Goliath, among other stories.

Like most large monasteries in Ireland, Seirkieran possessed an important scriptorium. It also appears to have been a centre for metalworking. According to local tradition, Daig MacCairill— 'a smith, a craftsman and excellent scribe' who later became the Bishop of Inishkeen, County Louth—was the *primcherd,* or chief artist, of Seirkieran. A passage from the *Life of Daig* offers an insight into the great demand for metal objects used in the daily life of the church. The passage tells us that Daig was remarkable for making:

> *... bronze bells, cymbals, crosiers, crucifixes, shrines, repositories or satchels, small boxes for the Sacred Hosts, chalices, patens, portable altars, chrism jars and book covers which were either plain or covered with gold or silver and encrusted with precious stones.*[9]

As the monastery at Seirkieran grew in strength and prestige, Ciarán's power inspired not only reverence, but also concern. The *Martyrology of Aengus* says that some monks worried that eventually Ciarán's monastery would have ruled over the whole of Ireland, at the expense of their own monasteries.[10] To prevent that from happening, the Irish monks fasted for the death of St Ciarán. The passage in the *Martyrology of Aengus* says 'the whole of Ireland would have been his had not that been done.'[11] According to legend, the cutting short of St Ciarán's life— through fasting for his death, and possibly also by more direct means— was an evil deed. It is counted as one of the 'three bad stories of the saints of Ireland.' (The other two are the expulsion of Carthage from Rahan, and the sending of Colum Cille into exile.)

Ciarán was such a highly regarded holy man that, as he was dying, many saints came to his bedside to honour him. One of these was Finnian, the founder of one of the most celebrated schools of Ireland at his monastery in Clonard, County Meath. Years earlier, Ciarán had served as Finnian's tutor. Finnian travelled from Clonard to be present for Ciarán's last days at Saighir because 'it was with him he studied his psalms and every kind of learning that he had.'[12]

On his deathbed, Ciarán tried to ensure that his monastery would continue to prosper. According to the *Lives of the Saints,* the dying Ciarán asked God to grant him three wishes. The first was that no one buried at his monastery should go to Hell. The second was that all those who celebrated his feastday should have successful and prosperous lives and enter the Kingdom of Heaven. The final wish was that God should favour in battle the men of Ossory and never allow them to be evicted from their territory because Ciarán was 'one of their race.'[13]

By supporting the monastery, and being buried there, the rulers of Ossory would gain prosperity, security and victory in battle. Furthermore, the gates of Hell would be closed to them.

Seirkieran after Ciarán

The first reference to Seirkieran in the *Annals of the Four Masters* is the death, in 739, of 'Laidhgnen, son of Doineannach, Abbot of Saighir.' In 867 the *Annals* record the death of 'Cormac, son of Eladhach, Abbot of Saighir, bishop and scribe,' indicating that there was a scriptorium at Seirkieran.

The *Lebar Brecc,* a fourteenth-century manuscript, contains a reference to an illuminated manuscript known as *Imirche Ciaráin* ('Ciarán's Penitential Journey'), which was kept at Seirkieran but has long since vanished.[14] This manuscript was illuminated by Cairnec Móel ('Cairnec the Bald'), a scribe in Seirkieran. It was still present at Seirkieran in the eleventh century.[15]

Between 839 and 842, the monastery was attacked by Vikings. In 916 the *Annals* record the death of Fearghal, son of Maelmordha, Abbot of Saighir, who is described as 'The Abbot of Saighir with multitudes; Fearghal, man of gentle exactions.'

The men of Munster attacked and plundered the monastery in the tenth century. However, by the eleventh century Munster was on friendlier terms with the abbot of Seirkieran, who also was in charge of the Munster monastery of Birr. In 1079, the *Annals of the Four Masters* describe Ceallach Reamha ('Ceallach the Lusty') as the 'successor of Brenainn of Birra, and of Ciarán of Saighir.'

Ciarán's monastery was the seat of the Bishops of Ossory until around 1052, when the see was moved to Aghaboe in County Laois.[16]

St Ciarán's Well

The name Seirkieran comes from Saighir— a word that may mean 'fountain'— and Ciarán. Today the water that flows from St Ciarán's Well may be the original 'fountain of life' from which the monastery received its name.

The well was described in 1834 as 'neatly faced with stone embankments of a quadrilateral form, and shaded with thorns, well hung with thorn scraps of calico dedicated to the titular saint.'[26]

It is the first station of the pattern held on 5 March, which is the Feastday of St Ciarán. In accordance with tradition, pilgrims attend mass, then go to the well, the holy bush and the graveyard.

In the 1930s, Margaret O'Neill of Clareen National School described the pattern at the well:

You do three rounds at the well on March 5th or within the octave of that date. You kneel down and say the rosary then go outside turn to your right and walk in again and do your second visit. Then go out again and do your third visit. It is usual to pay a visit to the Blessed Sacrament in the church now, but formerly this was not done.

At the well people often leave beads, pictures and even rags on the tree that is near the well. They take a drink of the water and take home a bottle full to use in case of illness. There is great faith in the water as a cure for sore eyes in particular and it is used to wash sores or it is drunk during illness and sprinkled when there is thunder and lightning. St Kieran's day is often the occasion of family reunions. Old residents never fail to do their rounds, if not on the feast day then some day during the octave and they pay a visit to the old home and see their friends.[27]

Sometime before 1170,[17] the monks of Seirkieran adopted the Rule of St Augustine. The monastery then became known as the Priory of St Ciarán. The walls of the large Augustinian priory built around this time can still be seen in the graveyard. Built up against the outer face of the northwest angle of these walls, it is possible to see the foundations of a twelfth-century round tower.

The monastery was taken over by Anglo-Normans around 1200-1220. When it was re-dedicated is uncertain, but by the fifteenth century it was known as the Priory of St Mary's.[18]

According to the *Annals of the Four Masters,* in 1548 the monastery was 'burned and destroyed by the English and O'Carroll.'

On 27 December 1568, the monastery was surrendered to the English crown as part of the Dissolution of the Monasteries. It was described thus:

> *. . . the prior was found to be seized of the site of the same, containing one acre, in which were the walls of a church, a small tower, a great stone house covered with thatch, now used as the parish-church, and two other houses, then the residence of the canons; worth, excluding repairs, 4s. 4d. yearly. The villa of Shyre belonged to the canons, in which were six cottages and forty acres of arable and pasture lands of the annual value of 17s. 8d. The rectory of Shyre, alias Shyre Keran, belonged also to the said priory; and the tithes and alterages were of the yearly value of 40s. besides the curate's stipend, taxes &c.*[19]

The lands containing Seirkieran then came under the ownership of James, Earl of Roscommon, who granted the priory and its grounds to Sir William Taafe.[20]

A small gun-tower that is entered from the priory and overlooks the graveyard appears to date from this period. The small, single-storey circular tower, with a conical cap and gun loops, was probably built during the sixteenth century to fortify the priory after it was taken from the local population and granted to the English planters.

By the eighteenth century, the church was in a poor and dilapidated state. According to Joseph Robinson, vicar of Seirkieran in 1777, the parishioners refused to enclose the graveyard after an act had been passed for the enclosing of church yards. This indicates that there was no boundary around the graveyard until the late eighteenth century, when the present wall was constructed.

In the nineteenth century the Church of Ireland built a church on the site. The builders used one of the original windows from the thirteenth-century priory as the east window for the new church.

In the late 1930s, the Rector of Seirkieran, Rev. Harold Gilling, undertook an excavation of the low square mound inside the ramparts of the early Christian monastery. The deep cavity one sees today on top of the mound is the result of this search for 'buried treasure.' Instead of finding treasure, Gilling came across a large flat stone, around which were deposited some fragments of quartz. This find led to his declaration that he had discovered 'the burial place of the pre-Christian kings of Ossory.'

In fact, this mound was probably built by the Anglo-Normans in the early thirteenth century as the foundation for a timber castle. Another possibility is that the mound may have supported a castle or fortified building for the first Bishop of Ossory in the tenth century.

Seirkieran has remained a holy place since Ciarán's time. Because of the deeds of its monks and its association with the Kings of Ossory, it has enjoyed both fame and wealth. The graveyard that was the burial place of St Ciarán and of warrior kings, such as Cerball, serves today as the final resting place for local people, both young and old, poor and rich.

The archaeological landscape at Seirkieran clearly illustrates that worship has continued on this same hallowed ground from the foundation of the monastery to the present day. The large crowds that attend the pattern day on the Feastday of St Ciarán (5 March), are a living testimony to the connection between the residents of Seirkieran and its founding saint. This link has been maintained for over 1500 years; hopefully, it will survive for future generations.

St Ciarán's Bush

St Ciarán's Bush has always occupied a special place for local people. According to tradition, this bush must be passed on the left-hand side; bad luck will befall anyone who does otherwise.

Since the nineteenth century—if not before—a rag bush has stood in the middle of two roads. Believers seeking help from the saint attach pieces of cloth to the bush. Pilgrims stop at the bush as part of the stations in the procession on St Ciarán's Feastday. A large flagstone lies at the base of the rag bush. According to local legend, this stone bears the impressions of St Ciarán's hands and knees.

THE CHURCH OF THE WELSHMEN

Gallen—Gaillinne na mBretann—Rocky Land of the Britons

Ireland in ould time . . . was well stored with learned men and colledges that people came from all partes of Christendome to learne therein . . .

In 492, Canoc (Mochanog), eldest son of the King of Brecknock, in Wales, founded a monastery at a place called Gallen, on the banks of the River Brosna, near the present-day village of Ferbane. The monastery was located in the Gaelic territory known as Delbna Bethra (Delvin Mac Coghlan), in the province of Meath.

In the *British Martyrology,* Canoc is described as 'illustrious for his sanctity.' In contrast, the surviving accounts of the monastery known as 'Gallen of the Britons' tell only of violent episodes related to the politics of the monastery's patrons. Unfortunately, the *Annals* are silent when it comes to portraying the everyday lives of the monks at Gallen.

However, a wonderful collection of cross slabs, most of which date from the eighth to tenth centuries, survive at Gallen. These grave covers offer a glimpse into the world of the monks. Furthermore, the similarities they bear to slabs found in Scotland and Northumbria (in Northern England) clearly demonstrate that Gallen was in contact with Irish monasteries in other parts of the world. Its monks travelled to and fro, transmitting ideas from sacred place to sacred place.

Like many monasteries of the Midlands, Gallen had a turbulent history. It was attacked and burned several times by Irish kings, Vikings, and by the English. One attack occurred in the year 820, when 'Gallen of the Welshmen was altogether burnt by Phelym McCriowhayne [King of Munster] both houses, Church & Sanctuaries.'[1]

After this episode, a band of monks from Wales restored the churches and established a school in the monastery, which became famous throughout Ireland. In his introduction to the translation of *The Annals of Clonmacnoise,* Connell Ma Geoghagan described the school:

> *Ireland in ould time . . . was well stored with learned men and colledges that people came from all partes of Christendome to learne therein, and among all other nations that came thither there was none soe much made of nor respected with the Irish as was the English & Welshmen, to whom they gave severall Collages to dwell and Learne In, as to the englishmen a collage in the towne of Mayo in Connaught, which to this day is called Mayo of the English, & to the Welshmen the town of Gallen in the Kings County, which is liekewise called Gallen of the Welchmen or Wales.*[2]

Its esteemed school did not prevent Gallen from being the scene of violence. In 949, the *Annals of the Four Masters* record 'the spoiling of Sil-Anmchadha, and the plundering of Cluain-fearta-Brenainn, by Ceallachan and the men of Munster. The plundering of Dealbhna-Beathra by the same party; and the Daimh-liag (stone church) of Gailine was burned by them.'

Another account of violence at the monastery comes from 1003, when a man named Iarnan was murdered in the 'doorway of the oratory in Gallen.'[3]

Like most early Christian monasteries in Ireland, the monastery at Gallen adopted the Rule of St Augustine in the twelfth century.[4] The monks replaced the old habit of their Celtic order with the long black cassock, white rochet (long white linen vestment) and cloak and hood of the Augustinians.

Referring back to this period at Gallen, a German planter, Matthew de Renzy, stated that the monastery enjoyed the patronage of the Anglo-Norman family of Tuites, who 'placed therein many Englisch fryers.'[5]

By the fifteenth century, the power of the Tuites had waned. Afterwards, the monastery was patronised by the Mac Coghlans, the Gaelic kings of this region. Several of Gallen's rulers were selected from this family; however the patronage of the Mac Coghlans embroiled the abbey in violent regional and kinship disputes.

During the early sixteenth century, Gallen was caught up in the middle of a conflict between rival Mac Coghlan kinsmen for leadership of the Gaelic territory known as Delbna Bethra. As a member of the Mac Coghlan tribe, the monastery's prior was eligible for the position of Chief of Delbna Bethra. This brought the clerical ruler into conflict with the secular Mac Coghlan chiefs, who also wished to lead their tribe.

In 1519, the *Annals* record that a great war broke out in Delbna Bethra between the descendants of Fergal Mac Coghlan and the descendants of Donnell Mac Coghlan. James Mac Coghlan, who was the Prior of Gaillinn (Gallen) and the heir apparent of Delbna Bethra, was killed by a ball shot from the Castle of Cluain Damha (Clonony).[6]

The violence waged on. In 1531, Murtough, the son of Conor Mac Coghlan, 'Prior of Gailinn (Gallen) and Vicar of Liath-Manchain (Lemanaghan),' was 'treacherously slain' by Turlough Oge O'Melaghlin and Rury O'Melaghlin. In 1543 the *Annals of the Four Masters* described this event:

> *A nocturnal irruption was made by Rury and his kinsmen into the plain of Gailinn, in Delvin, and burned and plundered the plain. Melaghlin Balbh O'Madden and Art Mac Coghlan pursued them, and gave them battle at the church of Gailinn, where Cormac O'Melaghlin, the brother of Rury, and thirteen of the chiefs of his people, were slain or drowned.*

In the late sixteenth century, all monastery lands were confiscated by Henry VIII and granted to English planters. In 1571 George Boucher received a grant from Elizabeth I of the 'sites of the monastery of Canoc of Gallen, the lands of Gallen and Rennagh (the modern parishes of Ferbane, Cloghan and Banagher).'[7] And in 1612, the lands of Gallen were granted again, this time by James I to Sir Gerald Moore. The grant included:

> *The site of this abbey, together with the church, cemetery, &c., five cottages and two gardens, in the town of Gallen; forty acres of arable land, thirty of pasture, wood and underwood in Gallen, and a moiety of the tithes and alterages of the rectories and vicarages of Feycorie (Wheery), Gallen, and Reynagh, in the King's County, parcell of the possessions of this abbey, were granted, 4th June, 1612, to Sir Ger. Moore, at the annual rent of £3 12s. 2d., who was to maintain an horse-man for ever on the same.*[8]

From then onwards, the church and town of Gallen entered a steady decline. By the early eighteenth century the site had probably been abandoned. Around 1820 George Petrie described its remains:

> *The ruins of a fifteenth century church, with its flamboyant east window, are still standing in Sir Edmund Armstrong's demesne near the village of Ferbane, in the King's County, at a distance of about two hundred yards from which is a low grassy mound, probably the site of the original foundation.*[9]

As late as 1929 the 'flamboyant east window' was still intact; today, however, only the lower parts of the abbey walls survive.

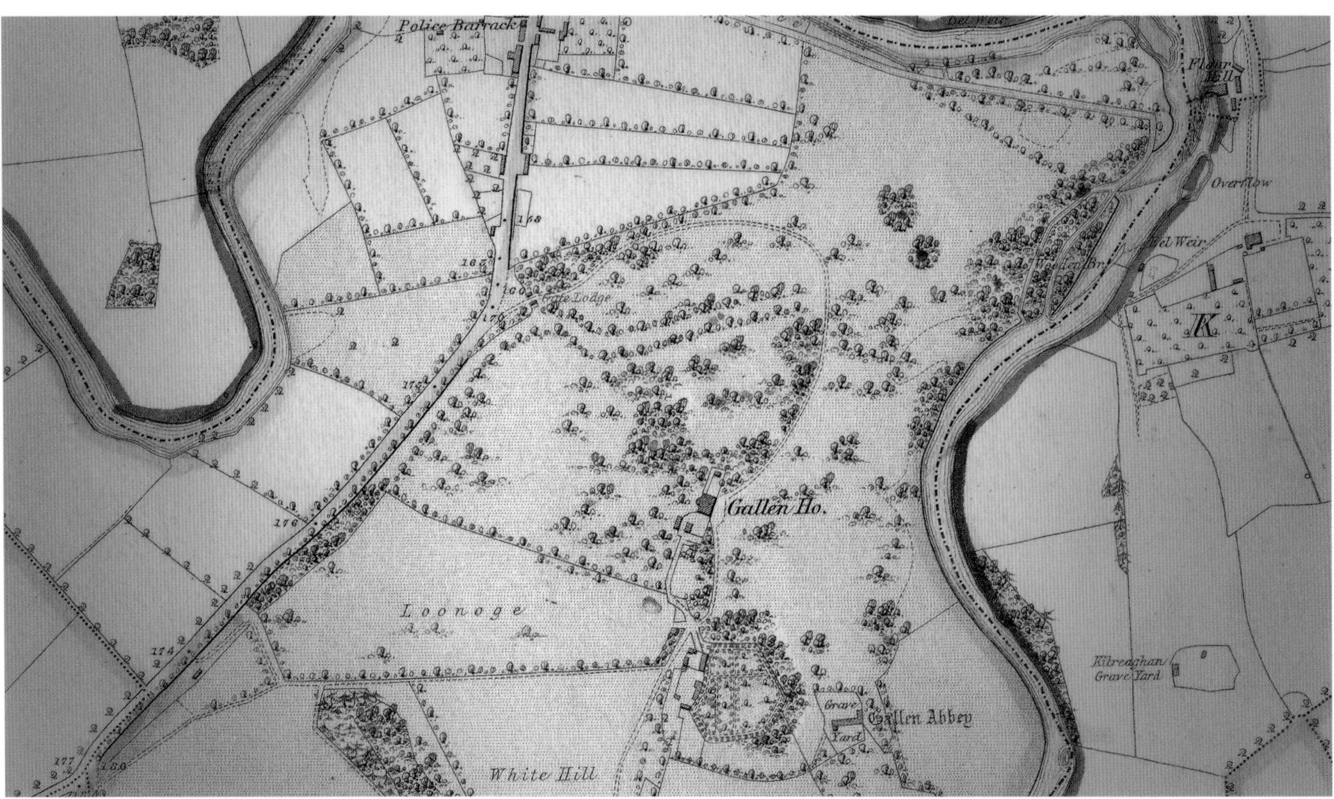

Crosses of Faith

The early monks were surrounded by an abundance of crosses in their monastic landscape. The ever-present crosses came to symbolise the way that Christ was present everywhere, as shown in this monastic poem written between the tenth and eleventh centuries.

Christ's Cross

Christ's cross to accompany me before me. Christ's
Cross to accompany me behind me. Christ's cross to
Meet every difficulty both on hollow and hill. . . .

Christ's cross up to broad Heaven. Christ's cross
down to earth. Let no evil or hurt come to my body or my soul.[23]

Excavations at Gallen in 1934-5

Excavation of the 'low grassy mound' noted by Petrie did indeed reveal the original site of Gallen monastery. Today, the monastic site at Gallen has two parts. One contains the ruins of the medieval abbey and its graveyard. About 200 metres away, in front of the nineteenth-century convent on the original site of Gallen monastery, stand the excavated remains of a church built in the early Middle Ages.

This long rectangular church was revealed during an excavation of the mound by T.D. Kendrick in 1934-35. The church had been built on top of the cemetery of the early Christian monks and some of their grave slabs were used in building its walls. Over twenty burials were also discovered in the church's interior. The overall pattern of burials suggests that the present church was built on the site of an earlier church that was contemporary with the monk's cemetery.

Today a newly built wall at the western end of the church displays a selection from more than two hundred early Christian cross slabs, most of which were found during excavation of the site. Dating from between the eighth and tenth centuries, these grave markers show 'an originality of design unequalled by those of any other site' in Ireland.[10] Several of these designs are also found in the North of England and Scotland, indicating that the monastery truly lived up to its name: 'Monastery of the Britons.'

The excavation also uncovered evidence of fire damage to the church building. In addition, the archaeologists discovered the remains of a coat of iron mail belonging to a medieval knight. The possibility that he met an untimely death in this church would certainly fit in with many violent accounts of the church at Gallen recorded in the *Annals*.

About 20 metres (nearly 23 yards) to the southwest of the building, Kendrick uncovered the bullaun stone that now stands in the centre of the church. He suggested that iron ore may have been crushed on this stone, forming the deep circular hollow within it.

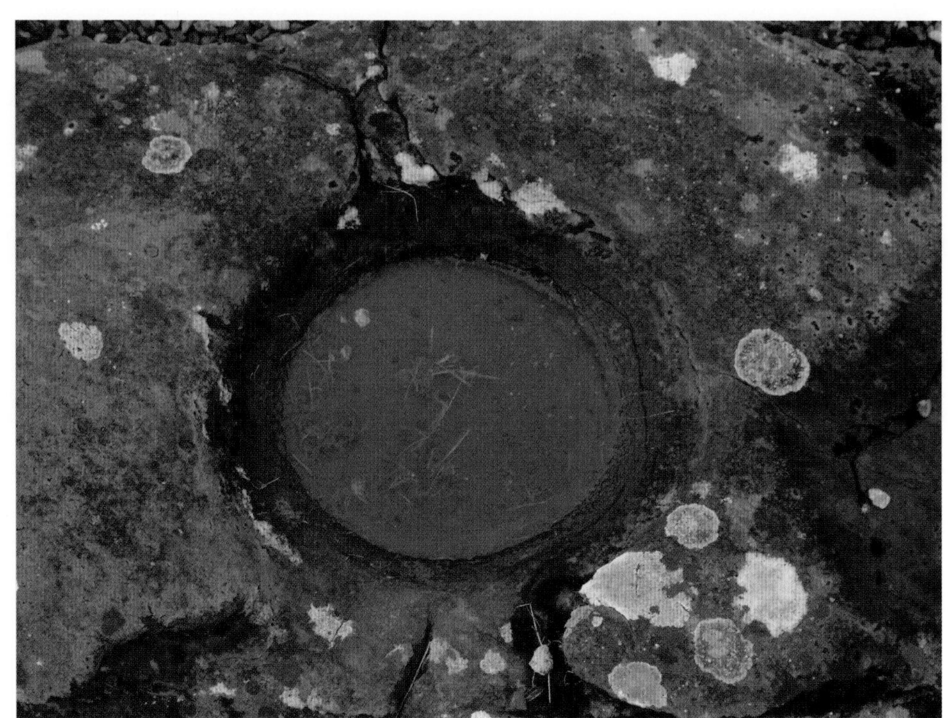

This headstone of blacksmith Thomas O'Connor (died 1799) is carved with an anvil, hammer, bellows and other tools of his trade. Metalworking at Gallen can be traced back to the early Christian period.

Symbols of Faith

After the excavations, some of the cross slabs were put on display at Gallen. The rest were moved to the National Museum of Ireland.

Originally, many of the cross slabs would have covered the graves of monks. Ornamentation on both sides of some slabs suggests that they stood upright and may have marked the graves of important men. Another possibility is that they were used in outdoor worship. And finally, an intriguing theory suggests that these slabs were commissioned by pilgrims who wished to commemorate their visits to the monastery.[11] Fulfilling these commissions would have provided income for the monastery.

Inscriptions on some of the cross slabs invoke the reader to pray for the soul of the named monk. Biblical scenes on other slabs may have been used to teach the scriptures to monks and to lay people.

The cross slabs display an extraordinary variety of Christian symbols. To understand what these symbols mean, it is necessary to examine their origins and the beliefs associated with them.

The veneration of the Cross and its adoption as a universal symbol of Christianity is a lasting legacy of the six Syrian popes, who ruled between the seventh and eighth centuries.[12] The Syrians used the cross as the main symbol of their faith so much that one commentator described them as a people who 'adore the vile wood of the Cross and you make this sign on your foreheads and you engrave it on the doors of your houses.'[13]

By the time that most of the Gallen cross slabs were carved (700-1000), monastic cemeteries would have been filled with cross after cross made from stone, wood and metal,[14] much like a twentieth-century military cemetery. The use of wooden crosses to mark burials is vividly captured in the *Annals of the Four Masters* in 871, when the body of Dunadhach, Lord of Cinel Cairbre Mor, is described as 'interred under hazel crosses at Druim Cliabh (Drumcliffe, County Sligo).'

Today the wooden and metal crosses have rotted away. Only the stone cross slabs survive.

At Gallen, the most common cross slab decoration is the ringed cross, known today as the 'Celtic Cross.'[15] Some of these ringed crosses have circles at the points where the arms intersect.

As well as being very common in Ireland, this type of design is widely found in the parts of England and Scotland that contained Irish monasteries, including Pictland (east Scotland) and Northumbria. The presence of this design at Gallen may indicate that its monks travelled from monastery to monastery.

The design is also found at the nearby monastery of Clonmacnoise, which may have inspired its use here.

The inscription of this interesting slab, with its decorated cross, reads: 'OR DO BRALIN' ('A Prayer for Bralin'). The slab probably covered the grave of a monk by that name.

This cross-inscribed slab is very similar to those found at Clonmacnoise, which from the ninth century onwards ruled a federation of monasteries that probably included Gallen. Dates for this type of slab range from ninth to tenth century.

Several broken pieces of a circular stone may once have been part of a tomb-shrine containing the bones of Canoc, the founding saint of Gallen.[16] To legitimise their foundation and create a link between Canoc and their homeland, it is possible that the monks gathered up the bones of St Canoc and re-interred them here.

At the monasteries, monks who worked on illuminated manuscripts were probably influenced by the designers of cross slabs, and vice-versa. This combination of an intricate interlaced cross within a circular slab is very similar to the circular discs containing crosses pictured in the *Book of Durrow*, folio 3v.[17]

Unearthed in 1907, this rectangular pillar appears to be the shaft of an upright cross. It features three decorated panels. The top panel contains a beautifully executed interlaced cross; trumpet-like spirals fill its four corners. In the middle panel, two horse-like animals, their tails interlaced, confront each other. The lowest panel is decorated with a Celtic fret pattern, with an unidentified animal at its centre.

The top of the shaft has a tenon, or tongue of stone, designed to fit into the mortise (hole) of another piece. Could this tenon have been intended to support the head of a cross?

Some commentators have suggested that this was an upright cross slab that marked the grave of the founding saint of the monastery.[18] The graves of the founding saints of some other monasteries were marked with two slabs, one covering the grave and the second upright.[19] Usually these important graves are located near the main churches of the monasteries.[20]

The symbols on this slab bear a strong resemblance to decoration on British crosses, particularly those from Pictland and Dál Riata in Scotland.[21] It is tempting to suggest that this slab may have been carved by the British monks who re-founded the monastery after it was burned in 820.

One intriguing cross slab is decorated with an incised ringed cross, flanked on either side by two smaller ringed crosses. This obviously depicts the scene at Calvary, in which the central cross of Jesus was flanked by those of the good and bad thief. This Cross of Thieves suggests that the slabs not only marked the graves of monks but also, like high crosses, illustrated stories from the Bible.

The ringed crosses may represent wooden crosses in which the arms were held in place by a supporting ring.

Eight cross slabs are decorated with a symbol that has been called the 'cross of arcs,' the 'marigold pattern' or the 'six-pointed star.' It may originally have been called the 'star of creation,' because each point could be seen to symbolise one of the six days of creation.

The symbol of the six-pointed star enclosed in a circle is commonly found in the Eastern Church, particularly in Syria. In the Eastern World the circle represented the sky or the heavens. This Christian symbol was much used in Byzantine Syria and may have been adopted by the Western Church in the seventh and eighth centuries, a time when it was deeply influenced by a series of Syrian popes.[22]

Throughout Syria the door lintels of the Christians were decorated with the pointed star within a circle. A similar lintel uncovered at Gallen may have come from the doorway of an early stone church.

On the cross slabs at Gallen, the six-pointed star is contained within a double or treble-lined circle; the latter may symbolise the Holy Trinity.

A sandstone slab offers an insight into the monks' belief in the power of prayer. Superimposed on a ringed cross is the extraordinary carving of a coiled, four-headed serpent. Its body wraps around the central boss of the cross and each of its mouths extends out into the arms of the cross, biting the heads of four humans.

The serpent probably represents Evil, while the four humans may symbolise the four evangelists, representing Good. The lowest figure stands upright with his hands held up and outwards, which may be the Orans position, a traditional prayer stance.

On this cross slab, the ringed cross represents the Crucifixion. The message of the slab may be that, by invoking the power of God through prayer, the monk will defeat Evil just as Christ did, through his death on the Cross.

THE CHURCH ON THE LONG RIDGE

Killeigh—Cill Aichidh—Church of the Field

Although St Sinchell was noted for his piety, in time the monastery at Killeigh—like those in the rest of Ireland—gained quite a different reputation.

A monk named Sinchell, who is said to be the first convert of St Patrick, founded a monastery in the lands of the Uí Failge during the sixth century. The place became known as Cill Achaid Dromafoda, meaning 'the Church in the Field of the Long Ridge.' This name was shortened to Cill Achaidh, which was later anglicised to Killeigh.

Sinchell was the son of Kennfinnain, grandson of Inchad, or Finchada, of the royal blood of Leinster.[1] His connection to the kingship of Leinster would have elevated the status of the monastery at Killeigh, which was located in this province.

The *Annals of the Four Masters* record the death of Sinchell in 548 at the age of 330 years. About the time of his death, the *Martyrology of Donegal* proclaims:

The men of heaven, the men of earth,
A surrounding host,
Thought that the day of judgment
Was the Death of Seancheall.
There came not, there will not come from Adam,
One more austere, more strict in piety;
There came not, there will not come, all say it,
Another Saint more welcome to the men of heaven.[2]

Today, just outside the village of Killeigh, a holy well and rag tree are dedicated to St Sinchell. His feastday is celebrated on 26 March.

In 799, the *Litany of St Aengus Céile Dé* extols the monastery at Killeigh by offering a list of its clerics, some from as far away as Armenia.[3] This list was copied from a manuscript in the archives of St Isidore's in Rome. The manuscript also contains 'The Pious Rules and Practices of the School of Senchil,'[4] which describes thirty-eight rules and practices of the monastery at Killeigh. According to the rules, offering Mass and hearing confession were two of the most important functions within the monastery.

In 800, the *Annals* record the burning of the monastery's new oratory, which was probably a wooden church. Another reference indicates that there was a scriptorium at Killeigh, for in 869 the *Annals of the Four Masters* record the death of 'Dubhthach, Abbot of Cill Achaidh, scribe, anchorite, and bishop.'

The region around the monastery was a frequent target of rival kings when they were raiding the lands of the Uí Failge. The *Annals of the Four Masters* record that in 937: 'The men of Munster, under Ceallachan, King of Munster, who had the foreigners [Vikings] along with him, plundered the churches of Cluain-eidhneach [Clonenagh, County Laois] and Cill-achaidh [Killeigh], and the territory of Meath.'

Another reference from the eleventh century reports: ' . . . the men of Teathbha [South Longford], of Muintir-Gearadhain [North Longford], and of the Cairbre-men, came upon a plundering excursion into Ui-Failghe; and they arrived at the Termon of Cill-achaidh.'[5]

THE MONASTIC ENCLOSURE AT KILLEIGH

The village of Killeigh probably originated as a town developed by monks of Sinchell's foundation. It sits in the middle of a large monastic enclosure encompassing 30 acres of land, which is bisected by the main Tullamore-Portlaoise road. Within the enclosure lie the ruins of an Augustinian priory, a Franciscan friary and an Augustinian nunnery.

The present Church of Ireland building incorporates the west end of the thirteenth-century Franciscan friary, which, in turn, may have been built on the site of the earlier monastic church. A castle and a mill once stood in the fields to the west of the church; the mill was powered by a stream flowing through the centre of the monastic enclosure.

The two earthen banks that made up the enclosure would have served as the walls of the monastic town. Although this boundary may date from the early Christian period, it could also have been created during the late twelfth century when the monastery adopted the Rule of St Augustine. A final scenario is that the monks first enclosed their monastery between the sixth and ninth centuries and then this boundary was re-built in the twelfth or thirteenth centuries.

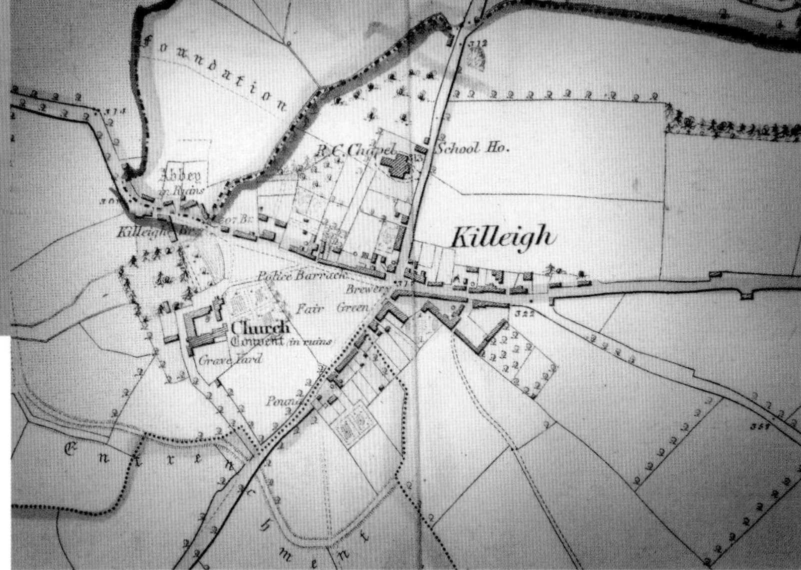

The Augustinian Priory

Although St Sinchell was noted for his piety, in time the monastery at Killeigh— like those in the rest of Ireland— gained quite a different reputation. Several letters from the eleventh and twelfth centuries describe practices that the Roman church looked upon with dismay.

A letter written in 1074 by Lanfranc, Archbishop of Canterbury, to Turlough O'Brien, King of Munster, describes the 'un-Christian state' of the church in Ireland. According to the archbishop, married couples would part and then live, as if married, with other partners. Children were baptised without consecrated chrism (sacred oil). And finally bishops were ordained without the sanction of the official church, and sometimes went on to confer holy orders in exchange for money.[6]

To combat this state of affairs, several synods were held by the Irish church, including the Council of Cashel in 1101 and the Synod of Rathbreasail in 1111. The latter aimed to establish a diocesan structure, to correct abusive conduct of both clergy and laymen and to free the church from the influence of the nobility who constituted its patrons.[7]

However, there was little change in the daily life of the church until Malachy, a monk from Armagh, made reform of the Irish church his primary mission.

On a visit to France, Malachy had been deeply impressed by the Rule of St Augustine, which he saw being practised at the monastery of Arrouaise, near Arras. The Rule requires adherence to strict personal poverty, celibacy and obedience,[8] none of which were qualities associated with the practices of the Irish church at that time.

On his return to Ireland, Malachy spearheaded a massive reform of the church. A Frenchman, St Bernard of Clairvaux, described the work of Malachy amongst the Irish:

> *Never before had he known the like, in whatever depth of barbarism; never had he found men so shameless in their morals, so wild in their rites, so impious in their faith, so barbarous in their laws, so stubborn in discipline, so unclean in their life.*
>
> *They were Christians in name, in fact they were pagans. They did not give first-fruits or tithes; they did not enter on lawful marriage, they made no confessions; nowhere was there to be found any who might either seek or impose penance. Ministers of the altar were few indeed; but what need was there of more when even the few lived idle lives among the laity? They had no prospect of fruitful work in their office among so wicked a people. In the churches was heard neither the voice of a preacher nor of a singer.*[9]

Another account details Malachy's reforms:

> *Barbarous laws disappeared, Roman laws were introduced; everywhere ecclesiastical customs were received and the contrary rejected; churches were rebuilt and a clergy appointed to them; the sacraments were duly solemnised, and confessions were made; the people came to the church, and those who were living in concubinage were united in lawful wedlock.*[10]

By the time of Malachy's death in 1148, most Irish monasteries had adopted the Rule of St Augustine. After adopting the Rule, the monastery at Killeigh became known as the Priory of the Holy Cross of Canons Regular of St Augustine.

As monks, the lives of the men at Killeigh had been devoted to their personal worship of God; they were not required to take an interest in the spiritual welfare of the lay community. However, once they became Augustinian canons regular, they were compelled to perform a pastoral role.

A canon regular was required to live in the community, where he would sing the praises of God by the daily recitation of the Divine Office in choir. At the same time, he had to preach and teach the Word of God to the lay people, administer the sacraments, offer hospitality to pilgrims and travellers, and tend to the sick.

Throughout the rest of the Middle Ages, the fortunes of the monastery at Killeigh would be inextricably linked to two families: the O'Conors, who were Lords of Uí Failge, and the O'Dempseys, the Lords of Clanmaliere.

The O'Conors were patrons of the monastery, while the O'Dempseys supplied some of its abbots. At times, this situation caused conflict. In 1162 the *Annals of the Four Masters* record that 'The Ui-Dimasaigh [O'Dempseys], i.e. Ceallach, Cubrogha, and Cuilen, were slain by Maelseachlainn Ua Conchobhair [O'Conor], lord of Ui-Failghe, in the middle of Cill-achaidh [Killeigh].'

By 1163 the O'Dempseys appear to have secured the abbotship, as the *Annals* record the death of Gillabrighte Ua-Dimusaigh [O'Dempsey], successor to the two Senchills.[11]

In the early thirteenth century, the Anglo-Norman settlers of this region probably constructed a building for the Augustinian priors on the outskirts of the monastic town of Killeigh. However, allegiance to the Anglo-Normans would ultimately prove to be the priory's downfall. As the power of its Anglo-Norman patrons waned, so too did the fortunes of the priory. At the same time there was a revival in the power of the local Gaelic aristocracy— and, in particular, the O'Conors of Uí Failge— who now endowed their wealth on a new religious foundation located in the heart of the monastic enclosure.

The Nunnery

The nunnery at Killeigh is just one of the hundreds of nunneries established throughout western Europe between 1080 and 1220.[23] The first nunnery in Ireland, which was established around 1144 at Clonard in present-day County Meath, was associated with the reform of the church by St Malachy. Most subsequent Irish nunneries were also Augustinian houses. They were usually located close to Augustinian monasteries, such as the one at Killeigh.

Originally the nunnery was under the patronage of the Warren family, Anglo-Normans who arrived in this region around 1200-1220.

Although geographically close to the monastery, the nunnery at Killeigh was in its own world, contained within its own enclosure. It has been suggested that some time after 1195 the community of nuns at Durrow monastery moved to Killeigh.[24]

During the Gaelic revival of the 1400s, the nunnery became a place of retreat for the widows and women of the Irish aristocracy, especially the O'Conors. In 1447, the *Annals of the Four Masters* record that:

> *Finola, the daughter of Calvagh O'Conor Faly, and of Margaret, daughter of O'Carroll, who had been first married to O'Donnell, and afterwards to Hugh Boy O'Neill, the most beautiful and stately, the most renowned and illustrious woman of her time in all Ireland, her own mother only excepted, retired from this transitory world, to prepare for life eternal, and assumed the yoke of piety and devotion, in the monastery of Cill-achaidh [Killeigh].*

The nunnery perished as a result of the Dissolution of the Monasteries by Henry VIII. By 1550, Walter Cowley described its ruins as no more than the 'walls where some time was a chapel wast.'[25] No trace remains of the nunnery, which was located where the post office stands today.

THE FRANCISCAN FRIARY

Around 1293, the O'Conors helped establish a new religious order, the Franciscan Minors, at Killeigh. A Franciscan friary was built on or near the centre of the early Christian monastery, thus linking it to both the first Christian foundation in the area and the original Gaelic patrons.

The friary at Killeigh was one of thirty Franciscan foundations established in Ireland by 1316. Most were patronised by the Anglo-Normans who had arrived in Ireland a hundred years earlier. However, a few Franciscan foundations, including the one at Killeigh, received patronage of the Gaelic lords.

Initially the friars were dependent on the generosity of their supporters and of the people in the towns where they preached. Because they were a mendicant order— a term derived from the Latin word *mendicare,* which means 'to beg' — the friars were forbidden from holding property. They had to survive on the offerings they received from their preaching and other work amongst the community.[12]

During the initial period of Christianity in Ireland, monks had been focused on their personal worship of God. With the introduction of the Rule of St Augustine, monks became canon regulars compelled to include a pastoral role as part of their vocation. The friars took this trend one step further: they were solely focused upon work in the community.

As followers of St Francis of Assisi, their mission was to preach to the people. In 1219 Pope Honorius III described them as 'sowers of the seed of the Word of God.'[13] Another writer from the thirteenth century describes the friars as:

> *. . . a sect of preachers called Minorites who filled the earth, dwelling in the cities and towns, by tens and sevens, possessing no property at all, living according to the Gospel, making a great show of the greatest poverty, walking with naked feet and setting a great example of humility for all classes.... No sort of food in their possession was kept for the morrow's use that the poverty of spirit which reigned in their minds might show itself to all in their dress and actions.*[14]

. . . friars are not pastors of the true flock but madmen, thieves and wolves.

Unlike monks, who spent their lives within a particular monastery, the Franciscan friars were a travelling brotherhood not tied to any specific geographical location. They moved from place to place, preaching in the urban churches established by their brotherhood. These churches, which were open to the public, were completely independent of the parish church system.

Because the Franciscans were so popular, the parochial clergy often resented them. They were concerned that friars would assume some of their tasks and revenues. In the fourteenth century, theologian John Whitehead commented that 'Friars asking the privilege of hearing confessions . . . are in mortal sin by so asking, and a Pope granting such privileges is also in mortal sin and excommunicated; friars are not pastors of the true flock but madmen, thieves and wolves.'[15]

Despite such opposition, in Killeigh the friary thrived, becoming a place of retreat for Gaelic leaders nearing the end of their lives, as well as a burial place for their families. In 1421, the *Annals of the Four Masters* record:

> *O'Conor (Murrough) then returned home; but he was attacked by a dangerous disease, whereupon he retired among the friars in the monastery of Killeigh, and took the habit of a friar; but before his death he appointed his own kinsman, Dermot O'Conor, in his place. O'Conor was only a month among the friars, when he died, after a well-spent life.*

Apparently, as this Irish warlord neared death he retired to the monastery built by his family, possibly to seek forgiveness from God for the deeds of his life. Before dying, he elected a member of his family to serve as abbot, thus ensuring that the O'Conors would continue to have an administrative role in the friary.

Several other members of the O'Conor family were buried within the Franciscan friary during the fifteenth century. They were joined by family members of their sometime rivals, the O'Dempseys of Clanmaliere, who were still being buried in the graveyard of Killeigh friary as late as 1690.[16]

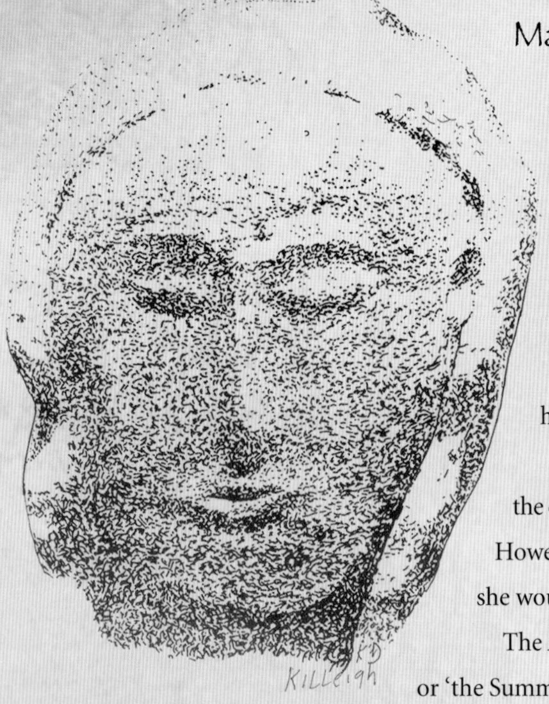

Margaret O'Carroll

Margaret O'Conor was described as the 'best woman of her time.' She was the daughter of Tadhg O'Carroll, ruler of Éile. Her marriage to Calvagh O'Conor, ruler of Uí Failge, was probably the result of a political alliance between the territories of Éile and Uí Failge. Famous for his military prowess, Calvagh was known as a 'Warlike Prince.'[26] Upon his death in 1458 the *Annals of the Four Masters* recorded that he had 'won more wealth from his English and Irish enemies than any other lord in Leinster.'

Throughout her life, Margaret was a patron of the arts and of the church, a builder of infrastructure and a skilled political negotiator. However, it was in a year of famine that she earned the name for which she would be known: 'Margaret, the hospitable O'Carroll.'[27]

The *Annals of Loch Cé* referred to this time as 'the summer of death' or 'the Summer of the quick acquaintance.' According to the *Annals of the Four Masters* of 1433: 'There was a famine in the Summer of this year, called, for a very long time afterwards, Samhra na mear-aithne, because no one used to recognise friend or relative, in consequence of the greatness of the famine.'

During that terrible year, Margaret hosted two great assemblies to provide food for the sick and starving people of Ireland. The festival at Killeigh was held on 26 March, Feastday of St Sinchell, patron saint of the monastery. It acted as a gathering not only for the educated people of Ireland and Scotland, but also for the poor people and the mendicant religious orders. Over 2700 people were listed in attendance.

The account below offers an insight into how the Irish nobility were obligated to provide help during times of distress, as well as to patronise the arts.

> *. . . it is an ungratious and unglorious year to all the learned of Ireland, both philosophers, poets, guests, strangers, religious persons, souldiers, mendicant or poore orders, and to all manner and sorts of the poor in Ireland. It is she [Margaret] that twice in one year proclaimed to and commonly invited (in the dark dayes of the yeare, to wit, on the feast day of Dá Sinchell, in Killachy[Killeigh]), all persons, both Irish and Scottish, to two general feasts of bestowing both meate and moneyes, with all manner of gifts, whereunto gathered to receive gifts the number of two thousand and seven hundred persons, besides gamesters and poor men, as it was recorded in a roll to that purpose, and that accompt was made thus, The cheife kins of each family of the Learned Irish was by Gilla-nanoemhe MacEgan's hand, the chief Judge to O'Connor, written in the roll, and his adherents and kinsmen, so that the aforesaid number 2,700 was listed in that roll with the Arts of Dan, or poetry, musick and antiquitie.*[28]

The *Annals* go on to describe Margaret, in a golden dress, as she supervised the feasting from the roof of her abbey:

> *And Margarett, on the garrots [attic-rooms] of the greate churche of Da Sinchell, clad in cloath of gould, her dearest friends about her, her clergy and judges too, Calvagh himself on horseback, by the churches outward side, to the end that all things might be done orderly, and each one served successively. And first of all she gave two chalices of gould [gold] as offerings that day on the Altar of God Almighty, and she also caused to nurse or foster two young orphans. But so it was. We never saw nor heard neither the like of that day, nor comparable to its glory and solace.*[29]

Two years later, Margaret went on a gruelling, four-month-long pilgrimage to the shrine of St James at Compostella in northwestern Spain.[30] She was accompanied by several members of the Gaelic aristocracy.

Margaret was an independent person who acted decisively, often without her husband's consent. The same year as her pilgrimage, she entered into negotiations with the English and secured the release of important hostages of the Irish aristocracy. She 'went to Bealathatrim [Trim Castle], and gave all the English prisoners for MacGeoghegan's son, and for the sons of Art, and that unadvised by Calvagh, and she brought them home.'[31]

She was also responsible for the construction of several bridges and roads, which resulted in improved communications throughout her territory. This show of civic spirit may be why historians have referred to her as 'the darling of all the Leinster people.'[32] In 1451, the *Annals of Connacht* record that 'she was the only woman that has made most of preparing high-ways and erecting bridges, churches, and mass-books, and all manner of things profitable to serve God and her soul and not that only, but while the world stands, her very many gifts to the Irish and Scottish Nations shall never be numbered.'

Margaret died in 1451. The reference to her death may suggest that she suffered from breast cancer. The *Annals of Connacht* state: 'Cursed be that sore in her breast that killed Margarett.'

In 1830 workmen who were pulling down part of the Franciscan friary discovered an upright female skeleton wearing a small iron cross of Spanish style. This may very well have been the body of Margaret O'Carroll, wearing a keepsake from her pilgrimage to Santiago de Compostela.

In a fifteenth-century eulogy entitled 'On a Warlike Prince,' court poet Sethfin Mór described Margaret with these words:

> *Margarets fame has established her protection; palm-branch who breaketh not her words, a lady who has not learned to refuse; darling of the blood of earls; flowing tresses whose fosterer is Jesus; heart bountiful and pious. To drink feasts she never forsook her prayers—a woman who lives by rule. She protects herself against our art, her words are on our side.*[33]

All of the religious foundations at Killeigh—the priory, the friary and the nunnery—went into serious decline after the Dissolution of the Monasteries by Henry VIII. In 1537 '. . . the Deputy, Lord Grey, plundered the Church of Killeigh and carried away a pair of organs and other articles fitted for the King's College, and as much glass as sufficed for the glazing of the College of Maynooth.'[17]

At the time the monastery was dissolved, it contained extensive lands and its abbot was also entitled to the revenues generated from at least five chapels within the region. An Inquisition taken in 1569 found that:

> *Phelim O'Connor, the last Abbot, was seized of the Abbey, containing half an acre of land, surrounded by a stone wall; also, an orchard and three gardens, with three messuages [dwellings], 124 acres of arable land, three of meadow, or moor, thirty-four of pasture, and three of wood and under-wood, in Fentyre and Killeigh; a small plot of ground in the town of Kylleigh, whereon was formerly a mill with a water-course; three messuages and six cottages in Dunfeigh; 20 acres of arable land, called Channon's land and seven acres of pasture and moor in Dunfeigh aforesaid; annual value of each acre, besides reprises, two pence halfpenny.*[18]

By 1576 the monastery property was included in a land grant to an English settler named John Lee. The grant consisted of 'three messuages, six cottages, twenty acres of arable land and seven of pasture, in the town of Donfeigh, in this county, with the tithes, etc., were granted for ever, in capite, to John Lee, at the yearly rent of 45s. 6d.'[19] An Act of Settlement dated 7 February 1679 confirms the land grant to Francis Lye (son of John Lee), of Rathbride, Esq. The lands were specified as: 'the scite, circuit, and precinct of the late monastery or priory house of ye Order of ye Holy Crosse of Killeigh. . . .'[20]

Today there is doubt over the exact location of the priory; fragments of a wall beside the community hall are believed to be the only remains of what Walter Cowley, in his *Survey of Offaly* in 1550, described as 'the Priorie of Chanons of Fyntyre.'[21]

The best surviving information on the friary buildings comes from a drawing by Rosemary Tarleton, dated 1896. It shows the friary as a long rectangular church with a south transept. A battlemented bell-tower stands over the centre of the church. To the north, there is a chapter house and a rectangular cloister enclosing a well. Off the cloister, a range of buildings probably served as dormitories for the friars.

The west end of the friary church is now incorporated into a Church of Ireland building, which was constructed in 1830. The remains of the friary's cloister, dormitory and chapter house are still used as part of a working farm and guesthouse, appropriately named 'Abbey Farm.'

Not much of the monastic town of Killeigh survives. However, as one looks at the houses that front on to the main road of the village, it is best to remember the words of the Rev. James Kinsella (a priest in Killeigh between 1819-1859):

The walls have been pulled down at different periods for building about the village. To the present day portions of cut stone, appearing to be the bases and capitals of columns, etc., are to be seen about the place. Many of these have been taken away to ornament the houses of the poor; some of the more opulent have worked them into their buildings. When first I took notice of these venerable ruins, I could not imagine that the same amount of destruction could have been effected in a century![22]

THE CHURCH OF THE ILLUMINATOR

Birr — Biorra — Land of Springs

Brendan's ability to foresee the future caused others to refer to him as the 'prophet of Ireland.'

Around the middle of the sixth century, a monk named Brendan founded a monastery on the banks of the Camcor River.

Brendan's monastery was located in the ancient kingdom of Munster, in the territory of Éile. Its frontier location, near the borders of the kingdoms of Meath, Leinster and Connaught, made it an ideal place for meetings between rival kings and churchmen. Many important royal assemblies and church synods were held at the monastery.

During its first three centuries, the monastery expanded and became an important religious foundation. Testimony to its wealth was the production, in the late eighth or early ninth century, of the illuminated manuscript known as the *Gospels of Mac Regol.*

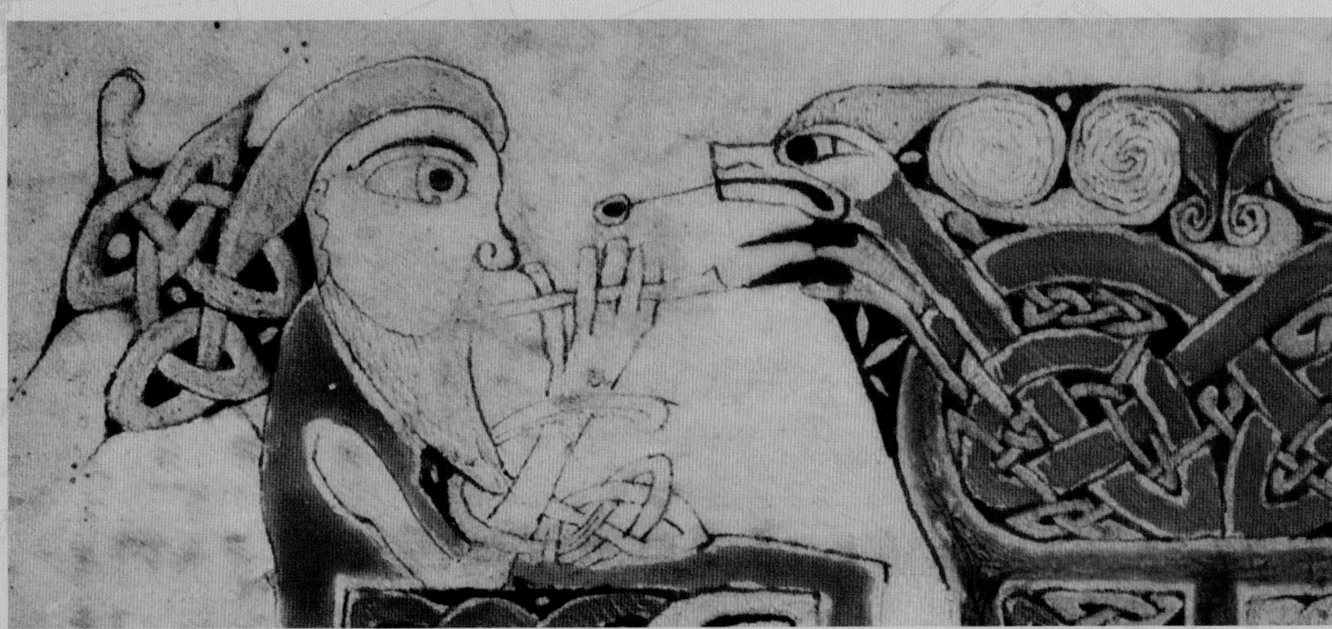

The Law of the Innocents

In the year 697, a meeting was convened at the monastery of Birr by Adomnán, the ninth abbot of Iona.[1] Attendees passed the Law of the Innocents, which provided for protection of the human being and assigned heavy penalties for those who caused death or inflicted injury on women and children. This law was also known as the Cáin Adomnáin. The Irish word *cáin* refers to a contract that not only regulates a person's behaviour, but also sets out the penalties for those failing to adhere to such regulations.

The Law of the Innocents allowed Adomnán to group women with clerics and youths, listing them all as non-combatants and exempting them from military service under their ruling kings.[2] This law was an attempt to ensure that women and young children would not be exposed to the horrors of battle.

The law also addressed other offences, including the injury or murder of clerics or boys, and damage to church property.

Ninety-one of the most important religious and secular figures in seventh-century Ireland, Scotland and northern Britain— all of whom either attended or sent their representatives to the meeting at the monastery at Birr— guaranteed the Law of the Innocents. It was also guaranteed by Coeddi, Bishop of Iona; Curetán, Bishop of Rosemarkie in Scotland; and by Uuictberct, an English cleric living in Clonmelsh, in present-day County Carlow.

In addition, attendees addressed an important issue that had brought the Celtic church into conflict with Rome: the proper date for the celebration of Easter. At this meeting, Fland of Febail, Bishop of Armagh, accepted the Roman date. His decision led the churches in the northern half of Ireland to adopt the Roman proposal.

An Angel Sends Adomnán to Ireland

Prior to passage of the Law of the Innocents '... the finest of women used ... to proceed to battle and battlefield, division and encampment, killing and slaughter,'[11] according to Adomnán. Because the law freed women from the obligation to serve in war, Adomnán became known as 'the liberator of women of the Gael.'[12]

According to legend, the release of women from military service was the result of divine intervention. An angel told Adomnán to go to Ireland and pass a law so that:

> *... women be not killed in any manner by man, whether through slaughter or any other death, either by poison or in water or in fire or by any beast or in a pit or by dogs, except [they die in childbirth] in lawful bed.*
>
> *You shall establish a law in Ireland and Britain for the sake of the mother of each one, because the mother has borne each one, and for the sake of Mary, the mother of Jesus Christ. And whoever kills a woman shall be condemned to a twofold punishment, that is, before death, his right hand and his left foot shall be cut off and after that he shall die and his kin shall pay seven cumals [value of three cows] and [the price] of seven years penance. For great is the sin when anyone kills the one who is mother, and sister to Christ's mother, and mother of Christ.*[13]

Brendan, Friend of Colum Cille

Brendan was one of the 'Twelve Apostles of Erin,' a name given to twelve early church leaders, all of whom were educated around 520 by St Finnian at his renowned monastic school at Clonard, in present-day County Meath. Four of these monks founded monasteries in Offaly: St Brendan of Birr, St Ciarán of Clonmacnoise, St Colum Cille of Durrow and St Ciarán (the Elder) of Seirkieran.

Brendan's ability to foresee the future caused others to refer to him as the 'prophet of Ireland.' He remained a close friend of Colum Cille, even after that saint was excommunicated in 561.

When Colum Cille was expelled from Ireland, he sent a messenger to ask Brendan where he should set up his monastery. Brendan looked up to the heavens, and then ordered that the ground be dug up where the messenger had stood. On that spot, the monks discovered a stone, which Brendan studied intently. On the stone, he discovered the shape of the letter 'Í.'

'Report this to your master,' he told the messenger. 'Í, that is, Go into the island of Í [Iona], where you shall find increase of virtue, and from where many souls will go to heaven, and the place will have great honour.'[14]

In another legend, senior monks questioned Brendan's loyalty to Colum Cille. Brendan retorted:

> *If . . . you had seen what the Lord has this day thought fit to show to me regarding this his chosen one, whom you dishonour, you would never have excommunicated a person whom God not only doth not excommunicate, according to your unjust sentence, but even more and more highly esteemeth . . .*
>
> *I have seen . . . a most brilliant pillar wreathed with fiery tresses preceding this same man of God whom you treat with contempt; I have also seen holy angels accompanying him on his journey through the plain. Therefore I do not dare to slight him whom I see fore-ordained by God to be the leader of his people to life.*[15]

Swayed by Brendan's vision, the churchmen revoked Colum Cille's excommunication and treated him, once more, with reverence.

The link between the two saints continued until Brendan's death, which occurred on 29 November, sometime between 565 and 573. Although in Iona, Colum Cille saw the 'holy angels who came to meet the soul of St Brendan, the founder of Birr, at his passing away.'[16]

BRENDAN
PRAY FOR US

PRAY FOR THE VEN. ARCHDEACON THOMAS PHELAN
V.G. P.P. BIRR. WHO IED MAY 30.1903. R.I.P.

The Gospels of Mac Regol

The monastery at Birr reached the height of its power around the beginning of the ninth century. It was during this period that its abbot and scribe produced the extraordinary illuminated manuscript known as the *Gospels of Mac Regol.*

The manuscript, which is signed by the author, reads:

> *Mac Regol depin Cxit hoc evangelium, Quicum que legerit Et intellegerit istam narrationem orat pro Macreguil scriptori.*[3] (*'Mac Regol illuminated this gospel. Whoever will read and understand the narrative, pray for Mac Reguil scribe.'*)

The manuscript contains the four Gospels with illuminated portraits of Mark, Luke and John; the figure of Matthew has probably been lost over time.

When compared to other scribes of his era, Mac Regol was not an outstanding artist. Within the book, the looseness of the spirals has been described as 'painfully rough.'[4] However, Mac Regol's inability to draw certain features, such as the drapery of the evangelists, did not stop him from producing a wonderful display of colours and frames.

To Professor Etienne Rynne, the *Gospels of Mac Regol* is the best example of how an Irish scribe's disregard for law and order, along with his lack of discipline, allowed for the purest expression of his spirit:

> *. . . the illuminated pages are few but once seen are never forgotten. Red and yellow predominate, purple and green playing a lesser role. There is a self-confident, slap-dash effect about the whole work, which is about as rough-and-ready and unsophisticated as any 'primitive' artist of the nineteenth or twentieth century ever managed. Everything seems to be left to chance, the artist seemingly letting himself go, not quite knowing what is going to happen but with the confidence of someone fully certain that only a masterpiece could result.*[5]
>
> *. . . his wild, free-hand spirals, his utter lack of restraint, the inconsequential way in which his lovely lettering is thrown together on the illuminated pages, and the garish effect of the finished result. Mac Regol was a born though not highly skilled artist, an individualist, perhaps self-taught, and, furthermore, a real Celt, every inch an Irishman.*[6]

By the end of tenth century, the *Gospels of Mac Regol* had found its way to the English monastery of Harewood, on the borders of Northumbria and Mercia, where two monks called Farman and Owun added an interlinear Anglo-Saxon text to the original Latin. In time, the book became known as the *Rushworth Gospels.*[7] This important text is second only to the *Book of Lindisfarne* in the clues it contains to the origins of the earliest English writing.[8]

Today the *Gospels of Mac Regol* is housed in the Bodleian Library at the University of Oxford. A copy of this book is on display in the library in Birr.

Everything seems to be left to chance, the artist seemingly letting himself go, not quite knowing what is going to happen but with the confidence of someone fully certain that only a masterpiece could result.

lu cas

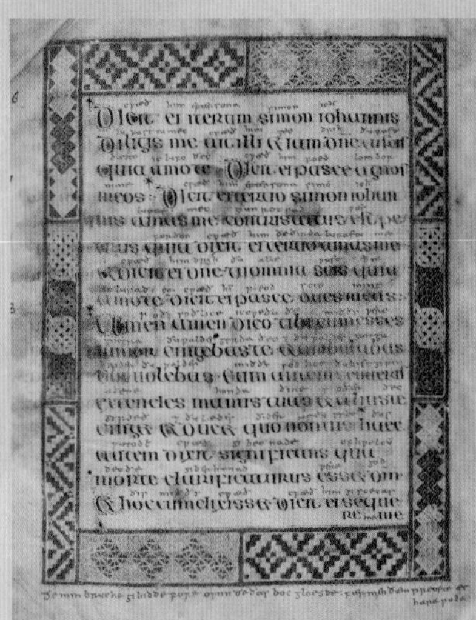

God's Word Made Text

According to the *Annals of the Four Masters,* books were among the most important things that St Patrick brought to Ireland; he left them behind at a church called Cell Fhine.

The written Gospels brought to Ireland by the first evangelists introduced the Latin alphabet to the Irish people. As these books were copied by Irish scribes (who were not native Latin speakers) a unique style emerged. Influences from Egypt, Syria and other far away places merged with the native Irish aesthetic.[17] This fusion of styles is exemplified in the illuminated manuscripts, in which the scribe combined picture, ornament and script to produce striking images.[18]

Scribes such as Mac Regol were often seen as having mystical powers. St Isidore of Seville compared the ink that flowed through the pen of a scribe to the blood that flowed from the pierced side of Christ to redeem all mankind. Giraldus Cambrensis ('Gerald of Wales') described illuminated manuscripts as 'works of angelic diligence.'[19]

A portrait in the *Gospels of Mac Regol* shows St Luke dipping his pen into an ink pot. This image symbolises the important evangelical role of the scribe in conveying the message of the Gospels through the illuminated pages.

Upon their completion, illuminated manuscripts became important relics of the monastery and were often attributed with supernatural powers.

The very difficulty in reading these heavily ornamented texts was seen as part of their mystery. The introductory pages of the *Gospels of Mac Regol* have been described as containing the 'grammar of illegibility.'[20] On each page ornamentation overwhelms the text. The fact that ornament is everywhere may symbolise that God is present everywhere and in everything.

The time-consuming process of deciphering each page was intended to lead the reader to a greater understanding of the Word of God. The interlace designs of these manuscripts have been described as 'a tool to focus reflection upon the multitude layers of meaning in the text, as a guide for conduct, life and salvation.'[21]

The function of this ornamental text has been beautifully described thus: 'the decorative veiling of the sacred text offers a metaphor of the art of spiritual reading to discern the hidden meaning within the literal letter of the four-fold Gospels.'[22]

Cap: 1.

From the ninth century onwards, the monasteries of the Midlands were attacked several times by the Vikings, more often by the Irish, and then by the English. During this period, the monastery at Birr went into decline, although it was host to a few more important meetings. In 851 the *Annals of the Four Masters* record an important 'royal meeting at Birra between Conchobhar, son of Donnchadh, King of Ireland, and Feidhlimidh, King of Munster.' The *Annals of Ulster* record the holding of 'The Synod of Birr' in 1174 at which West Meath was transferred to the See of Clonmacnoise.[9]

Soon, however, the monastery became little more than a pawn in battles in which one warring faction after another tried to assert its dominance over the region.

In 1213 the *Annals of the Four Masters* record that the 'English of Ireland [the Anglo-Normans] erected the castle of Kinnitty, the castle of Birr, and the castle of Durrow. The castle at Birr was constructed beside the monastery, because the church was the centre of politics and power.

The next year (1214), the *Annals of Loch Cé* record that Cormac, son of Art O'Maelsechlainn, King of Meath, 'went to the castle of Birr, and burned its bawn, and burned the entire church, and took all its food out of it, in order that the Foreigners of the castle should not get food in it.'

By the fifteenth century, the Gaelic rulers of Ireland had regained their power. The O'Carrolls, who were the Lords of Éile, built a new castle on top of or near the earlier timber castle. Known as 'Black Castle,' this stronghold was a symbol of their lordship in this region. During this time period, the O'Carrolls also had a great influence over the church at Birr. The priest of Birr was selected from the ranks of their family members.

In the sixteenth century both the castle and the church suffered when a dispute broke out among various O'Carrolls over who should be chief of their tribe. In 1532, the sons of John O'Carroll attacked 'the castle of Birr, and plundered the country out of it. The son of the parson O'Carroll was slain on the Green of Birr by Teige Caech, the son of O'Carroll.'[10]

The English crown seized the lands of the O'Carrolls during the seventeenth century and granted them to Laurence Parsons in 1620. Parsons replaced the Black Castle of the O'Carrolls with the castle that one sees at Birr today. The old monastic church became a place of worship for the new community of settlers.

Today the archaeological evidence shows that worship continued for 1500 years on the site of old St Brendan's Church. The monastery became the nucleus of the town of Birr. And today St Brendan's Well, which was possibly used by the monastic community, and then by the town, lies within the walls of Birr castle.

Old St Brendan's Church contains architecture from several time periods. The oldest part of the church dates from the thirteenth century, when the Anglo-Normans ruled Birr. The building was widened in the seventeenth century, probably during the time that the Parsons became the ruling family of this area.

In the nineteenth century a new Church of Ireland building was constructed at the end of Oxmantown Mall, and the old church was abandoned. Since then, the church and its graveyard have fallen into ruins.

As Birr expands beyond its historic boundaries, Brendan's monastery will continue to remain at its centre, forging a link between the modern town and its monastic past.

As Birr expands beyond its historic boundaries, Brendan's monastery will continue to remain at its centre, forging a link between the modern town and its monastic past.

CIARÁN'S SHINING CITY

Clonmacnoise—Cluain Mhic Nóis—Meadow of the Sons of Nós

. . . many souls shall leave this place to enter the kingdom of God.

When Ciarán arrived at Clonmacnoise he said 'Here will I live; for many souls shall leave this place to enter the kingdom of God, and this will be the place of my resurrection. . . .

A shinning and saintly city grew up in that place in honor of Saint Ciarán, and the name of the City was Clonmacnois.[1]

Many of the men and women who became the first saints of Ireland came from noble families; Ciarán was the son of a carpenter. The *Chronicon Scotorum* records that he was born in the year 512.

Various annals suggest that he was of the Latharna Molt tribe, a branch of the Dál nAraide in Ulster; others suggest that his father was from Connaught.[2] Little else is known about Ciarán's life before he entered the famous monastery and school of St Finnian at Clonard in present-day County Meath. One of his fellow students, Colum Cille, wrote of Ciarán:

Noble the youth who goes westward from us
Ciarán, the son of a carpenter;
Without envy, without pride, without contention,
Without jealousy, without satire.[3]

Temple Kieran

According to tradition, the little church known as Temple Kieran was the mortuary chapel of St Ciarán. Until the seventeenth century this building contained the relic known as the 'Hand of St Ciarán.' It may also have contained the Imleach Chiaráin ('the Bed of St Ciarán').

It is possible that this chapel was built after Ciarán's death, on the site of his cell. According to legend, the saint 'promised immediate entry into heaven to every soul that would die on the hide of St Ciarán's cow.' The opportunity to die on that relic became one of the main reasons for pilgrimage to Clonmacnoise, especially for kings on the threshold of death.

Even the soil around this small church was said to be soaked in miraculous powers. Describing the area around Temple Kieran, Caesar Otway, a nineteenth-century chaplain, wrote:

> *Beside it was a sort of cavity or hollow in the ground, as if some persons had lately been rooting to extract a badger or a fox: but here it was that the people, supposing St Kieran to be deposited, have rooted diligently for any particle of clay that could be found, in order to carry home that holy earth, steep it in water, and drink; and happy is the votary who is now able amongst the bones and stones to pick up what has the semblance of soil, in order to commit it to his stomach, as a means of grace, or as a sovereign remedy against diseases of all sorts.*[25]

As late as the seventeenth century Clonmacnoise remained the burial place of choice for some of Ireland's nobility. The *Annals of Loch Cé* record the death of Brian Óg, Lord of Magh-Luirg, Airtech and Tir-Tuathail, who died of dysentery in 1636. This ruler is described in the same annals as 'the best man of his age, and estate, and high lordship, that came of the Gaeidhel of the West of Europe in his own time. . . .' It goes on to say that he was buried at 'Cluain-mic-Nois, under the protection of God and Ciarán, on the festival day of Brigid. (And twenty lords of his kindred were interred, moreover, in that cemetery before him.)'

The *Chronicon Scotorum* records that 'Ciarán mac an tSaoir [son of the wright], founded a monastery on the banks of the River Shannon at a place known as 'Cluain-maccu-Nois.'

The place-name Cluain Mhic Nóis suggests that there may have been a pre-Christian settlement on this spot. In fact, evidence of Iron Age activity was uncovered during excavations at Clonmacnoise in 1998.[4]

Nós, whose sons gave the monastery its name, has been described as the 'son of Fiadhach [Feeagh], a chief of the tribe of Delbna, in whose territory Clonmacnoise was situated.'[5]

The monastery of Clonmacnoise was located on the border of the ancient kingdom of Meath, looking across the Shannon into the province of Connaught. Within Meath, Clonmacnoise was situated in the Gaelic territory of Delbna Bethra.

The monastery was founded at the meeting point of two important routes: the Shannon River and the Eiscir Riada. This gravel ridge formed part of an ancient road known as the Slighe Mór, one of the five great roads in ancient Ireland.

Within a year of establishing his foundation at Clonmacnoise, Ciarán died, at the age of thirty-three.

Almost immediately, tales of Ciarán's compelling personality and his absolute devotion to God caused the growth of a cult of St Ciarán. The fact that both Ciarán and Jesus Christ were the sons of carpenters who died at the age of 33 may have been emphasised by monastic historians. Creating a link between the lives of Jesus and Ciarán could have been the monastery's way of suggesting that burial in Clonmacnoise would guarantee resurrection on the Day of Judgement.

Attracted by Ciarán's story, rulers and aristocratic people alike wished to be associated with his foundation. The population of the monastery soared as people came to join the followers of Ciarán. Kings and wealthy families created allegiances to the monastery by granting large donations of land to Clonmacnoise.

Just fifty years after Ciarán's death, Clonmacnoise had begun to change from a haven of spiritual contemplation into a bustling coenobitic (community-based) monastery. Before long its material wealth threatened to overwhelm its spiritual role.

In time, the great monastic settlement of Clonmacnoise would drive the economic development of this entire region. Hundreds of monks would live and work here, producing elaborate works of metal, illuminated manuscripts and fine stonework. In a remarkably short time, Clonmacnoise would change from a cluster of huts on a riverbank into one of the great literary and artistic centres of Ireland.[6]

THE EARLY MONASTERY

In the early years after Ciarán's death, at a time when the monastery was under Abbot Alither (circa 585-599), Colum Cille paid a visit to Clonmacnoise. A story in *Adamnán's Life of Columba* describes the scene:

> *... the blessed man ... was pleased to pay a visit to the brethren who dwelt in St Ceran's [Ciarán's] monastery, Clonmacnoise. As soon as it was known that he was near, all flocked from their little grange farms near the monastery, and, along with those who were within it, ranged themselves, with enthusiasm, under the abbot Alither; then advancing beyond the enclosure of the monastery, they went out as one man to meet St Columba [Colum Cille], as if he were an angel of the Lord.*[7]

There is no surviving surface evidence of the early Christian monastic enclosure mentioned in this story. However, the remains of such an enclosure were revealed during excavations conducted in the year 2000 in a field east of St Ciarán's National School.[8] The ditch had been deliberately filled in sometime between the late eighth and early ninth century,[9] possibly when a new enclosure was dug to accommodate expansion of the monastery.

An archaeological survey of the riverbed next to the monastery has revealed the remains of an enormous wooden bridge dating to 804.[10] The bridge measured more than 120 metres (about 131 yards) in length and was five metres (about 5½ yards) wide. Its height was more than ten metres (about 11 yards).[11] By connecting the kingdoms of Connaught and Meath, this bridge linked the east and west of Ireland.

Excavations performed elsewhere on the monastic site support the theory that the ninth century was a time of rapid expansion for Clonmacnoise.[12]

During this period, Clonmacnoise became an attractive target for raiding warriors attracted by the material wealth accumulated by the monks. Over a period of three hundred years, the monastery was raided and burned thirty-five times by rival Irish kings, the Vikings and the Anglo-Normans.

The *Annals of the Four Masters* described an attack in 832 by the King of Cashel: 'A great number of the family of Cluain Mic Nois were slain by Feidhlimidh, son of Crumhthan, King of Caiseal; and all their termon (land) was burned by him, to the door of the church.'

Throughout its early history Clonmacnoise had an uneasy and often violent relationship with rival monasteries. In the year 760 the *Annals of Ulster* record a battle at Móin Choise Blae ('the Bog at the Foot of the River Blai') between the Munster monastery of Birr and the community at Clonmacnoise.

Although the Kings of Munster briefly supported the monastery, by the mid-ninth century they had become the arch-enemies of Clonmacnoise. In 832 and 833 Feidlimid, a Munster king, carried out two violent attacks on the monastery. During his final raid in 846, Feidlimid was struck with a crosier and eventually died as a result. St Ciarán is said to have risen from the grave and thrust the crosier himself.

Clonmacnoise continued to be a favourite target of the Munster kings until the eleventh century.

The year 841 saw the first attack by the Vikings. The *Annals* mention 'The plundering of Cluain Mic Nois by the foreigners of Linn Duachaille.'

By the eleventh century, the local tribe of the Delbna had taken on the role of defenders of Clonmacnoise. The *Annals* record:

> *... [two tribes from north Munster—the Éile and the O Fogartys—made] a predatory excursion to Cluain-mic-Nois; and they took prisoners from Cros-na-screaptra (Cross of the Scriptures), and killed two persons, i.e. a student and a layman. God and Ciarán incited the Dealbhna, with their lord, i.e. Aedh Ua Ruairc, to go in pursuit of them; and they defeated and slaughtered them, killing, among others, the Tanist of Ui-Forgga, who had slain the student. The Dealbhna arrived at rising-time on the following morning, bringing the prisoners to the place whence they had been taken.*

Patron kings and ecclesiastical dynasties

Throughout its history, two sets of people shaped the fortunes of the monastery at Clonmacnoise: the kings who sustained it by their patronage and the families whose men filled its offices of abbot, bishop, vice-abbot and priest.

Because of its frontier location, Clonmacnoise received patronage in the seventh century from both the Kings of Connaught and the Kings of Meath. There was also a brief period during the early ninth century when the Kings of Munster were associated with the monastery. Their patronage was quickly replaced by that of the Kings of Meath, who remained patrons of Clonmacnoise until the twelfth century. Afterwards, the Kings of Connaught were the monastery's primary patrons until their decline in the fifteenth century.

The monastery's leaders inevitably came from families loyal to the patron king. When Clonmacnoise was patronised by the Kings of Connaught, men from families of Connaught ancestry filled its administrative positions. When patronage of the monastery shifted to the Kings of Meath, the families of Meath took control.

Burial Place of the Kings of Ireland

> *The life of Kyran thus sett downe that the best bloode have choosen their bodyes to be buried in Cluainemacnoise, for that Kyran had such power, being a holy Bishop, through the will of God, that what souls harboured in the bodies buried under that dust may never be adjudged to Damnation; wherefore those of the same blood have divided the churchyard amongst themselves, by the consent of Kyran and his holy clearkes.*[27]

For centuries, Irish rulers and nobles believed that burial within Clonmacnoise would guarantee entrance into Heaven. This made the monastery the chosen burial place of several kings of Ireland. Income from the burial of Irish aristocracy was one of its main sources of wealth.

The *Registry of Clonmacnoise* lists the families who had burial rights within this hallowed ground. They include the Uí Maelsechlainn (Maeleachlainn), Kings of Meath; the Uí Ruairc, Kings of Bréifne; the O'Kelly family, Kings of Uí Máine; the Mac Carthaigh family of North Munster, and most importantly, the O'Conors, Kings of Connaught.

In return for burial rights, these families donated large tracts of land to the monastery. As a result, Clonmacnoise possessed thousands of acres encompassing several tribal territories.

The last two High Kings of Ireland were buried inside the Cathedral at Clonmacnoise. Both came from the O'Conor family and were Kings of Connaught.

In 1156, Turlough O'Conor was interred beneath the altar of St Ciarán. Upon his death he made a donation to the monastery of 160 ounces of gold, 60 marks of silver, and all his treasures—except his sword, drinking horn, shield and weapon.

Ruaidrí, the son of Turlough O'Conor, was the last High King of Ireland. After his death in 1198 at the Abbey of Cong, his body was taken to Clonmacnoise and buried on the north side of the altar of the Cathedral.

In 606 the *Annals of Tigernach* make the earliest reference to a pilgrim in Ireland. They record the death of Aedh, an Irish chief, while on pilgrimage at Clonmacnoise. This account establishes Clonmacnoise as Ireland's oldest pilgrimage site.[13]

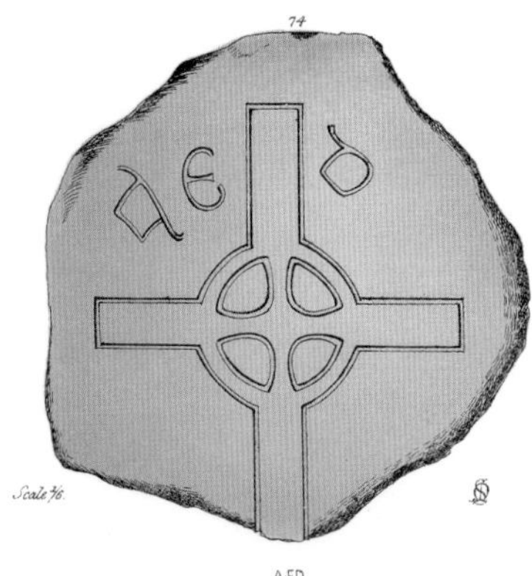

AED

Four years later, in 610, the *Annals of the Four Masters* record the death of Gorman who was living on 'the water of Tibraid Fingin [Fingin's Well], on his pilgrimage at Cluain Mic Nois.' In 756 the *Annals of Tigernach* records that another Gorman, Abbot of Louth, came on pilgrimage to Clonmacnoise and stayed for a year fasting on bread and water from 'Fingin's Well.'

By the eighth century the Kings of Meath had taken over patronage of the monastery. This resulted in tension between rival monasteries within Meath. After Domnall, King of Meath, was buried at Durrow in 763, the monasteries of Durrow and Clonmacnoise went to war over which monastery would hold the burial rights—and secure the revenues from—the future Kings of Meath. Two hundred people perished in the Battle of Argaman (764) before Clonmacnoise emerged as the dominant monastery of the region.[14]

In the tenth century, the Kings of Meath appear to have commissioned the high crosses and the first stone buildings at Clonmacnoise, including the one that became its cathedral.

In 904 the *Annals of the Four Masters* records the construction of the first stone church at Clonmacnoise: 'The Daimhliag (stone church) of Cluain-mic-Nois was erected by the king, Flann Sinna, and by Colman Conailleach.'

Clonmacnoise Cathedral

The Cathedral at Clonmacnoise is a multi-period structure that may have been first built in the tenth century by the King of Meath and Colman, Abbot of Clonmacnoise. The *Annals* mention the church in 924 as part of the record of Colman's death: 'Colman, son of Ailill, Abbot of Cluain-Iraird and Cluain-mic-Nois, a bishop and wise doctor, died. It was by him the Daimhliag [stone church] of Cluain-mic-Nois was built.'

During the reign of Elizabeth I (1558-1603) the Cathedral became a parish church and was united to the Bishoprick of Meath.[28] According to 'Bishop Dopping's Visitation Book' of 1682-85, the Cathedral had been repaired in 1647 by the 'Popish Dean' Charles Coghlan, but had since fallen into disrepair.[29]

Corporate Monasticism

From the sixth to the late thirteenth century, various Irish *Annals* offer the following count of clerics at Clonmacnoise: eighty-three abbots, twenty-nine bishops, twenty-six vice-abbots and sixteen priests.[30] Analysis of each of these positions offers an insight into the working life of the monastery.

Although the abbot held the most important position, he was not necessarily concerned with spiritual leadership. In fact, he had more in common with local kings than with the monks beneath his care. As administrator of an enormous monastic estate, the abbot managed the income of Clonmacnoise, which derived from taxes gathered from affiliated churches, and the donations of kings and wealthy families.

The Irish *Annals* indicate that the vice-abbot helped the abbot to run the estate of the monastery, especially when donated lands occupied a large geographical region. This was the case at Clonmacnoise, which owned extensive tracts of donated land in Counties Galway, Roscommon, Westmeath, Offaly, Leitrim, Sligo, Fermanagh, Cork and Limerick.

However, often the main function of a vice-abbot, who was sometimes referred to as the 'prior,' was as a tax or tithe collector. Because of this, he was often disliked by the lay people. The vice-abbot was responsible for ensuring that all the churches under the rule of Clonmacnoise collected their taxes and sent them back to the chief foundation. In return, they received the protection and prestige that came from being associated with such a powerful monastery.

The following record from the *Registry of Clonmacnoise* details the taxes collected from dependent churches in south Leitrim. It also tells of how O'Rourke, the local king, took responsibility for maintaining the church buildings:

> *. . . whence it came that a comharb or corbe [vice-abbot] was sent from Cluain to Kill Tachuir [Kiltoghert], Dubsuileagh O'Conoil, who used to receive the Bishop of Cluain's rents, and it was this, viz. Three Beeues and 3 hoggs at every St Martin out of Kill Tachuir, and two beeues and a hogg from every one of the other sixe churches or chaples mentioned before in O'Ruairk's country, and the same O'Ruairk of his devotion towards ye church undertooke to repayre those churches and to keep them in reparation during his life upon his owne chardges.*[31]

Serving beneath the abbot, the bishop was responsible for the spiritual needs of the monastic community. Sometimes, the abbot also acted as bishop, as in the case of Colmán, son of Ailill, who, according to the *Annals* in 924, served as abbot and bishop of Clonmacnoise.

The priest served beneath the bishop. Only one priest served at a time, administering the sacraments to the monastic community and possibly to the lay people of the region.

The monastic town of Clonmacnoise contained many more positions of importance, including Supervisor of the Little Church and Master of the Guesthouse.

These years also saw the emergence of one of the most important ecclesiastical families ever to reign at Clonmacnoise: the Meic Cuinn na mBocht ('the sons of Conn of the Poor').

This family emerged from the Céili Dé ('Companion of God') movement, which sought a return to monastic life based on the core principles of the founding saints, in particular devotion to God and self-denial. Members of this reform movement were often referred to as culdees or anchorites. Living within or near the monastery, they shunned the secular world. Very often an anchorite would become *Anmchara* ('spiritual adviser') to the monastic community.

One such person was Conn na mbocht ('Conn of the Poor'), who was the leader of the Céili Dé at Clonmacnoise. In 807 the *Annals of the Four Masters* state:

> *. . . of these was Conn na mbocht, who was at Cluain Mic Nois, who was called Conn na mbocht from the number of paupers which he always supported.*

Over the next four hundred years, Conn's descendants would provide the majority of abbots, bishops and spiritual leaders of Clonmacnoise. During their long tenure as abbots of Clonmacnoise, the family accumulated great personal wealth from the income of the church. From time to time, the family made public displays of their concern for the poor; in one instance, they donated over twenty cows to paupers. However, the very fact of their wealth contradicted the philosophy of the Céili Dé movement.

The death of a namesake of the original Conn is mentioned in 1059, when the *Annals of the Four Masters* records that 'Conn-na-mbocht, the glory and dignity of Clonmacnois died.'

Several of his sons became abbots known for improving the infrastructure of the monastery. They built part of the Cathedral of Clonmacnoise and also constructed several roads into the monastery. The same *Annals* from 1070 report that Maelchiarain, Abbot of Clonmacnoise, constructed 'the causeway from Cros-Chomhghaill ['Cross of Congall'] to Uluidh-na-dTri-gCross ['Carn of the Three Crosses'], and thence westwards to the entrance of the street.'

The Book of the Dún Cow

Around the eleventh or twelfth century, Maelmuire, a family member of the Conn na mBocht, wrote the *Leabhar na hUidhre (The Book of the Brown Cow)* at Clonmacnoise. This manuscript, which is written in Irish, takes its name from a sixth-century relic said to be the hide of the cow that belonged to St Ciarán.

The manuscript contains the oldest surviving versions of the 'Táin Bó Cuailgne,' the 'Voyage of Bran,' the 'Feast of Bricriú' and other religious, mythical and historical tales. It is presently housed in the Royal Irish Academy, Dublin.

The Nun's Chapel

This beautiful Romanesque church was constructed under the patronage of Derbforgaill, daughter of Murchadh Ua Maeleachlainn and wife of Tigernán Ua Ruairc. Her abduction in 1152 by Diarmait, King of Leinster, led to war between the Uí Briuin and the Kings of Meath.

The *Annals of the Four Masters* record that in 1167 'The church of the Nuns at Cluain-mic-Nois was finished by Derbforgaill, daughter of Murchadh Ua Maeleachlainn.' This church probably replaced the earlier Nuns' Church, which burned down in 1082. Some of the foundations of that church can be seen in a southern part of the boundary wall around the Nuns' Chapel.

Around 1837 Caesar Otway described the role played by the beautiful Romanesque Arch of the Nuns' Chapel on the Pattern Day:

> *. . . part of an expiating penance for the pilgrim to creep on his bare knees under this arch while approaching the altar-stone of this chapel, where sundry paters and aves must be repeated as essential to keeping the station; adjoining this is a holy stone on which St Kieran sat, and the sitting on it now, under the affiance of faith, proves a sovereign cure for all epileptic people.*[32]

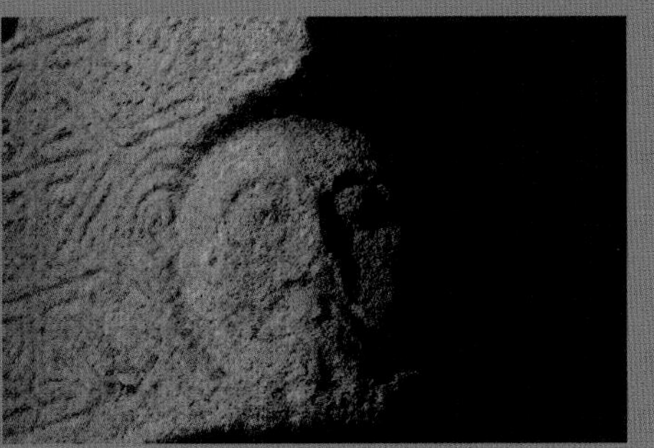

Sheela-na-Gigs

Sheela-na-gigs appear to be fertility images that may have originated with the Celts.

The term 'sheela-na-gig' is derived from the Irish Síle na gCíoch, meaning 'Sheela of the Breasts.'[33] Some have suggested that this term is derived from the Irish Síle i na giob meaning 'Sheela on her hunkers,'[34] which refers to the fact that most of these figures are shown in a squatting position, with their legs wrapped around their heads. The figures are usually females with their genitalia exposed or emphasised.

These pagan symbols were incorporated into the imagery of Romanesque churches, possibly to promote the moral teachings of the church. A sheela in the chancel arch of the Nuns' Chapel at Clonmacnoise is found in a similar position to that of a worn carving in the east window of the church at Rahan. They may be the work of the same master craftsman.

In Offaly, sheela-na-gigs are as often found on tower houses as they are on churches. Scholars believe that they were placed on these residences for superstitious reasons, such as to ward off evil spirits.

As their wealth grew, so did the family's desire to establish an independent church free from obligations to the community of Clonmacnoise and the Kings of Meath. They achieved this freedom in 1093 when Cormac, son of the abbot of Clonmacnoise, bought Íseal Chiaráin ('Ciarán's Low Place') from the monastery.

This place has been identified as Twyford, in the modern parish of Ballyloughloe, in County Westmeath.[15] It was the site of a church where St Ciarán stayed before founding Clonmacnoise, as well as the burial place of his brothers Lúchran and Odran. It included a residence for the poor and a church; it also appears to have been the headquarters of the Céili Dé.

After the purchase, Íseal Chiaráin became the family residence of the Meic Cuinn na mBocht ('the sons of Conn of the Poor'), as well as their proprietary church, free from the obligations of Clonmacnoise and secular rulers.[16]

By the twelfth century the O'Conors, Kings of Connaught, re-established their patronage of Clonmacnoise. At this point the O'Malones, a family with close connections to the O'Conors, appear to have taken over the role previously played by the Conn na mBocht family.

The O'Malones were responsible for construction of the twelfth-century round tower overlooking the River Shannon. In 1124 the *Chronicon Scotorum* records that 'The great bell-tower of Cluaín moccu Nóis was completed by Gilla Críst ua Maíleoin (O'Malone) and Tairdelbach ua Conchobuir [King of Connaught].'

This structure was similar in function and form to the minarets of the Muslim world. When it was time for prayers, a bell was rung from the top storey of the tower to alert monks working in the fields. Such towers also served as places of refuge when monasteries were under attack and may have been storage places for valuables.

This round tower was put out of use not by violence, but by natural causes. In 1134, the *Chronicon Scotorum* records that 'lighting took the roof from the tower of Cluain moccu Nóis.'

By the twelfth century Clonmacnoise had become an extremely wealthy monastery, owning extensive tracts of donated land throughout Ireland. It contained fabulous treasures of untold value. For example, the *Chronicon Scotorum* records that in 1114 the King of Meath 'offered three treasures to Ciarán in Cluain i.e. a glided horn and a glided silver goblet and a bronze vessel with gold and silver.'

The fortunes of Clonmacnoise began to change during the twelfth century reform of the Irish church. Part of this agenda was to remove power from the ecclesiastical families and to establish celibacy among the rulers of the monastery.

However, the Connaught kings were not keen supporters of this initial reform movement, which was led by people with no links to the monastic community of Clonmacnoise, such as the King of Munster and Malachy, who represented the Church of Armagh.

As reform became established throughout the country, most Irish monasteries adopted the Rule of St Augustine. The presence of the Augustinian nunnery (the Nuns' Chapel) suggests that Clonmacnoise may have adopted this Rule as well, but if so, this was only done as a matter of lip service. Prosperous and secure in its position as one of the leading power centres in the Irish church, the great foundation continued on with the old monastic ways.

The consequences were dire. Excluded from the politics of the reformed church, Clonmacnoise eventually became fossilised. It began a decline that would remain unchecked for centuries.

The Divine Metalworkers of Clonmacnoise

An inscription on this beautiful eleventh-century book shrine, or *cumdach,* states that it was made by Donnchadh Ua Taccáin 'of the community of Cluain (Clonmacnoise).' The shrine contains a Mass Book written at the monastery of Lorrha in what is now County Tipperary during the late seventh or early eighth century.

The metal shrine demonstrates the exquisite craftsmanship of the metalworkers of Clonmacnoise. Other examples of their work include the wonderful Crosier of Clonmacnoise, a bronze crucifixion plaque (see page 87) and a kite-shaped brooch. This workshop may also have produced the Shrine of St Manchan of Lemanaghan.

The great monastic settlement of Clonmacnoise drove the economic development of the entire region. Hundreds of monks lived and worked there, producing elaborate works of metal, illuminated manuscripts and fine stonework. In a remarkably short time, Clonmacnoise changed from a cluster of huts on a riverbank into one of the great literary and artistic centres of Ireland.

The Final Centuries

As well as being the century of reform, the twelfth century also saw the first attack by the Anglo-Normans on the monastic town that surrounded Clonmacnoise. The monastic buildings were spared because they were the property of the Bishop of Clonmacnoise. The *Annals of the Four Masters* record that in 1178:

> *The Constable of the King of England in Dublin and East Meath (namely, Hugo [Hugh de Lacy]) marched with his forces to Clonmacnoise, and plundered all the town, except the churches and the bishop's houses. God and Kieran wrought a manifest miracle against them, for they were unable to rest or sleep, until they had secretly absconded from Cuirr Cluana on the next day.*

Then, in the year 1200 Clonmacnoise was attacked when 'Meyler [Meiler Fitzhenry], and the English of Leinster, marched to Clonmacnoise against Cathal Carragh [O'Conor], where they remained two nights: they plundered the town of its cattle and provisions, and attacked its churches.'

Clonmacnoise Castle

To the west of the monastery lie the ruins of the stone castle of Clonmacnoise, which protects an important crossing point on the River Shannon. Its construction was recorded in 1214 in the *Annals of Loch Cé*: 'The castle of Cluain-mic-Nois and the castle of Durmhagh [Durrow] were built by Foreigners [Anglo-Normans].' The first castle on this site may have been built of timber, which was replaced by the stone structure one sees today.

Two years later King John of England paid compensation to the Bishop of Clonmacnoise for 'his land occupied in fortifying the castle of Clonmacnois, for his fruit trees cut down, his cows, horses, oxen and household utensils taken away.'[35]

The castle appears to have had a short life as a military base for the Anglo-Normans. It was probably abandoned in the 1300s during the upsurge of the power of the Gaelic kings.

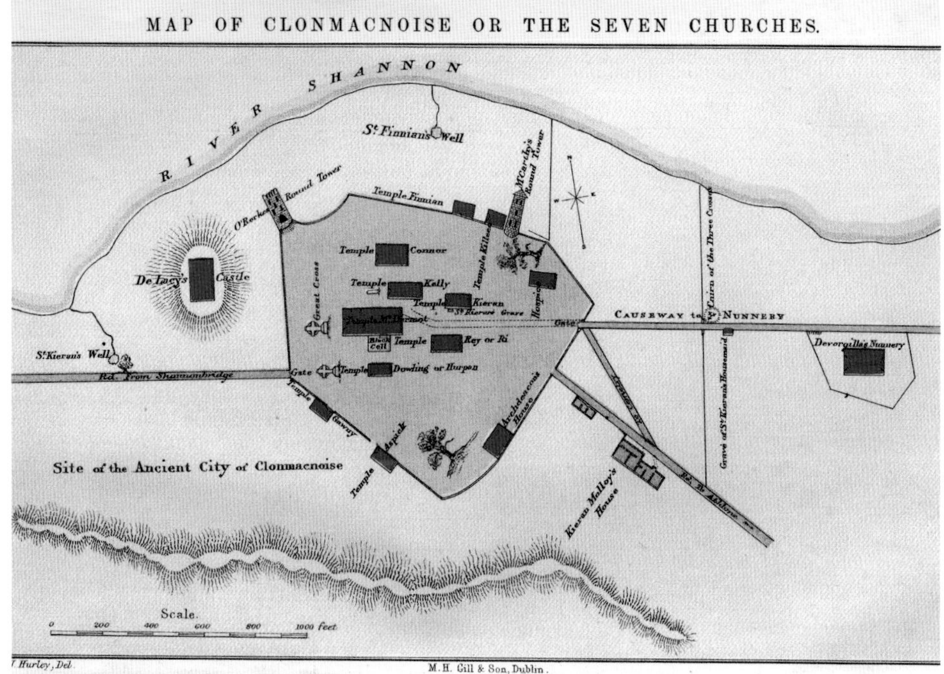

In 1684, Bishop Dopping described the Cathedral and eight other churches at Clonmacnoise. All were in ruins, except for two small churches (Temple Kieran and Temple Hurpan). Today the other surviving ruins are: Temple Finghin, Temple Connor, Temple Kelly, Temple Dowling, Mac Laffey's Church, Temple Melaghlin and the Nuns' Chapel.

Three high crosses stand proudly around the Cathedral. The North Cross and South Cross are located to the north and south of the Cathedral, while the Cross of the Scriptures stands to the west.

By the time of the Gaelic Revival in the fifteenth century, the once great monastery of Clonmacnoise had shrunk to a small foundation patronised by the Mac Coghlans, Kings of Delbna Bethra. From this time onwards the politics of Clonmacnoise and of the Mac Coghlans would be intertwined.

Seeking to become the secular as well as the spiritual ruler of the Delbna Bethra, in 1444 Cormac Mac Coghlan, Bishop of Clonmacnoise, went to war against his kinsmen. His political ambitions ended when he and his supporters were defeated by the sons of David and Felim Mac Coghlan.[17]

As a religious foundation, Clonmacnoise had shrunk quite considerably by the time that Henry VIII began to execute his policy of dissolving the monasteries. However, that policy gave licence to the English forces to take what was left at the once great monastery.

In 1552 the English army plundered the churches of Clonmacnoise. The *Annals of the Four Masters* say: 'There was not left moreover, a bell, small or large, an image, or an altar, or a book, or a gem, or even glass in a window, from the wall of the church out, which was not carried off.'

Following the Reformation, Clonmacnoise became a place of worship for a smaller community adhering to the beliefs of a new church. Then, after the Catholic Rebellion of 1641, the Catholic clergy regained Clonmacnoise. Charles Coghlan, a member of the Mac Coghlan family, took control as Vicar General of the monastery. He made repairs to the Cathedral in 1647; this work is commemorated on a plaque in the north wall of the chancel.[18] In 1649, the Catholic clergy assembled in this newly repaired structure. From there, they denounced Cromwell and his supporters.

However, this period was short-lived. Throughout the rest of the seventeenth century, the power of the Mac Coghlans declined and so did the fortunes of Clonmacnoise.

Place of Pilgrimage

By the late 1600s, Clonmacnoise had become a collection of tumbling monastic ruins. Only two roofed churches remained: Temple Kieran and Temple Hurpan.[19] Yet it was during this time that the monastery—and in particular, its holy wells—became a focus of worship that sustained the persecuted Catholic faith.

As mentioned earlier, the first recorded pilgrimage in Ireland took place at Clonmacnoise in 604. People continued to take solitary pilgrimages to the monastery throughout the subsequent centuries. Most were following the example of pentitential pilgrims, such as Colum Cille, who exiled himself to Scotland in atonement for his sins. Their philosophy is described in the *Book of Lismore,* which says that the pilgrim 'leaves his fatherland completely in body and in soul.'[20]

However, in late sixteenth-century Ireland, the practice of the penitential pilgrimage became fused with other popular communal practices, such as visiting a holy well on the feastday of a particular saint or a patron saint.

It appears that these practices were at odds with the beliefs of the official church. As early as 1614, clerics of the Catholic Church expressed their unease. During synods that year in Armagh and Dublin, they called for reform of 'certain abuses and superstitious usages practised by ignorant persons assembling at wells and trees.'[21]

Then, in 1697, during the Williamite era (1688-1702), the Irish Parliament introduced the Penal Laws. These laws attempted to banish the Catholic clergy from the country and restricted the rights of the Catholic lay population.

The Penal Laws were in force from 1691-1760. During these years, popular religious practices gained greater significance. 'Patterns'—a corruption of the term 'patron'—took on a new meaning for a people whose clergy had been banished from the country and prohibited by law from saying Mass. Pilgrimages to holy wells became the core symbol of Catholic devotion to a persecuted faith.

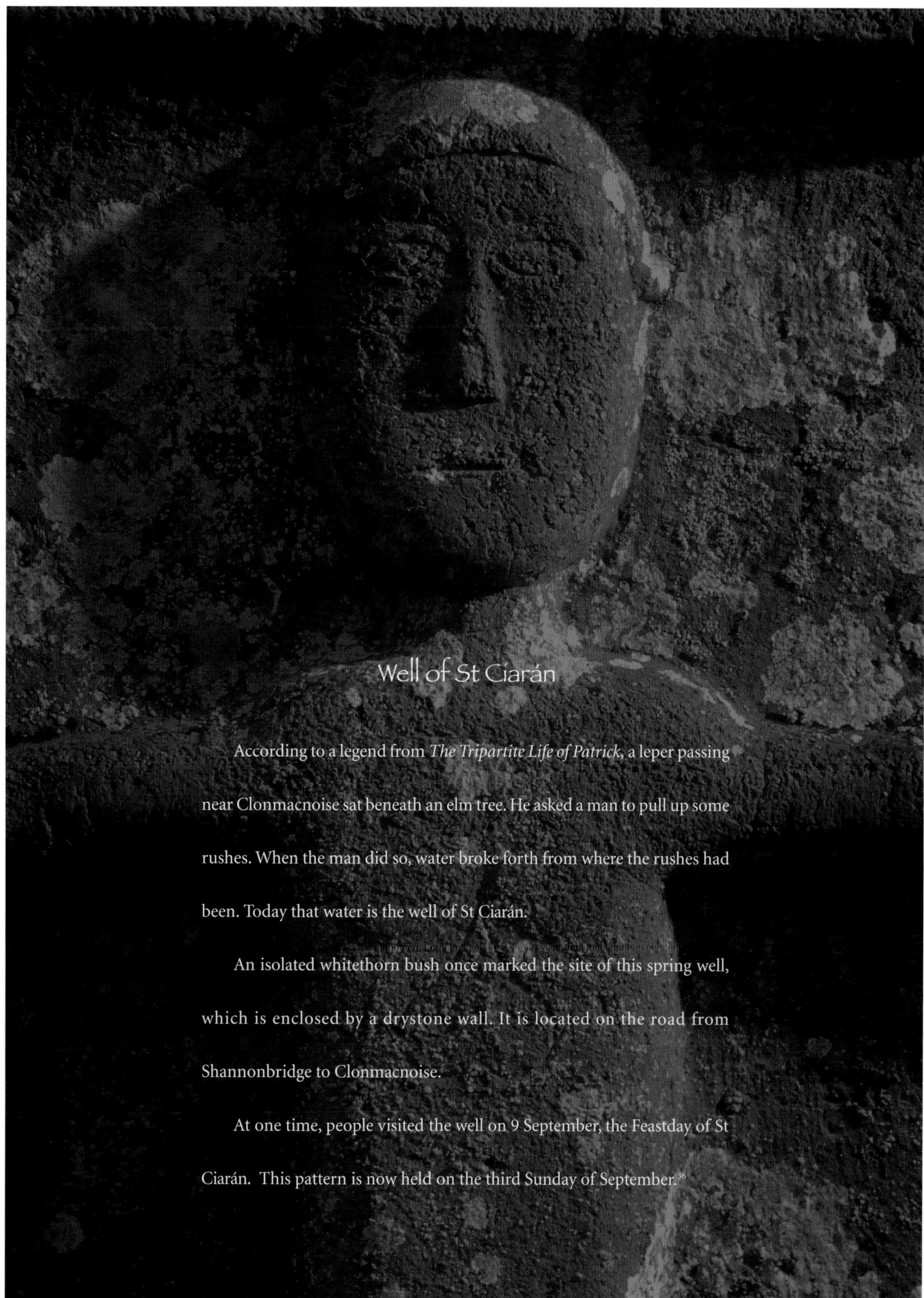

Well of St Ciarán

According to a legend from *The Tripartite Life of Patrick*, a leper passing near Clonmacnoise sat beneath an elm tree. He asked a man to pull up some rushes. When the man did so, water broke forth from where the rushes had been. Today that water is the well of St Ciarán.

An isolated whitethorn bush once marked the site of this spring well, which is enclosed by a drystone wall. It is located on the road from Shannonbridge to Clonmacnoise.

At one time, people visited the well on 9 September, the Feastday of St Ciarán. This pattern is now held on the third Sunday of September.[36]

The Long Station

The pilgrimage route at Clonmacnoise is known as 'the Long Station.'[37]

The first in a series of stops, or stations, is St Ciarán's Well. Bare-footed, the pilgrim circles the well. She or he stops and says prayers at the three stones lying around the well, then kneels down to kiss the face of the crucified Christ on the upright stone, which is inscribed with the words: 'Repent and do penance.' It was once a tradition to leave behind a votive offering in the well or on its whitethorn tree.

From here the pilgrim walks up to the monastery to say prayers at various buildings and at the high crosses. The pilgrim makes three clockwise circuits around the graveyard.

Next the pilgrim proceeds along the Pilgrim's Road, passing by the Cairn of the Three Crosses en route to the Nuns' Chapel, where more prayers are recited. After walking around this church three times, the pilgrim proceeds to the last stop on the circuit, which is Fingin's Well.[38]

During the early 1700s, the Catholic Church continued to express its opposition to these patterns. Official opposition continued throughout the eighteenth century. In 1771 the Bishop of Ferns urged his clergy to 'put back and discourage as much as ye can patrons or pilgrimages, or meetings of pretended devotion, or rather of real dissipation and dissoluteness.'[22] However, the bishop's mandate fell on deaf ears. Patterns grew ever more popular, particularly amongst the country people.

By the early 1800s, the Pattern Day had become an important festival in rural Ireland, much to the continued disapproval of the Catholic Church. The pattern at Clonmacnoise in 1816 was reputed to have attracted up to four thousand people.[23]

What was once a tradition of solitary pilgrimage and penitence by a holy site had been transformed into an occasion for merriment, play and certain unruly drunken social behaviour. One observer described these practices as 'orgies of a Bacchanalian licentiousness mixed up with the devotions of a religious rite.'

Around 1837 Caesar Otway, a Church of Ireland chaplain, described the pattern held in a large field known as the patron-green to the north of the old graveyard at Clonmacnoise:

> *... thousands had assembled, after doing their stations and performing their vowed penances, to commence a new course of riot, debauchery, and blasphemy; to run up a new score, which St Kieran was, in the following 9th of September, to wipe out; and so on the year's sins and the day's expiation....*[24]

Eventually, under pressure by local parish priests and reformers, such as the temperance crusader Father Mathew, the Catholic Church outlawed patterns in the mid-1800s.

Today the pattern at Clonmacnoise is once again an expression of reverent personal devotion. On the first Sunday in September people come to participate in 'The Long Station,' a walk of penitence and prayer around the remnants of the many buildings that once made up Ciarán's shining city, Clonmacnoise.

The Dead at Clonmacnois

In a quiet watered land, a land of roses,
Stands Saint Kieran's city fair;
And the warriors of Erin in their famous generations
Slumber there.

There beneath the dewy hillside sleep the noblest
Of the clan of Conn,
Each below his stone with name in branching Ogham
And the sacred knot thereon.

There they laid the seven kings of Tara,
There the sons of Cairbre sleep
Battle-banners of the Gael that in Kieran's plain
Of crosses
Now their final hosting keep.

And at Clonmacnois they laid the men of Teffia,
And right many a lord of Breagh;
Deep the sod above Clan Creide and Clan Conaill
Kind in hall and fierce in fray.

Many and many a son of Conn the Hundred-fighter
In the red earth lies at rest;
Many a blue eye of Clan Colman the turf covers
Many a swan-white breast.[39]

— *Angus O'Gillan, translated by T. W. Rolleston*

THE CHURCH OF THE ABBESS RYNAGH

Banagher—Beannchar—Pointed Hills or Pointed Rocks

Having no water to baptise the baby, they prayed to God for help. Then they scraped the soil, and a fountain sprang up under a tree.

In the sixth century, a widow named Rynagh (also Reynagh, Rinagh) founded a convent on a hill overlooking the banks of the River Shannon.

Legend says that Rynagh was descended from the ancient kings of Connaught. Her early life was marked by tragedy and drama. Rynagh lost her husband before she gave birth to their child.

Her cousin King Cormac became jealous after a prophecy foretold that Rynagh's heir would surpass in greatness all others of his illustrious line. Afraid that Cormac might try to kill her and her unborn child, Rynagh fled from her home. However, Cormac's soldiers were in hot pursuit. They seized the young pregnant woman, tied a heavy stone around her neck, and threw her into the Kiltartan River, near present-day Gort, County Galway.

Miraculously, Rynagh was saved. Today the stone intended to drown her is an object of devotion in the old parish church in Kiltartan.

Soon after she survived the attempt on her life, Rynagh gave birth to a son. As she lay with the child, feeling anxious and isolated, two pilgrim monks approached. One of them was blind; the other was lame. Having no water to baptise the baby, they prayed to God for help. Then they scraped the soil, and a fountain sprang up under a tree.

The pilgrims christened the child 'Colman.' Afterwards, they washed in the waters of the fountain and were healed. In gratitude for their healing, the monks asked Rynagh to entrust them with the safety and education of the child. She readily agreed and Colman grew up to become the saintly first bishop of what we know today as the Diocese of Galway and Kilmacduagh.

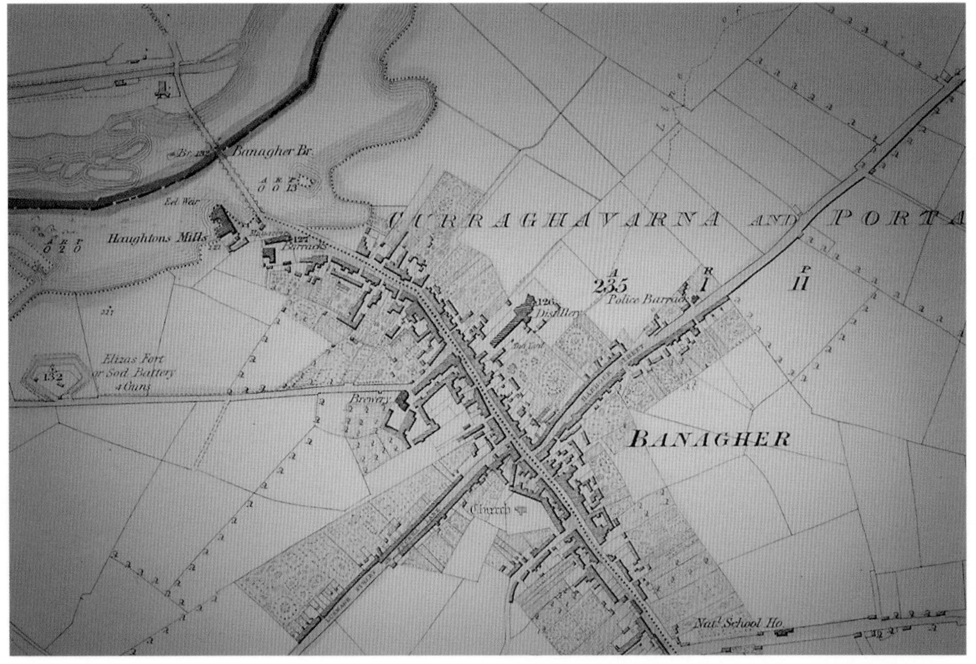

The *Annals* record that Rynagh visited her brother, Finnian, at his famous monastery and school at Clonard, in present-day County Meath. She remained with Finnian for some time.

Later she entered the nunnery at Clonmacnoise. From there she founded a convent at Banagher in an area that today is part of Church Street. Rynagh became the first abbess of the new convent and was noted for her love of the poor. Her convent developed into a seat of piety and great learning.

Rynagh died around 610. She was probably buried in Banagher or at Kilmacduagh near Gort, which was the monastery founded by her son.[1] Today St Rynagh is patron saint of the combined parish of Banagher and Cloghan.

The town of Banagher developed around Rynagh's convent. There are a number of different theories about the origins of the town's unusual name. 'Banagher' has been interpreted as meaning 'the pointed hills or pointed rocks.' Local historian Valentine Trodd

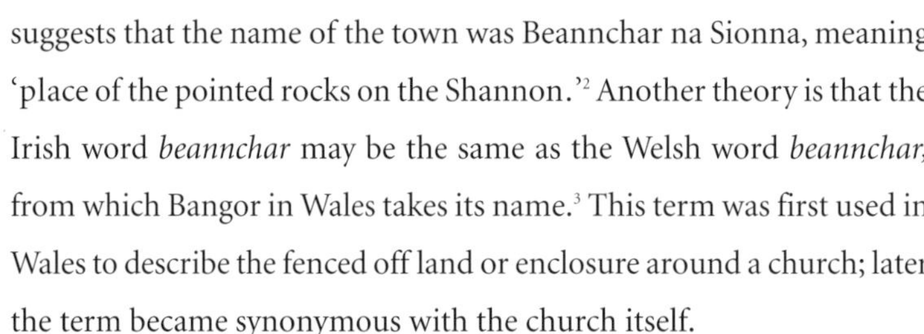

suggests that the name of the town was Beannchar na Sionna, meaning 'place of the pointed rocks on the Shannon.'[2] Another theory is that the Irish word *beannchar* may be the same as the Welsh word *beannchar,* from which Bangor in Wales takes its name.[3] This term was first used in Wales to describe the fenced off land or enclosure around a church; later the term became synonymous with the church itself.

Before founding his monastery at Clonard, Rynagh's brother Finnian studied for about thirty years in Wales. During that time, he would have become familiar with the Welsh term *beannchar* associated with the early churches in that country. It is possible that Finnian and other early Irish saints educated in Wales brought back the term *beanncha,* among other Welsh words, when they returned to Ireland.

The monastery of Killrignaighe (Cill Ríonaí or 'Church of Rynagh') is mentioned in the *Life of St Finnian.*

In 1875, local historian Thomas Lalor Cooke described the ruins 'called Kill-Righnaighe, the church of Rignacia' as being located nearly in the centre of Banagher, and surrounded by the parish burial ground and possible enclosure. The enclosure that Cooke describes may have been the same early Christian enclosure from which the town Banagher received its name.

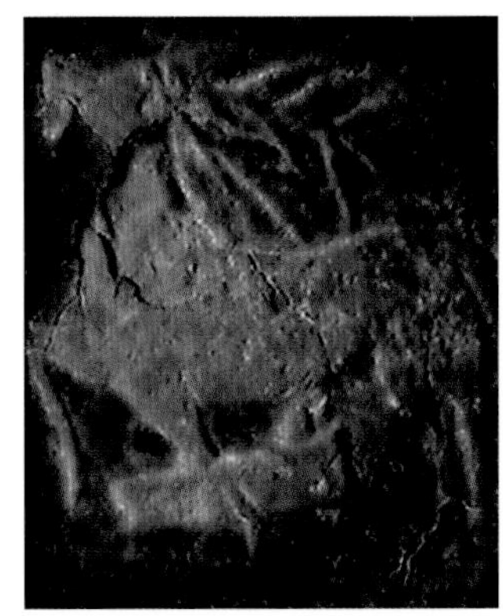

Today, on top of the hill where Rynagh founded her religious community, are the ruins of a nave and chancel parish church dedicated to St Mary that was probably built in the fifteenth or sixteenth century. This church is located in the Diocese of Clonmacnoise, in a territory once known as Delbna Bethra (Delvin Mac Coghlan), which was part of the ancient kingdom of Meath.

Records indicate that there is a well— now covered over— in the old market square near this church. This well may have been associated with the early Christian monastery of St Rynagh, later becoming the town well for the inhabitants of medieval Banagher.

Probably from the time that Rynagh founded her monastery, it received the patronage of the Mac Coghlan family. This Gaelic family were the secular rulers of the territory of Delbna Bethra.

The Mac Coghlans were constantly feuding with their neighbours the O'Maddens, who ruled a territory known as Síl Anmchadha, near the present-day village of Lusmagh. Not only was this area the frontier zone between two Gaelic territories (Síl Anmchadha, ruled by the O'Maddens, and Delbna Bethra, ruled by the Mac Coghlans), it was also the border between the kingdoms of Meath and Connaught.

Records indicate that one of the Mac Coghlans was murdered by an O'Madden at the church founded by Rynagh, but the date of this incident is uncertain.

According to the *Annals of Connacht,* in 1436 'Feidlim Mac Cochlain, king of Delbna Bethra, was killed in the church of Cell Rignaigi, at the Mass on Sunday, by the sons of O Matadain (O'Madden).'

The *Annals of the Four Masters* give the date of this event as more than one hundred years later, in 1539, when 'Mac Coghlan (Felim, the son of Meyler) was slain at Beannchor, by the sons of O'Madden . . . after he had heard mass on Sunday, the second of the Nones of July.'

Whatever the year of this event, it is interesting to note the changing name of the church. The *Annals of Connacht* refer to the site of the killing as the church of 'Cell Rignaigi' and the *Annals of the Four Masters* refer to the site as the church of 'Beannchor.' This suggests that the church now known as Banagher church was previously known as Cell Rignaigi ('Rynagh's Church').

Today the ruins of the chancel of that church contain the beautiful grave slab of Sir John Mac Coghlan (died 1590), decorated with a floriated cross. Here is a translation of its incomplete Latin inscription:

> *[Here lies buried] Sir John C[oghlan] Knight, sometime chief of [his people] who caused to be made. . . . in the 19th year of the reign of Queen Elizabeth, the year of the termination of the exactions of Imaileac . . .*[4]

Sir John Mac Coghlan was Knight of Cloghan and Chief of Delbna Bethra. In his will, he left instructions that he was to be interred in the 'church of the Blessed Virgin of Raonach [Rynagh].'[5]

In a feuding society marred by frequent, violent battles between rival families, the Mac Coghlans entered into a period of intense castle-building. The castles of Clonlyon, Leitra, Doon, Lemanaghan, Clononey, Kilcolgan, Lisclooney, Fadden, Coole, Garrycastle, Streamstown, Kincora and Cloghan (Cloghan village) were all residences of the Mac Coghlan chiefs of Delbna Bethra. The abundance of castles led an ancient Irish poet to describe this tribe as 'Mac Coghlan of the Fair Castles.'[6]

In 1612 John Mac Coghlan established a market at Banagher every Thursday. Later the market moved to Monday; by the nineteenth century it had moved again and was being held every Friday.[7]

As part of the English plantation of the Mac Coghlans' territory, Sir Arthur Blundell built Fort Falkland in 1624. This fort was able to control the important crossing over the River Shannon at Banagher.

Another significant change occurred on 28 September 1628, when Banagher received a charter of incorporation. Its new title was the Borough and Town of Banagher, which consisted of a sovereign, twelve burgesses and free commons. More importantly, the town was to hold two fairs, both of two days duration. One occurred on the Feast of Saints Philip and Jacob (1 May), the other on the Feast of Saints Simon and Jude (28 October).

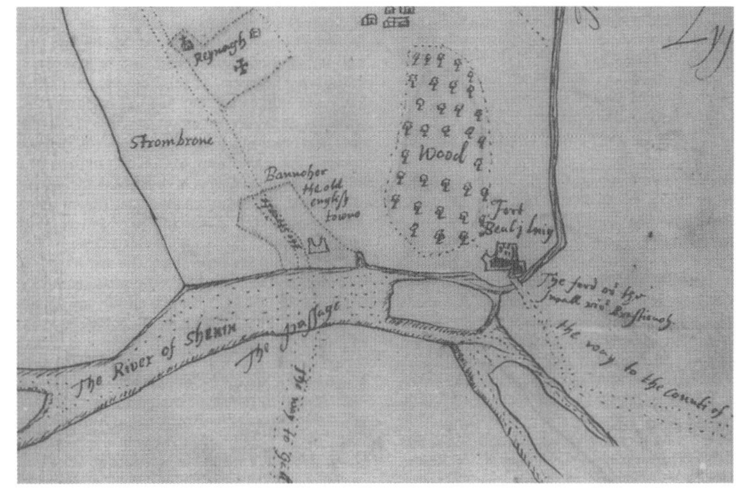

Another important condition of the settlement was that 222 acres in the townlands of Leacarrow, Reynahan, Coolreagh and Ballingowen be given over to the purpose of supporting a 'preaching minister,' who was to reside in the town.

During this period it is likely that the church was taken over by the settlers. Within its vault, a memorial dating from 1680 indicates that the Armstrong family began using the church at Banagher as their final resting place around that time.

The church continued to be a place of worship until the nineteenth century, when the Church of Ireland constructed a new building in the town. Empty of parishioners, the church entered its present life as a ruin in the centre of Banagher, overlooking the backyards of the properties that flank the main street of the town.

The Banagher Pillar

Visiting the monastery around 1850, Thomas Lalor Cooke, a famous local antiquarian, made a remarkable discovery amongst the overgrown grass and weeds of the graveyard. He described this finding as '. . .the shaft of an ancient stone cross, erected to commemorate Bishop O'Duffy, who was killed in the year 1297 by a fall from his horse. . . .'[8]

Local people informed him that the cross had once stood beside a natural spring in the old market square, but that this well had been covered over many years before.

The shaft of the cross is carved with scenes contained within a framed panel. The image of a three-tailed lion is located over a carving of a bishop, with his crosier, riding a horse. Below the cleric an animal, resembling a horned deer, is caught in a trap. The bottom of the pillar contains four naked bearded human figures. Their legs are interwoven and each figure pulls the beard of one behind him. Decorative interlaced tracery can be seen on the sides of the pillar, while the back of the stone has a carving of a mythical beast or serpent.

Believing that the cross was being vandalised by some 'gothic foes,'[9] Cooke took it to Birr. From there, the shaft was moved to Clonmacnoise.[10] Today it is in the safe hands of the National Museum of Ireland.

Although Cooke identified this shaft as being a memorial from the thirteenth century, it is more likely that this pillar dates from the eighth century and depicts hunting scenes, as suggested by Francoise Henry.[11] It was just a co-incidence that the motifs on the pillar resembled an historical event recorded in the *Annals* some 500 years later. As Cooke rightly observed, the carvings on the Banagher Pillar were trying to tell a story, the meaning of which has since been lost through the passage of time.

THE CHURCH ON THE PLAIN OF OAKS

Durrow—Darú—Plain of Oaks

I shall bear a son . . . and his teaching shall reach throughout the borders of Ireland and Scotland.

In the sixth century a monk named Colum Cille (also known as Columba) established a monastery at Durrow. It flourished, becoming one of the most important monasteries he founded in Ireland and Scotland, second only to Iona.[1]

The boy who would become Colum Cille was born a nobleman in the year 521 in what is now Gartan, County Donegal. He was a member of the Uí Néill dynasty and part of the tribe known as the Cenél Conaill, rulers of Tír Conaill. His parents were described as 'Fedlimith, son of Fergus, son of Conall Gulban, son of Niall, of the Nine Hostages. His mother was of the Corprige of Leinster, to wit, Ethne the Great, daughter of Dimma mac Noe.'[2]

Legend says that at the baptism of the boy's ancestors, St Patrick prophesised the saint's birth and his vocation. Patrick said:

A manchild shall be born of his family,
He will be a sage, a prophet and a poet, etc.
He will be a sage, and he will be pious,
He will be an abbot with the King of the royal ramparts.[3]

Before the boy's birth his mother Eithne also made a prophecy. She said: 'I shall bear a son . . . and his teaching shall reach throughout the borders of Ireland and Scotland.'[4]

When the baby was born, he was immediately christened by the priest Cruithnechán with the name 'Crimthann,' meaning 'deceitful one' or 'fox.' An angel instructed the priest to foster the boy, according to the custom of the time.[5] The priest followed these instructions, taking the boy into his own home. Soon the angels intervened again to give the child a new name:

The angels of God, King of heaven,
Took 'Crimthann' away as his name,
And 'Colum Cille' ['Dove of the Church'] to him then was given.[6]

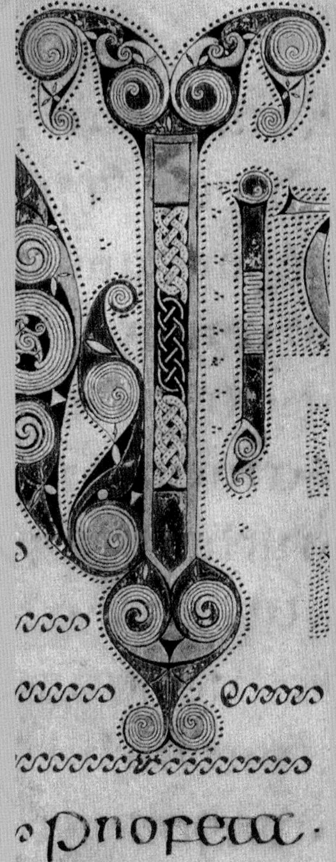

Colum Cille's birthright was to become one of the ruling kings of Ireland. Instead, he became a priest. According to the *Leabhar Breac:* 'He had in right of kin, a choice of the sovranty of Ireland, and it would have been given to him had he himself not put it from him for the sake of God.'

Attending the renowned monastic school of St Finnian at Clonard, Colum Cille became one of the twelve early church leaders known as the 'Twelve Apostles of Erin.' Afterwards, he travelled throughout Ireland preaching the Word of God and setting up many monasteries.

Colum Cille gained a reputation as a poet, a scribe and a lover of nature, as well as a founder of monasteries. In the words of his biographer, Adomnán of Iona:

> *He had the face of an angel; he was of an excellent nature, polished in speech, holy in deed, great in counsel . . . loving unto all.*

Possibly because of his noble birth, Colum Cille's ministry had tremendous appeal to the warlords and kings of sixth-century Ireland. Their enthusiastic patronage enabled the Columban monasteries (those founded by Colum Cille and his followers), including the foundation at Durrow, to outstrip others in both wealth and prestige.

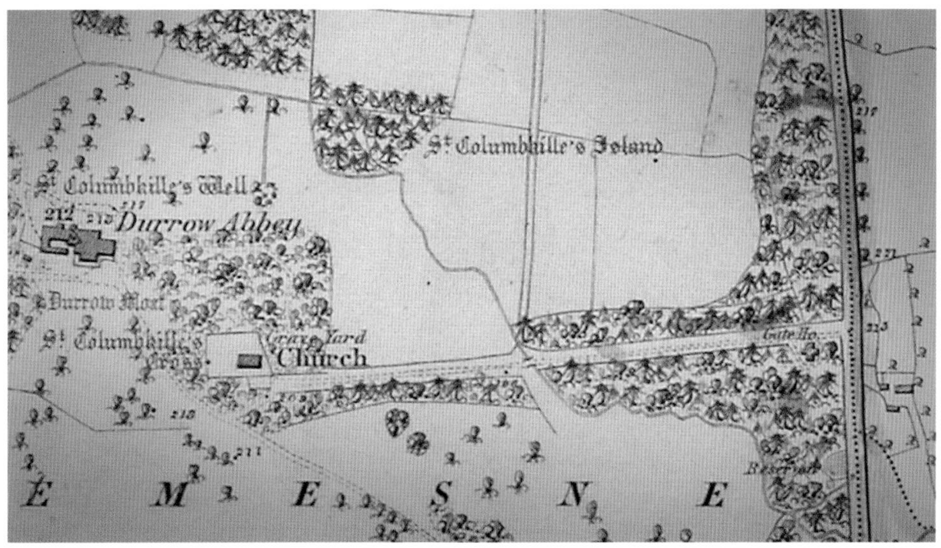

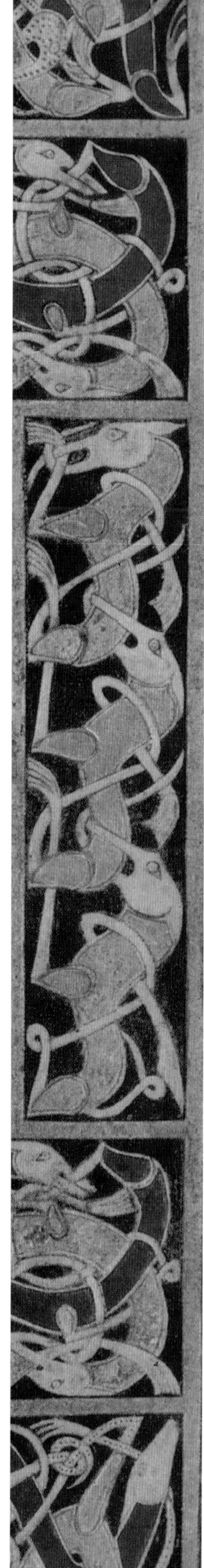

Colum Cille's Monastery at Durrow

While in exile Colum Cille yearned for his monasteries in Ireland, and in particular, the one at Durrow. 'An Exile's Dream,' a poem attributed to the saint and written down in the eleventh century, vividly describes his love for the landscape surrounding Durrow:

> *Happy for Dimma's son in his holy abbey, where I might*
> *hear what would delight my mind in Durrow in the west:*
>
> *The Sound of the wind in the elm making music for us,*
> *and the startled cry of the pleasant grey blackbird when*
> *she has clapped her wings;*
>
> *Listening early in Ross Grencha to the stags, and to*
> *Cuckoos calling from the woodland on the brink of summer.*[10]

At the time that Colum Cille founded the monastery at Durrow, its lands were part of the territory of Tethba, which today mainly consists of County Longford.

Durrow was located near the Slighe Mór, one of Ireland's five main roads. It connected Tara in County Meath to the West of Ireland, in places following another ancient route, the Eiscir Riada. The High Wood to the north of the monastery is probably a remnant of the section of the Slighe Mór that passed nearby.

No accounts survive of what Colum Cille's monastery was like when it was founded. It probably included a wooden church, surrounded by huts in which the monks lived and worked.

One story from the *Life of Colum Cille by Manus O'Donnell* refers to an enclosure around the monastery, which was put in place after Colum Cille went into exile. In the book, Colum Cille tells his monk Cormac Ua Liatháin: 'I won't like it if you don't go back to Ireland and instruct Laisrén, the abbot of Durrow, to improve and enclose the monastery well.'[11]

The enclosure in this story may refer to the two earthen banks in Durrow Demesne that were described in the nineteenth century by local antiquarian Thomas Stanley.[12] He also noted that a prehistoric standing stone was located on top of one of the monastic banks, but no trace of it remains.

Over the past two hundred years, the great monastic enclosure of Durrow has been reduced to a cropmark. It can be seen, measuring around 500 metres (about 547 yards) in diameter, in aerial photographs of the lands around the church.

Ordnance Survey maps show that there was also a burial mound—marked as Sheean, possibly meaning 'fairy mound'—in the field to the south of the monastery. An excavation of this mound in the mid-1980s by the National Museum of Ireland revealed several early Christian burials.

Over its lifetime, the monastery at Durrow appears to have had several important patrons: the Kings of Meath, the Kings of Tethba, and the MacGeoghegans, who were the chieftains of the region known as Cinél Fiachach. It also had the support of the tribe known as the Foxes (Catharnach Sinnach), rulers of the territory of Muintir Tadhgain in the kingdom of Tethba.

Though the ruling secular families patronised the monastery, they were not permitted to appoint its abbot. At first, the abbots of Durrow were selected from Colum Cille's own extended family, as was common practice for all of the Columban foundations.

This arrangement is described in the *Life of St. Columba* in the *Leabhar Breac:* 'So, therefore Colombcille blessed Durrow, and left therein a warden (one) of his household, namely, Cormac descendant of Liathan.'[13]

Later on, rule of the Columban monasteries became dominated by certain families, who passed down their positions to their children. These hereditary rulers formed ecclesiastical dynasties that governed the monasteries.

Association with the Uí Néill dynasty made Durrow an important monastery. After a member of the southern Uí Néill dynasty, Domnall, King of Meath, died in 763, he was buried in the graveyard at Durrow.

At that time, the wealth and prestige of a monastery were inextricably linked to the people buried within its confines. Domnall's burial at Durrow probably sparked the outbreak of the Battle of Argaman the following year (764). The monasteries of Clonmacnoise and Durrow went to war over which one would hold the burial rights of future kings of Meath. Another factor in the fight was the struggle over which monastery would be the most powerful in the kingdom.[14] Over two hundred people were killed before Clonmacnoise emerged victorious.

Today at Durrow, just inside the graveyard gate, several early Christian cross slabs are set into the east face of the graveyard wall. One bears an inscription to Domhnaill (Domnall), King of Meath (died 763). Another slab is dedicated to Aigidiu, the father of Aed mac Aicidi, a tenth-century chief of Tethba.[15]

Even kings could not find sanctuary from the political violence that was a fact of life both outside and within Irish monasteries during this era. In 1019 the *Annals of Loch Cé* record that: 'The stone-church of Dermhagh [Durrow] was broken open by Muirchertach [Ua Maelsechlainn], grandson of Carrach, against Maelmhuaidh [O'Molloy], king of Feara-Ceall [Fir Chell], who was taken out of it by force, and afterwards slain.'

Around 1144, an Augustinian priory dedicated to St Mary was established at Durrow, possibly by St Malachy under the instigation of Murchad Ua Maelsechlainn, King of Meath.[16] This appears to have been a double monastery, containing an Augustinian nunnery as well as a priory for regular canons.[17]

Colum Cille the Scribe

A twelfth-century monastic poem attributed to Colum Cille captures the spirit of the monk at work. One can almost imagine him dipping his goose quill into an inkhorn and writing for hours.

My Hand is Weary with Writing

My hand is weary with writing; my sharp great point is
not thick; my slender-beaked pen juts forth a beetle-
hued draught of bright blue ink.

A steady stream of wisdom springs from my well-coloured
neat fair hand; on the page it pours its draught of
ink of the green-skinned holly.

I send my little dipping pen unceasingly over an assemblage
of books of great beauty, to enrich the possessions
of men of art–whence my hand is weary with writing.[22]

The High Cross at Durrow

During the ninth century, the Kings of Meath commissioned the construction of the High Cross at Durrow. Originally the cross was located to the west of the church, but it has recently been moved inside the building for conservation purposes.

The panels of the cross illustrate stories from the scriptures, including Eve presenting Adam with the apple and Cain slaying Abel.

The east face depicts Christ with sceptre and cross-staff, which is associated with the last judgement. On his left there is a piper and David with his harp. Also on the east face, the bottom of the shaft shows Christ flanked by two angels, who hover above St Peter and St Paul. The central panel contains beautiful Celtic interlace, while the top panel illustrates the Sacrifice of Isaac.

The west face of the cross depicts Christ's arrest and the Crucifixion.

The top of this cross is crowned with a small church with a shingled roof. This carving was probably modelled on one of the wooden churches at Durrow.

An eroded inscription seems to suggest that this cross was erected for Maelsechnaill, King of Tara, who ruled from 846 to 862.[23]

Commissioning stone sculptures, such as the High Cross at Durrow, was one way that early Christian rulers associated themselves with a monastery. They may have believed that through paying for these sacred sculptures, they would also purchase salvation for themselves and their family members. The commissioning of the High Cross could also symbolise the power and control by a king and his kin over a particular region. Rulers believed that association with a particular monastery enabled them to pass through the secular world armed with the spiritual and moral support of the church. For example, when the Leinster King, Diarmait mac Máel na mBó was defeated by the Kings of Meath at Durrow in 1059, this victory was attributed to 'the miracles of God and Colum Cille.'[24]

When the Anglo-Normans came to Ireland, one of their leaders, Hugh de Lacy, built a castle on the grounds of Durrow. It was the site of his assassination in 1186. Today remnants of this motte-castle survive beside the eighteenth-century house known as Durrow Abbey.

Just northeast of Durrow monastery, in the townland of Ballybought, lie the remains of an unusual stone castle, which is marked on the Ordnance Survey map as Shancourt ('Old Court') or Meenaglish. This may be one of a series of castles built in 1213 by the English to secure their territory following their defeat of Cormac, son of Art O'Melaghlin, in 1213.[18]

During the Gaelic Revival of the fifteenth century, the MacGeoghegan family took over the administration of the monastery at Durrow and its church. At least one leader of that tribe retired to the monastery. In 1454 the *Annals of the Four Masters* record that 'Farrell Roe Mageoghegan resigned his lordship, and retired into the monastery of Durrow-Columbkille, having lost his sight; and Niall Mageoghegan assumed his place.'

The links between the MacGeoghegan family and Durrow monastery were maintained until the Dissolution of the Monasteries in the sixteenth century. The family were also the hereditary keepers of the Crosier of St Columba, which is now housed in the National Museum of Ireland.

In 1562 the dissolved monastery was leased to Nicholas Harbert. It was described in 1569 as consisting of an abbey that contained: 'a church, a hall and other buildings, the possessions including a ruined castle, two rectories, several messuages [dwellings] and cottages, with over 1,000 acres value given as over £18.'[19]

Around 1680 the church was described as the parochial church of Durrow. A description of its interior, written between 1682-1685, makes it clear that the church had fallen upon hard times. The account says the building contained a reading desk, a pulpit and an unrailed table, but no carpet, chalice, flagon or font. By this time, a stone wall enclosed the graveyard.[20]

The church appears to have been damaged in the political upheaval of the region in 1693 and then poorly repaired the following year.[21]

Today the only intact structure that remains on the site of the monastery at Durrow is the Church of Ireland building. It probably stands on the site of an earlier medieval nave and chancel church. To the north of the graveyard are the remains of St Columbkille's Well at which a pattern is held each year on the saint's feastday, 9 June.

Hugh de Lacy's Assassination

After the Anglo-Normans came to Ireland, Henry II made his warrior, Hugh de Lacy, King of Meath.

In 1186 de Lacy began building a timber castle on land next to the monastery of Durrow. As he surveyed the nearly completed castle, de Lacy was assassinated by a lad known as Gilla-gan-Inathair ('the Gutless Lad') O'Miadhaigh.[25] The boy was a foster-son of the Sinnagh (Foxes), who had ordered the killing.

Under the year 1186, the *Annals of the Four Masters* describes this event:

> *Hugo de Lacy, the profaner and destroyer of many churches; Lord of the English of Meath, Breifny, and Oriel; he to whom the tribute of Connaught was paid; he who had conquered the greater part of Ireland for the English, and of whose English castles all Meath, from the Shannon to the sea, was full; after having finished the castle of Durrow, set out, accompanied by three Englishmen, to view it.*
>
> *One of the men of Teffia, a youth named Gilla-gan-inathar O'Meyey, approached him, and drawing out an axe, which he had kept concealed, he, with one blow of it, severed his head from his body; and both head and trunk fell into the ditch of the castle. This was in revenge of Columbkille.*
>
> *Gilla-gan-inathar fled, and, by his fleetness of foot, made his escape from the English and Irish to the wood of Kilclare. He afterwards went to the Sinnagh (the Fox) and O'Breen, at whose instigation he had killed the Earl.*

The Book of Durrow

The *Book of Durrow* is the earliest surviving fully decorated insular Gospel-book. It predates the *Book of Kells* by over a century.

It was probably written and illuminated in the scriptorium of Durrow monastery sometime in the first half of the seventh century,[26] though some scholars would argue that it was created in a Columban monastery in northern Britain or in Iona and then brought to Ireland in the tenth century.[27] Whatever its origins, the *Book of Durrow* was created in one of the Columban monasteries in Ireland, Scotland or Britain.

The book contains 248 pages. Each folio measures about 245 mm by 145 mm (9½ by 6½ inches).[28] Its written text and its painted pages would each have taken about sixty days to produce.[29]

The shrine that originally contained the book was lost during the seventeenth century.[30] It bore an inscription stating that Flann, King of Ireland (879-916) had the shrine made in honour of St Columba (St Colum Cille).

According to Bernard Meehan, the book was: 'written in a superb majuscule script, accompanied by pages of ornament by an artist who produced some of the most striking images in insular art.'[31]

The Book of Durrow

The *Book of Durrow* is the earliest surviving fully decorated insular Gospel-book. It predates the *Book of Kells* by over a century.

It was probably written and illuminated in the scriptorium of Durrow monastery sometime in the first half of the seventh century,[26] though some scholars would argue that it was created in a Columban monastery in northern Britain or in Iona and then brought to Ireland in the tenth century.[27] Whatever its origins, the *Book of Durrow* was created in one of the Columban monasteries in Ireland, Scotland or Britain.

The book contains 248 pages. Each folio measures about 245 mm by 145 mm (9½ by 6½ inches).[28] Its written text and its painted pages would each have taken about sixty days to produce.[29]

The shrine that originally contained the book was lost during the seventeenth century.[30] It bore an inscription stating that Flann, King of Ireland (879-916) had the shrine made in honour of St Columba (St Colum Cille).

According to Bernard Meehan, the book was: 'written in a superb majuscule script, accompanied by pages of ornament by an artist who produced some of the most striking images in insular art.'[31]

The *Book of Durrow* consists of the four gospels. Each gospel is preceded by two illuminated pages. One contains the symbol of the evangelist, while the other is a page of pure ornamentation, known as a carpet page. Three main colours are used throughout the book: a vivid yellow known as yellow arsenic, often used as a gold substitute; a red derived from red lead, and a faded green that comes from acetate of copper.[32]

In this Gospel-book, the symbol of the man represents St Matthew and that of the calf stands for St Luke. However, the usual symbols for Saints Mark and John are reversed, with the eagle representing St Mark and the lion representing St John.

Art historian Francoise Henry vividly described the manuscript:

> *The ornaments vary from page to page. On one page wide ribbons, yellow, red and green, zig-zag and twist on a background of deep black, on another they are knotted to form a series of circles. Elsewhere spirals of the same simple, well-harmonized colours swirl, whirl and curl around hissing animal heads. And finally a whole page is made of fantastic animals, sinuous bodies plaited and interwoven together, wan, worm-like heads seizing everything within reach in soft, prehensile jaws.*
>
> *Nearly every page is surrounded by a border of interlacing, and these also frame the symbols. The man, the eagle, the calf and the lion boldly drawn, speckled with dazzling spots of yellow, red and green float each in the middle of a great rectangle of vellum bound by the frame, more startling by reason of this isolation.*[33]

Similarities to manuscripts from Syria, Mesopotamia and Egypt led Henry to conclude that this part of the world inspired the monks who illuminated the *Book of Durrow*.[34]

In 1661 Henry Jones, Bishop of Meath and Vice-chancellor of Trinity College, acquired the illuminated manuscript, which today is on display in the magnificent library of the university.

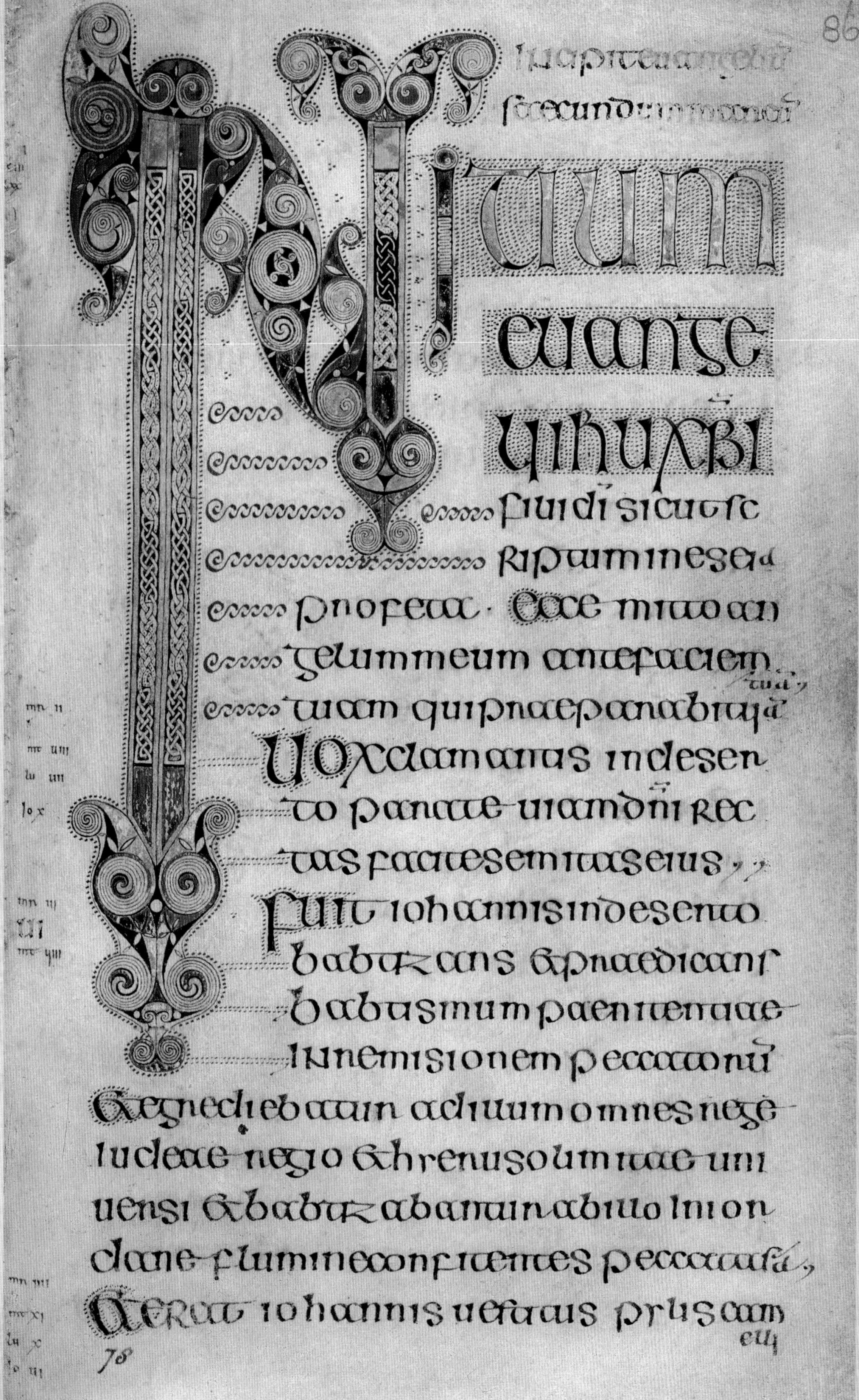

The Power of Sacred Relics

Sacred relics, such as the *Book of Durrow,* were believed to contain the power of God. Early Christians in Ireland believed that divine power passed through the angels, providing the inspiration for the saint or scribe. That power travelled through the scribe's quill as he made the Word of God manifest on the pages of the religious texts. When the scribe or saint died, the divine power within him came to rest in the relics he left behind: his bones, his clothing and the manuscripts that he created.

The *Life of St Columba* contains a story that illustrates the belief that these sacred relics possessed miraculous powers.

> *About fourteen years before the date at which we write, there occurred during the spring a very great and long-continued drought in these marshy regions . . . fearing the impending calamity, [we] took counsel together, and resolved that some of the senior members of the community should walk round a newly ploughed and sowed field, taking with them the white tunic of St Columba, and some books written in his own hand, that they should raise in the air, and shake three times the tunic which the saint wore at the hour of his death; and that they then should open the books and read them on the little hill of the angels now called Sithean Mor, where the citizens of the heavenly country were occasionally seen to descend at the bidding of the blessed man.*
>
> *When these directions had been executed in the manner prescribed, then, strange to relate, the sky, which during the preceding months of March and April had been cloudless, was suddenly covered with dense vapours that arose from the sea with extraordinary rapidity; copious rain fell day and night, and the parched earth being sufficiently moistened, produced its fruits in good season, and yielded the same year a most abundant harvest. And thus the invocation of the very name of the blessed man, by the exhibition of his tunic and books, obtained seasonable relief at the same time for many places and much people.*

When Conell MacGeoghegan was translating the *Annals of Clonmacnoise* in 1627, he gave an eyewitness account of how the *Book of Durrow* was used by the people of Offaly:

> *. . . when sickness came upon cattle, for their Remedy putt water on the booke & suffered it to rest there a while & saw alsoe cattle returne thereby to their former or pristine state & the booke to receave no loss.*[35]

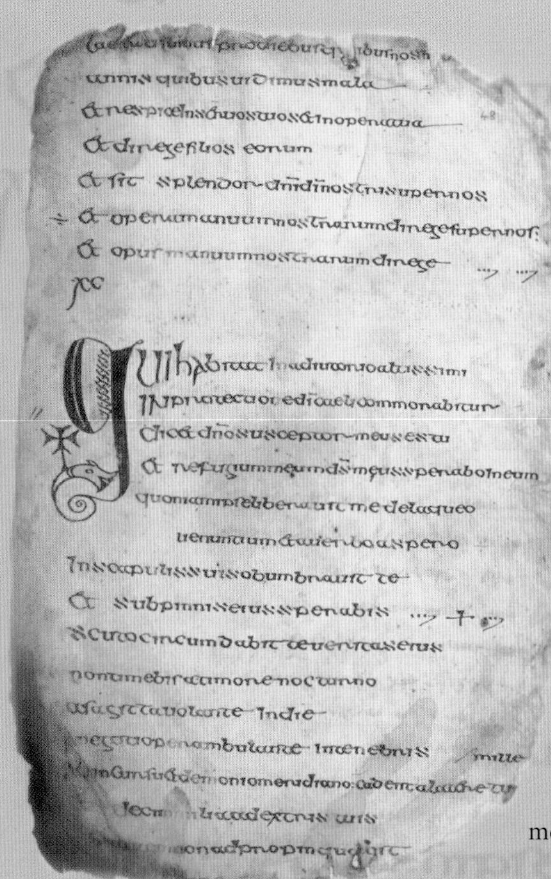

The Cathach of St Columba

Although Colum Cille did not write the *Book of Durrow,* he is believed to be the author of a late sixth- or early seventh-century manuscript known as the *Cathach of St Columba (St Colum Cille).* The manuscript of this psalter (book of Psalms) is the oldest surviving example of Irish majuscule writing.

The word *cathach* means 'battle or champion,' which refers to how the manuscript was used. Contained within a metal shrine known as a *cumhdach,* the *Cathach of St Columba* was carried into battle by the O'Donnells to ensure victory.

In the sixteenth century, Manus O'Donnell, son of a chieftain of Tír Conaill, described the significance of the *Cathach of St Columba:*

> *It is the chief relic of Colum Cille in the territory of Cinél Conaill Gulban. And it is enshrined in a silver gilt box, which it is not lawful to open. And whenever it be carried three times, turning towards the right, around the army of the Cinél Conaill when they are going into battle, the army usually comes back victorious.*[36]

Today the *Cathach* can be seen in the library of the Royal Irish Academy, Dublin.

The Church on the Holly Ridge

Drumcullen—Druim Chuilinn—Hill of Holly

Location on this important territorial boundary made the monastery a suitable place for provincial kings to meet and—sometimes—to murder each other.

In the sixth century a monk named Barrind (Barrindeus, Bairfhinn or Barron) founded a monastery at Drumcullen, a day's journey from the monastery at Rahan.

Little is known about Barrind other than that he came from Tír Conaill (Donegal) and was a kinsman of St Colum Cille. He was born of the race of Conall Gulban, son of Niall of the Nine Hostages.

In the early days of the church in Ireland, the monastery was described as 'a cell called Drum Cuilinn [Drumcullen], on the confines of Munster, Leinster, and Clanna Neill . . . which was in the territory of Fearceall [Fir Chell]. . . . In Drum Cuilinn dwelt the holy abbot, Barrfhinn [Barrind], renowned for miracles.'[1]

Barrind gave his name to the most prominent landscape feature in the region, Knockbarron Hill. Its name is derived from cnoc bairfhinn, meaning the 'Hill of Barrind.' From the top of this hill there are commanding views of the Slieve Bloom Mountains and the territory of Éile, known as Ely O'Carroll.

The frontier monastery of Drumcullen was located on the banks of the Camcor River— then known as Avonchara ('the Terrible River')[2]— which forms part of the boundary of the ancient province of Meath, in the Gaelic territory known as Fir Chell. Across this river was the rival kingdom of Munster.

Location on this important territorial boundary made the monastery a suitable place for provincial kings to meet and—sometimes—to murder each other. This latter role was highlighted in the *Annals of Loch Cé* when, in 1184, Art O'Maelsechlainn, King of Midhe, was slain by Diarmaid O'Briain, King of Thomond, at a meeting in Druim-Chuilinn [Drumcullen].[3]

St Barrind's Voyage

According to legend, Barrind was a great traveller. In one story Barrind and his son Mernoc discovered the 'Land of Promise of the Saints.'[16] In the *Life of St Brendan of Clonfert,*[17] Barrind recounts the story of this fantastic voyage:

> *. . . my dear son . . . led me to the western shore, where there was a small boat, and he then said: 'Father, enter this boat, and we will sail on to the west, towards the island called the Land of Promise of the Saints, which God will grant to those who succeed us in the latter days.'*
>
> *. . . clouds over-shadowed us on every side, so dense that we could scarcely see the prow or the stern of the boat. After the lapse of an hour or so, a great light shone around us, and land appeared, spacious and grassy, and bearing all manner of fruits. And when the boat touched the shore; we landed, and walked round about the island for fifteen days, yet could not reach the limits thereof. No plant saw we there without its flower; no tree without its fruit; and all the stones thereon were precious gems.*
>
> *But on the fifteenth day we discovered a river flowing from the west towards the east, when, being at a loss what to do, though we wished to cross over the river, we awaited the direction of the Lord. While we thus considered the matter, there appeared suddenly before us a certain man, shining with a great light, who, calling us by our names, addressed us thus: 'Welcome, worthy brothers, for the Lord has revealed to you the land He will grant unto His saints. There is one-half of the island up to this river, which you are not permitted to pass over; return, therefore, whence you came.'*
>
> *Hearing this we were moved to tears, and having rested awhile, we set out on our return journey, the man aforesaid accompanying us to the shore, where our boat was moored. When we had entered the boat, this man was taken from our sight, and we went on into the thick darkness we had passed through before, and thus unto the Island of delights.*
>
> *. . . the brethren . . . rejoiced with great joy at our return, as they had long bewailed our absence, and they said: 'Why, O fathers, did you leave us, your little flock, to stray without a shepherd in the wilderness?'*
>
> *. . . I tried to console them, and said: 'Do you not know, by the fragrance of our garments, that we have been in the paradise of God?'*

After Brendan heard Barrind's story, an angel appeared in his dreams, saying, 'Arise Brendan, that which thou hast requested, thou shalt receive of God, that is to visit the Land of Promise.' Legend has it that Brendan set sail with fourteen of his followers and that the place he discovered is known today as America. Scholars suggest that this story symbolises the quest for enlightenment.

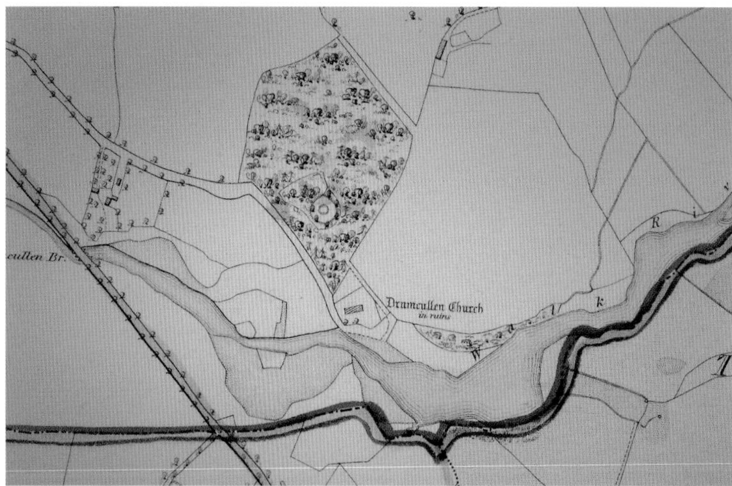

In 1205 King John granted to Meiler Fitzhenry the lordship of a vast geographical region that included Drumcullen. The administrative centre of this holding was at Ardnurcher (Horseleap), in present-day County Westmeath. St David's Church at Ardnurcher was the parish church for the entire region, with Drumcullen as one of its daughter-chapels.[4]

At this time, St Barrind's monastery changed to serve the spiritual needs of the Anglo-Norman lord and his followers. It was common for Anglo-Normans to re-dedicate Irish churches to their favourite saints. Therefore, it is likely that Fitzhenry was involved in removing the church's original patron saint, and re-dedicating the church at Drumcullen to St John.

It appears that Fitzhenry granted one-third of his land to the church at Drumcullen. Today the field to the north of the church contains the impressive remains of the foundation mound, or *motte,* of a wooden castle erected by the Anglo-Normans between 1180-1220. The timber castle constructed on top of this mound was known as a *bretasche,* French for 'timber tower.' The anglicised version of this word is 'brittas,' which appears in townland names including, possibly, the nearby townland of Ballybritt.

The bailey— a courtyard attached to the timber tower— acted as a garrison for the Anglo-Norman lord. From this stronghold Fitzhenry was able to control and pacify the Gaelic kings whose land the Normans had confiscated. However, Anglo-Norman control over the area was short-lived. Within a hundred and fifty years the church was back in the hands of the local Irish chieftains.

In the first part of the 1400s, Drumcullen was a chapel of ease attached to the parish church of Lynally. For part of that time, it was controlled by the O'Lynams, a family that were an ecclesiastical dynasty in the Diocese of Meath. In 1466, the *Calendar of Papal Letters* records that Patrick Oluoneym (O'Lynam), son of unmarried parents, was appointed clerk of the parish church of Lynally. He would also have served at Drumcullen.

Sometime before 1500, the church's status changed to that of a fully-fledged parish church. During this time, a two-storey priest's house was inserted into the west end of the church. The ground floor chamber appears to have been the sleeping quarters that connected to the upper storey by a stone stairs.

One can imagine the priest in his first floor apartment, reading his book by the light that flowed through the window in the west gable of the church, and then retiring downstairs to sleep under the barrel-vaulted stone roof. Upon wakening, he could pass through the doorway into the west end of the church to administer the sacraments to his congregation.

Rory O'Conebaghe (Conboy) was listed as 'vicar of Dromcollyn' in 1547.[5] Three years later, the church was once again served by the O'Lynams. Records state that the 'vicarage of St Berryn,' (the church at Drumcullen) was served by the priest Ruaidhrí Ó Laidheanáin (O'Lynam).[6]

Between 1536 and 1547, Henry VIII initiated a policy of suppressing the Irish monasteries. This suppression continued during the reign of Elizabeth I (1558-1603) and the church at Drumcullen fell upon hard times. Its ultimate demise probably occurred between 1649-58, when English forces under Oliver Cromwell embarked on a campaign to stamp out the remaining centres of Catholic faith.

By the late seventeenth century 'Bishop Dopping's Visitation Book' (1682-1685) described Drumcullen church as 'unusable.' The Bishop wrote that the Protestant curate was preaching in a private house at Eglish. The Catholic priest, as well as offering services in private houses, offered mass in the open air on mass rocks.[7]

The Mystery of the Kinnitty High Cross

In the grounds of Kinnitty Castle there is a high cross, known locally as the Kinnitty High Cross, which may originally have come from the monastery at Drumcullen. It bears a dedication to Maelsechnaill mac Maelruanaid, who was King of Meath from 846-862. The inscription reads:

OR DO RIG MAELSECH NAILL M MAELRUANAID
OROIT AR RIG HERENN
('A prayer for King Maelsechnaill son of Maelruanaid
A prayer for the King of Ireland')
OR DO COLMAN DORRO... INCROSSA AR RIG HERENN
OR DO RIG HERENN[18]
('A prayer for Colman who made the cross for the King of Ireland
A prayer for the King of Ireland')

It is highly unlikely that the monastery at Kinnitty, which was located in the province of Munster, would have commissioned a high cross for a rival king. A far more likely scenario is that the cross was taken from Drumcullen, which is located in the province of Meath.

Further evidence that the cross was moved is that its golden brown sandstone shaft and head have been clumsily set into a grey-coloured limestone base. Obviously, this base and cross were not designed for each other. It seems likely that the base belongs to a limestone cross, the head of which lies in the graveyard at Drumcullen.

There may have been three high crosses at Drumcullen, two of limestone and one of sandstone. The partial remains of two of these crosses could have been fitted together when, as legend says, the Bernard family (builders of Castle Bernard, now known as Kinnitty Castle) took the cross from Drumcullen churchyard in the nineteenth century.

Even today, the subject of the cross can still come up between the communities of Kinnitty and Drumcullen, as shown in the following story told by Fr. Moorhead, Parish Priest of Eglish:

At the village of Kinnitty one evening in 1992, during an under-sixteen hurling match between Drumcullen and Kinnitty, a foul was committed on a Drumcullen player. The foul gave rise to an argument on the sideline between the rival supporters. During the argument a Drumcullen supporter shouted out to the Kinnitty people: 'When are you going to give us back our Cross?'

During the early nineteenth century, the abandoned church at Drumcullen was noted for its impressive Romanesque doorway, an indication that the stone church was built sometime in the mid- to late twelfth century, possibly before the arrival of the Anglo-Normans. In 1801, Charles Coote described the doorway of Drumcullen church as a 'very fine arch of curious workmanship.'[8] However, he also noted that the church was 'rapidly falling to ruin, as at every funeral in the adjacent burial ground, it [was] plundered for a headstone.'[9] By the end of the century, Rev. John Healy would write: 'Not many years ago there was a handsome doorway to be seen. Not a vestige of it now remains, though some carved stones are to be found scattered here and there through the graveyard.'[10]

By 1900, fragments of the beautiful doorway, along with remnants of the head of a high cross, lay broken on the ground of the graveyard at Drumcullen.

However, even as the church fell into decay, local people continued to observe rituals on Knockbarron Hill. In his report on the monastery in 1839, John O'Donovan observed that local people did not observe the Feastday of St Barrind, which is 21 May. Instead, 24 June, the Feastday of St John, was the Patron Day of the parish. On that day people visited St John's Well and St John's Rock on top of Knockbarron Hill. They placed votive offerings in the crevices of the holy rock and tied offerings onto the tree overhanging the well.

Peering into the crevice of the rock in 1918, Olive Purser described seeing:

> *. . . rosary beads, little devotional images and cards, buttons of all kinds down to the linen variety, clasps, brooches, pipe bowls, staples &c. The offerings included even money; a brass farthing dated 1790.*

A local girl told Purser: 'If you say a prayer at the rock and leave something there, you leave your sins behind you.'[11]

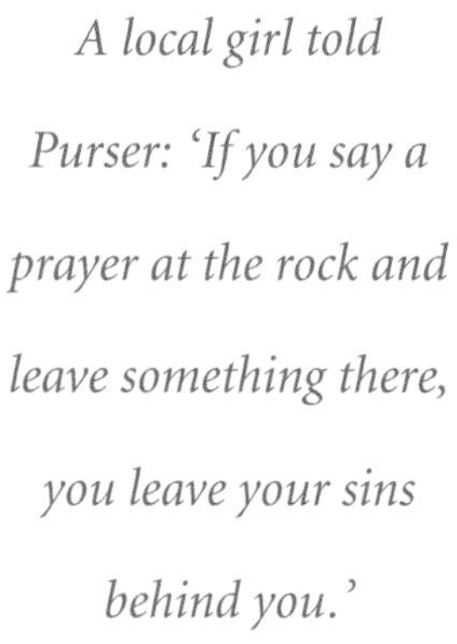

A local girl told Purser: 'If you say a prayer at the rock and leave something there, you leave your sins behind you.'

Purser recorded that the date of celebration on the top of Knockbarron Hill was 23 June; this date coincides with the pagan festival of Midsummer's Eve.

The practice of converting pagan customs and festivals into Christian celebrations was common in the early church. In fact, in a letter from 601, Pope Gregory gave Bishop Augustine the following advice:

> *... because they [the English] are in the habit of slaughtering much cattle as sacrifices to devils, some solemnity ought to be given in exchange for this. So on the day of the dedication or the festivals of the holy martyrs, whose relics are deposited there, let them make themselves huts from the branches of trees around the churches which have been converted out of shrines and let them celebrate the solemnity with religious feasts. Do not let them sacrifice animals to the devil, but let them slaughter animals for their own food to the praise of God, and let them give thanks to the Giver of all things for His bountiful provision.*[12]

Midsummer's Eve, known locally as Oíche Fhéile Eoin ('Night of St John's Festival') or St John's Eve, was originally one of several important pre-Christian festivals that marked the change of seasons. Rituals on this day were attempts to invoke the will of the gods or of St John to protect livestock and crops from bad weather or disease.

During the nineteenth century, it was the custom to light a communal bonfire on top of a hill, like Knockbarron Hill, at sunset on 23 June. This festival was often referred to as Bonfire Night. In a ritual that could be interpreted as a fusion of Christian and pre-Christian beliefs, the community would often gather around the fire where a local priest recited a decade of the Rosary. During his recitation the people would walk in a clockwise direction around the bonfire.

In the recent past bonfires were lit on this night in the area around Drumcullen. Local people would scatter ashes from the bonfire on their crops to ensure a bountiful harvest. Another belief was that driving cattle over the embers of the bonfire would ensure a high milk return.[13]

During her visit in 1918, Olive Purser noted that: 'In a neighbouring field [near the church] are what seemed very like the remains of a circle of sacred stones.'[14]

Remains of this possible stone circle can still be seen in a field to the north of the church and motte.[15] Its presence near the monastery may support the theory that this was a pre-Christian ritual centre taken over by the early Christian monks. The same process may have occurred at other monasteries throughout the county; for example, records of standing stones on the monastic enclosures at Rahan and Durrow could indicate that these monasteries were also founded on pre-Christian ritual sites.

Since the seventeenth century, Barrind's monastery at Drumcullen has been used only as a burial place for the people of Drumcullen. However, the tradition of worship at this site still continues each year with the pattern that is held on 23 June, St John's Eve. This may be the latest manifestation of a tradition that extends back for millennia at the monastery of St Barrind and on Knockbarron Hill.

THE CHURCH OF SWANS

Lynally—Lainn Eala—The Church of Swans

. . . my relics shall be with you,

and I will bequeath evil to them that encroach upon you.

Around 590 a monk named Colman mac Béognae erected a church at a place called Fiodh Elo ('Elo Wood') in the Gaelic territory of Fir Chell, part of the kingdom of Meath.[1] Ever after he was known as Colman of Elo.

Colman was born around 555 at Glenelly, County Tyrone. He was a nephew of St Colum Cille and was successor to Mac Nise, the founding bishop of the Diocese of Connor. Colman studied in Iona, leaving this monastery after the death of Colum Cille in 597.[2] As well as the monastery at Lynally, Colman founded a church at Muckamore, in present-day County Antrim. He was also a missionary to the area around Galloway, in southern Scotland, where three churches are dedicated to him.[3] In the year 611, Colman died at the age of 56.

Today the monastery of Lynally sits on the flat floodplains of the Clodiagh River with good views of open flat countryside. Ballycowan Castle is visible in the distance. However, Colman would not have known this landscape.

He founded his monastery in what was probably a small clearing or meadow, surrounded by one of the great oak forests of Ireland. The *Annals of Loch Cé* called this place 'the Green of Lann-Eala.' There may have been a small lake beside the church; in the *Life of Colman* it is called Lough Ela ('Swan Lake').

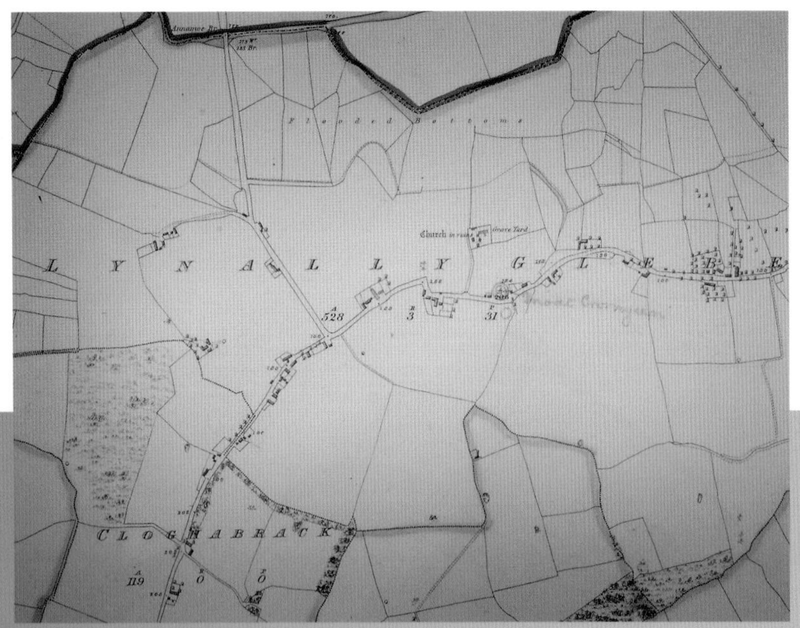

St Patrick and Mac Nise had already declared that a monastery would be established at this location. They 'saw above it a hole in the heavens and angels passing to and fro.'[4] Early church leaders considered the site at Lynally, like those at Seirkieran and Rahan, to be a hallowed place chosen by God, which would act as a portal to heaven.

When Colman arrived in the territory of Fir Chell, his first task was to convince its rulers to abandon their Celtic gods for the one Christian God.

However, the rulers of Fir Chell did not welcome the evangelist.[5] In one story, they set Colman the task of defeating a monster, which lived in the lake of Lough Ela. This monster had terrorised the people and caused pestilence and disease throughout the territory. Neither the Celtic priests nor the warriors of the tribe had been able to destroy it, and its continued existence undermined the authority of the king.

Skeptical about the new religion, Donnchad, the King of Fir Chell, said to Colman: 'It would be better for us to set you holy man called Colman Ela to fight the monster, and it would be better [still] in our opinion that neither . . .[of you] should return.' In other words, if Colman, as well as the monster, were to perish, then two problems would be solved.

The Singing Swans

According to a legend from the *Life of Colman*, when the monks built the stone enclosure around Colman's monastery, they also built a great causeway (road) that linked Lynally to Kilclare on the present-day Westmeath-Offaly border.

As the monks engaged in the gruelling work of building this great road, a flock of swans began to arrive every hour on the hour. The swans sang songs that relieved the exhaustion of the monks, allowing them to continue work without tiring.

Because of this story, the land around the monastery became known as Lainn Eala, meaning 'Swans' Land'[13] or 'Church of the Swans.'

In the seventeenth century the church of Lynally was also known as Dullenally,[14] which may refer to the monastic enclosure. *Dull* is a corruption of the Irish word *dun,* meaning 'enclosure' or 'fort.'

Today at Lynally only the slightest remains of this enclosure can be seen surrounding the church and graveyard. No remains of the great causeway have ever been discovered.

The Alphabet of Devotion

Colman was the author of the *Alphabet of Devotion*, an A-to-Z guide book of how a monk should live. Because Colman was a disciple of his uncle, Colum Cille, his *Alphabet* offers an insight into the mindset of the monks at Durrow, Iona and other Columban (associated with Colum Cille) monasteries in Ireland and Scotland.

In his *Alphabet* Colman identifies three enemies of the soul: the world, the devil and an unholy teacher. To combat these threats, he points out the three things that drive out a restless spirit and create a stable mind: vigil, prayer and labour. For Colman, this approach was the essence of a monastic life. These principles are clearly echoed in the *Rule of St Carthage* of Rahan.

Before sending him to confront the monster, the king decided to test Colman's powers of persuasion. He ordered his followers: 'Bring Colman to us that he may preach to us, so that we may know how many among us he can convert.'

Eloquence—specifically the ability to boast—would be essential if Colman were to convince the native rulers of the power of the Christian God. This pre-Christian warrior aristocracy placed high value on physical prowess, fighting skill, and the ability to defend one's honour and that of one's tribe with a quick wit and a ready tongue.[6] Boasting was an integral part of the tales they composed about their heroic past. To convert the Fir Chell, Colman would have to match them, skill for skill, in word and in deed.

It is little wonder that, when asked to speak before the Lords of the Fir Chell, Colman decided to invite his uncle Colum Cille and Manchan of Lemanaghan to join him. As the three evangelists began preaching from their Latin books and offering eloquent praise to God, the Lords of the Fir Chell were deeply impressed. Almost to a man, they abandoned their Celtic gods and became supporters of Colman and his religion.

The sons of Donnchad offered land so that Colman could build a monastery, declaring that their descendants would be its patrons. Duinecha, heir to the chieftainship of the territory, swore that he would follow Colman to the four corners of the world.[7]

Impressed though King Donnchad may have been, he still demanded that Colman slay the monster in the lake. If Colman defeated this beast, the king said he would donate in return: 'the place in which it (the monster) is, and I will give my seed after me, and (any of) my assistants that he prefers to have given to him, shall be given to him.'

Cuineda and Duinecha, two sons of the king, accompanied Colman to the lakeside. As he stood on the banks, Colman addressed the monster: 'If God permit, I would permit the reeds of the lake to bind thee for me, that I may slay thee.'

Then Cuineda and Duinecha entered the lake and struck off the monster's head. They presented its lifeless body to Colman. In return, Colman said to Cuineda: 'Thou and thy seed shall be with me till doom as stewards; and my relics shall be with you, and I will bequeath evil to them that encroach upon you.'

Duinecha stepped forward and pledged his life to Colman as well, saying: 'I will be thy servant, till thy habitation and labour be all ready.'

Then Colman and his followers proceeded to the land which now belonged to him as a gift from the king.

There the monks built a monastery surrounded by a stone enclosure. Inside was a wooden church, built by Colman, along with circular houses made of wattle, in which the monks lived.

In the *Life of Colman,* Baithin, a disciple of Colman, describes these buildings:

With wattles the round house is made;
The dwelling that is pleasing to God.
Its family increases more and more.[8]

As well as being a 'city of refuge' for those who chose the religious life, Colman's monastery at Lynally grew to become a centre of evangelism, commerce and industry.

Because Colman was not only an abbot, but also a priest and a bishop, he could perform every function within the monastery at Lynally. His triple role enabled him to administer the diocese (as bishop), run the secular affairs of the monastery (as abbot), and perform clerical duties as a priest. Colman could do everything from administering the sacraments to managing the financial affairs of the monastery.

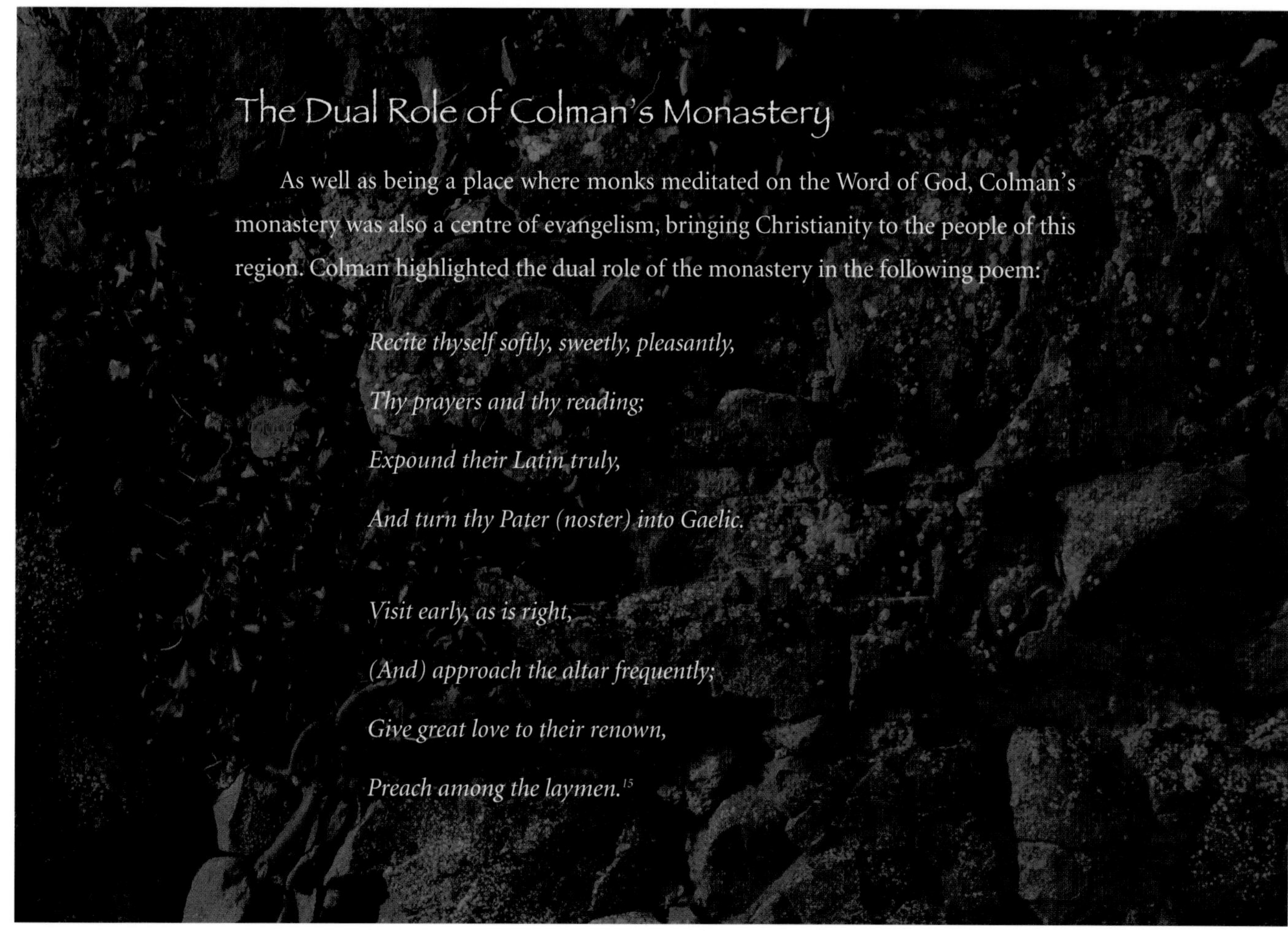

The Dual Role of Colman's Monastery

As well as being a place where monks meditated on the Word of God, Colman's monastery was also a centre of evangelism, bringing Christianity to the people of this region. Colman highlighted the dual role of the monastery in the following poem:

Recite thyself softly, sweetly, pleasantly,
Thy prayers and thy reading;
Expound their Latin truly,
And turn thy Pater (noster) into Gaelic.

Visit early, as is right,
(And) approach the altar frequently;
Give great love to their renown,
Preach among the laymen.[15]

Different areas within the cemetery were reserved for the monks and for the people of Fir Chell. A passage from the *Life of Colman* contains a legend that may show why ordinary people were willing to pay for the privilege of burial within the lands of Lynally monastery.

As a young priest, Colman had been tutored in Rome by 'Gregory the Golden-Mouthed.' When he learned of Gregory's death, Colman was stricken with grief. A day later, he saw seven donkeys carrying seven sacks of soil from Rome, which had been sent by Gregory as he lay dying.

As they unloaded the sacks, the attendants of the donkeys said to Colman: 'Here is the help which thy tutor sent to thee; shake it over the length and breadth of thy cemetery, and any one who is buried in it shall not see Hell.'

When this was done Colman said: 'The first part of the cemetery shall be thine, O Duinecha; and the middle of it shall be thine, O Cuineda. And the rest of the cemetery shall belong to the Fir Cell [Fir Chell] and to the men of Erin.'

Today the graveyard and the church are the only surviving reminders of Colman's monastery.

The stone church is a multi-period structure; its earliest part dates from around the tenth or eleventh century. Originally this church was a small rectangular undivided building, with

The first part of the cemetery
shall be thine, O Duinecha;
and the middle of it
shall be thine, O Cuineda.
And the rest of the cemetery
shall belong to the Fir Cell
and to the men of Erin.

sidewalls projecting beyond the gables. It may have been a copy, in stone, of an earlier wooden church that it replaced.

It is possible that there was once a small house-shaped shrine in the graveyard near the stone church. The *Annals of Ulster* record that in 1122 on Spy Wednesday (the Wednesday before Good Friday, on which Judas is said to have betrayed Jesus), the shrine of Colman, son of Luachán, was found in the burial place of Lann Ela. Unfortunately this shrine, like many shrines from Offaly monasteries, has disappeared.

In 1207 the Anglo-Normans attacked the territory of the Fir Chell. Around this time they also constructed a timber castle across the field to the south of the church. The remains of a *motte,* or earthen foundation for the castle, are still visible.

Until the fifteenth century, the parish church of the people of the Fir Chell was St David's Church in Horseleap (Ardnurcher) in modern Westmeath. In 1400, the people petitioned Pope Boniface IX, stating that they needed a parish church closer to home because access to St David's Church was difficult 'especially in the winter and rainy season as it was eight English miles away.' Finally, in 1424, the pope confirmed the elevation of the status of St Colman's church at Lynally to that of a parish church.

A Ministry of Obligations

Like many monasteries, Colman's foundation at Lynally became a centre of industry and commerce in a region that remained largely agricultural. During the Middle Ages, one of the three great fairs of Ireland was held annually at Lynally (the others were at Clonmacnoise and at Teltown, County Meath).

To prosper, the monastery needed the financial support of lay people. The following narrative poem, from the *Life of Colman,* describes the obligations of lay people to Colman's religious community. If the people paid their dues to the monastery, they would receive bountiful and prosperous lives and the salvation of their souls. Failure to support the material needs of the monastery would result in famine, illness and eternal damnation.

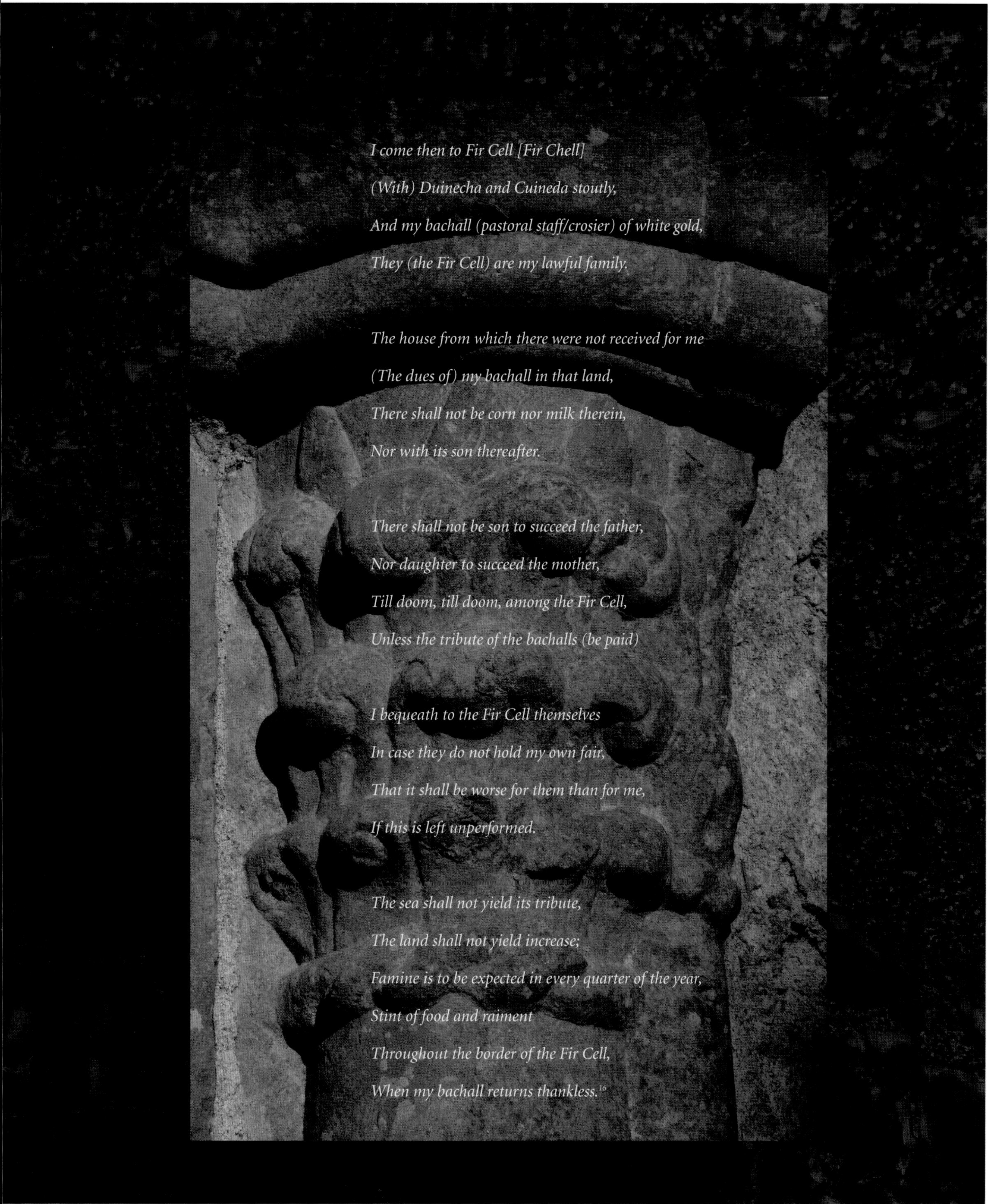

I come then to Fir Cell [Fir Chell]
(With) Duinecha and Cuineda stoutly,
And my bachall (pastoral staff/crosier) of white gold,
They (the Fir Cell) are my lawful family.

The house from which there were not received for me
(The dues of) my bachall in that land,
There shall not be corn nor milk therein,
Nor with its son thereafter.

There shall not be son to succeed the father,
Nor daughter to succeed the mother,
Till doom, till doom, among the Fir Cell,
Unless the tribute of the bachalls (be paid)

I bequeath to the Fir Cell themselves
In case they do not hold my own fair,
That it shall be worse for them than for me,
If this is left unperformed.

The sea shall not yield its tribute,
The land shall not yield increase;
Famine is to be expected in every quarter of the year,
Stint of food and raiment
Throughout the border of the Fir Cell,
When my bachall returns thankless.[16]

After it became a parish church the small building was enlarged and extended to the east. To accommodate the newly created parish priest of Lynally, the church added on a two-storey wing with a barrel-vaulted ground floor to the south. The priest's sleeping quarters were on the ground floor and his living quarters were upstairs. An internal doorway gave him access to the church.

In the graveyard, there are the remains of a floriated grave slab decorated with a traceried window. It was made sometime between 1350 and 1600. The window depicted on the slab may represent the original east window of Lynally church.

Like other monasteries in Offaly, Lynally was the site of turmoil and bloodshed. The *Annals of the Four Masters* records that in 1557 the English army burned the church and devastated the great woodlands that surrounded it in an act of revenge against Art O'Molloy, one of the Lords of Fir Chell:

> *Another hosting was made by the Treasurer into Fircall, to take vengeance upon O'Molloy (Art) for his protection of the wood kerns and other insurgents. On this occasion the whole country, from the Wood of Coill mor eastwards, was ravaged; Baile-mhic-Abhainn (Ballycowan) and Lynally, both houses and churches, were burned; and Calvagh, son of O'Molloy, was killed at Bel-atha-glaisi, by the Treasurer and his army, on that occasion. He came a second time, and burned the territory, and cut down its woods, and gave neither peace nor rest to O'Molloy, but chased and banished him, and proclaimed him a traitor, and gave the lordship to Theobald O'Molloy, who delivered up to him his son as a hostage in his own place.*

Despite similar episodes, this extensive woodland was still intact in the seventeenth century, when it was known as the Great Wood of Fircall.

After the Reformation, the church at Lynally became a Protestant place of worship. In 1684 Thomas Coffey, Vicar of Fir Chell, constructed his burial vault inside the church and inserted his armorial plaque into the west wall of the building. Its inscription reads: 'This monument was made for Thomas Coffey, clearke, and his deare wife Anne Hide and their posterite Anno Dom 1684.'

An account from that time describes the church as being in good condition, containing a small chancel with glazed windows and a clay floor. It also possessed a desk, pulpit, and railed-in table, but it had no font, carpet, cloth, chalice or flagon.[9] The church stood within a graveyard that had been enclosed by a stone wall since at least the seventeenth century.[10]

A second burial vault beside the Coffey vault probably belongs to the Forth family, who lived in Redwood Castle (now Charleville Castle) in the late seventeenth century.[11]

In 1690 Bishop Dopping of Meath re-roofed the church at Lynally with a shingle roof taken from the nearby church at Rahan.[12] The church at Lynally continued to be used until the early nineteenth century, when a new Church of Ireland building was constructed nearby. At that point, the church at Lynally ceased to be a place of worship.

Early church leaders

considered the site at

Lynally to be a hallowed

place chosen by God,

which would act as

a portal to heaven.

THE CHURCH ON THE LAND OF FERNS

Rahan—Raithin Ui Suanaigh—the Ferny Land of the O'Swanys

It was he (Mochuda) that had the famous congregation consisting of seven hundred and ten persons; an angel used to address every third man of them.

In about 594, a priest named Carthage founded a monastery at Rahan, on the flat fern-covered land by the banks of the Clodiagh River.

Carthage was the son of a chieftain from what is now north Kerry. To the delight of his parents, as a young boy he spent time in the court of Maoltuile, King of Ciarraige Luachra. The king was very fond of the child. One day when the young boy was out herding pigs, he came across some monks, who were chanting and singing hymns. Compelled by the music, Carthage left the pigs with a swineherd and followed the monks back to their monastery. He remained there until the king, who missed the company of the young boy, sent a messenger to bring him back.

When the king asked Carthage where he had been, the boy replied: 'Sire, this is why I have stayed away— through attraction of the holy chant of the bishop and clergy; I have never heard anything so beautiful as this; the clerics sang as they went along the whole way before me; they sang until they arrived at their house, and thenceforth they sang till they went to sleep. The bishop however remained by himself far into the night praying by himself when the others had retired. And I wish, O king, that I might learn [their psalms and ritual].'[1]

Soon Carthage joined the monastery under the tutelage of its bishop. He learned to read and write, and eventually became a priest. The bishop called him 'Mochuda,' a term of endearment derived from the Irish *mo chuidig,* meaning 'my portion.'[2]

Carthage founded his first church at Kiltallagh in south Kerry, but he soon left it and went on a pilgrimage to the northern part of Ireland. Before this journey he visited the monastery of Ciaran Mac Fionntan at Rosgiallan (present-day Rostellan, County Cork). When Carthage asked Ciaran where he should establish his monastery, Ciaran replied:

> *You shall go first to Meath where you will found a famous church in the territory of Ibh Neill and there you will remain for forty years. You shall be driven thence into exile and you will return to Munster wherein will be your greatest and most renowned church.*[3]

Leaving Ciaran, Carthage travelled along the ancient road called the Slighe Dhála ('Dala's Road') to the monastery of Colman Elo at Lynally, in the province of Meath. On his arrival, Carthage said to Colman: 'Father I would remain here with you.'

'Not so,' replied Colman, 'but go you to a place called Rahan in this vicinity; that is the place ordained by God for your dwelling and you shall have there a large community in the service of God.'[4]

Colman told Carthage that he would find a bundle of timber rods in Rahan and on that spot he should set up his monastery. And so Carthage built his first cell with the timber rods that Colman had left behind. Over the next forty years, the monastery developed into a thriving community of over 800 monks, led by Carthage.

Today the monastic landscape at Rahan offers visitors a tantalising glimpse of what life must have been like for the monks. The ancient boundary of the monastic town can still be traced around the large site, which measures over 380 metres (415½ yards) in diameter. On top of the earthen bank, a timber palisade or a hedgerow would have defined the limits of the monastic community.

Rahan may have been a sacred place before Carthage used it to build his 'City of God.' In 1870-71, Thomas Stanley, a local antiquarian, visited the site and recorded that: 'A stone stands between the two banks which encircled old Rathan, [Rahan] and beside its Southern entrance, I take it to be monumental. It is a slab and is arranged upon the meridian.'[5]

Nothing survives of this standing stone, but its presence suggests that Rahan may have been a pre-Christian ritual centre. Whatever the site's previous importance to local people, Carthage's monastery turned Rahan into a hive of activity.

The community that lived within the enclosure would have included not only monks, but also artisans, farmers and their families. Tradesmen of every type would have come to the monastery seeking employment.

At Rahan, carpenters built wooden buildings and crosses. Stonemasons constructed churches and hewed crosses from stone. Herdsmen tended the calves that yielded vellum used in the monastic scriptorium. Metalworkers created chalices, agricultural tools and other metal items.

The *Life of Mochuda* paints a portrait of a diverse, self-sustaining community that includes a famous school, a hospital for the sick, a mill, cells for the monks, and a church with a cemetery.

The economic world outside the monastery revolved around cattle. In stark contrast, the monastic way of life, as revealed in the *Life of Mochuda,* revolved around arable farming. Carthage's life story contains numerous references to tillage, cereal production and milling.[6]

Carthage was a strict disciplinarian. He forbade the monks to eat anything but vegetables grown by themselves, and placed a premium on hard work as integral to the life of a monk. His rigorous approach to monastic life found its fullest expression in prayer. Carthage preferred to pray with arms fully extended in the crucified position, known as the 'Cross-Vigil.' The agony caused by this position was thought to bring the penitent closer to an understanding of the sacrifice and suffering of Christ.

Rule of St Carthage

After Carthage left Rahan, he founded a monastery at Lismore in Waterford. In the eighth century, a monk from that monastery wrote the *Rule of St Carthage,* which outlines the teachings of Carthage as followed by the monks at Rahan and Lismore.

The *Rule* consists of 135 four-lined stanzas. It starts with the Ten Commandments, and then it lists the obligations respectively of bishops, abbots, priests, monks and culdees (anchorites). These are followed by a section on the order of meals for the monks, and finally, on the obligations of a king.

Carthage's *Rule* identifies the various hours of the breviary (prayer and hymn book used by monks) that are still observed by the religious orders today.

The following stanzas outline the way a monk should live:

The Rule of St Carthage

If you be a clerical student under government,
Be active in resisting evil,
Abide in the law of the Church,
Without laxity, without fault.

With modesty, with meekness,
With constancy in obedience:
With Purity, with faultlessness
In all acts however trivial.

With patience, with simplicity,
With gentleness to everyone:
With groaning, with prayer,
Unto Christ at all hours . . .[17]

Accounts of the monastery refer to several crosses associated with the community. One account of the saint's life tells of how Carthage spoke to the dead in the cemetery of Rahan, saying: 'I will come on the Judgment Day with all my monks to the Cross of Constantine in front of the Church.'[7] Another story refers to the Cross of Ua Suanaig,[8] which was located in the townland of Roscore near Rahan.

None of these crosses survive. Whether they were built of timber or stone, it is clear that the crosses marked important locations within and outside the monastery. The Cross of Ua Suanaig in Roscore may have acted as a boundary marker for the lands of Rahan monastery, while the Cross of the Angels and the Cross of Constantine within the monastery could have been assembly points for the monks within the 'City of Refuge.'

Not much of the monastery from Carthage's time survives above the ground. However, a local place-name preserves the folk memory of a hermitage that belonged to one of his monks. A field in the grounds of the old Jesuit College has long been known locally as the Crann Field. The *Life of Mochuda* tells of the foundation of a small hermitage known as 'Cluain da Chrann,' which was established by Carthage for Mochua Mac Mellain, the first monk to enter the monastery at Rahan.

According to the story, Carthage built this cell for the monk as a reward for his virtuous youth, and so that he might have some comfort in his old age. Carthage said to the monk: 'Your place of resurrection will not be here (Rahan) but in another place which God has given you.'[9]

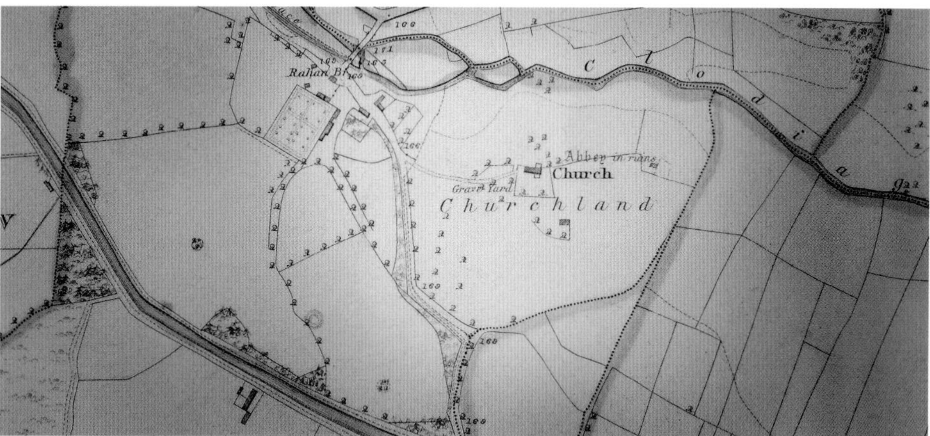

The story of the Crann Field helps us imagine the large monastic town of Rahan, with its isolated hermitages in the surrounding fields. The hermitages were near enough to allow monks to visit Rahan, but far enough away from the monastery to allow them to contemplate the Word of God in splendid isolation.

This arrangement appears to have been the model for early Christian monasteries in Offaly. Within the large monastic town, a Christian community could carry out its daily chores. Yet outside this monastic community, isolated hermitages offered individuals solitude in which to pursue their personal devotion to God.

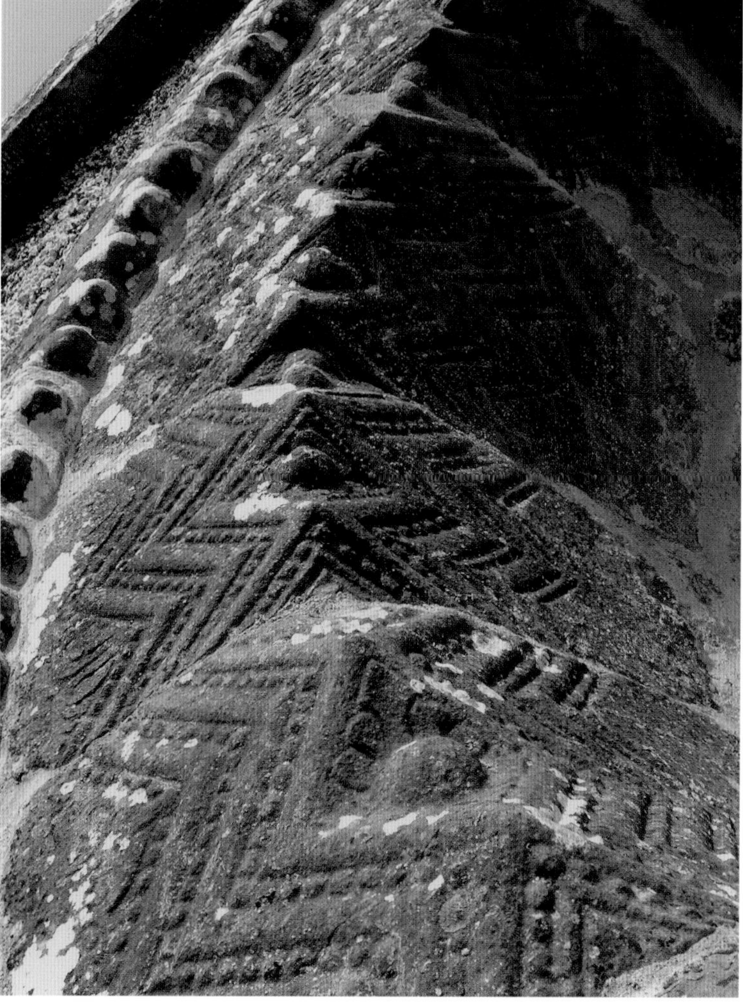

Despite its great spiritual and economic success, eventually Carthage's great monastery at Rahan succumbed to local politics. As a native of Munster, Carthage's allegiance would have been to the kings of that province. However, the monastery at Rahan was located in Meath, near the ancient Munster-Meath boundary. Eventually, the Kings of Meath decided to expel Carthage because they did not believe a man from Munster would act in their best interests. He was the 'wrong man, in the wrong place, at the wrong time.'

Another reason for his expulsion may have had to do with the famous conflict in the Irish church over the date of Easter. At the Synod of Magh Léne (Moylena) held near Durrow in 630, the leading churches in the southern half of Ireland adopted the Roman date for the Easter celebration.[10] However, churches of the northern half of Ireland would not agree to give up the traditional Easter date. This led to conflict between Irish monasteries. It also caused tension between the Irish church and the church in Rome.

It is possible that Carthage may have allied himself with the southern churches. Adoption of the Roman date for Easter at Rahan could have led to tension between Carthage's monastery and the monasteries of Durrow and Clonmacnoise, which might explain why they participated in the expulsion.

The expulsion of Carthage was foretold by Colum Cille (also known as Columba), a sixth-century saint who founded a number of famous monasteries, including Durrow in County Offaly and Iona in Scotland. The story is told in detail in *The Lives of Irish Saints.* In this account, Colum Cille tells Carthage: 'Let not what I say to you trouble you—this will not be the place of your resurrection, for the king of Erin and his family will grow jealous of you owing to machinations of some of the Irish clergy, and they shall eventually drive you hence.'

In 635, Blathmac, the King of Tara, and his brother Diarmuid, along with monks from the monastery of Clonard carried out the eviction. They said to Carthage: 'Leave this monastery and region and seek a place for yourself elsewhere.' [11]

Carthage and his disciples met at the Cross of the Angels in front of the church door and from there he cursed the King of Tara. Monks from Durrow also attended the expulsion and Carthage cursed them as well, saying: 'Contention and quarrelling shall be yours for ever to work evil and schism amongst you—for you have had a prominent part in exciting opposition to me.' [12]

Afterwards, Carthage left the monastery with his followers, never to return. They went to Waterford, where Carthage founded another monastery at Lismore. He died there two years later.

Rahan after Carthage

Following the departure of Carthage, there is no known mention of the monastery until the year 740, when the *Annals of Clonmacnoise* report that the monastery was under the rule of the Uí Suanaigh family. In 751, Finoyne O'Swanaye (Uí Suanaigh) of Rahan died, and from then on Rahan was known as Rahan O'Swanaye (Uí Suanaigh).

The O'Swanaye family ruled as abbots of the monastery until the twelfth century. In 1205, the *Annals* record the death of Moyle Kieran O'Kelly, Coarb ('Successor') of Rahan O'Swanaye, an indication that the O'Kellys had replaced the O'Swanayes as abbots of Rahan. It is likely that the two families were related and that the abbot of Rahan was an hereditary position shared between them until the thirteenth century.

Before the Anglo-Normans arrived in Ireland, Rahan also appears to have enjoyed the patronage of the O'Molloys, the Lords of Fir Chell. Whatever wealth this patronage brought to the monastery, it also involved the religious community in turbulent—and often violent—politics. At least two of the O'Molloys met their deaths in the church at Rahan. In 1139 the *Annals of the Four Masters* record that Muircheartach Ua Maelmhuaidh (O'Molloy) was burned to death by the Feara-Ceall (Fir Chell), by the Uí-Luainimh in the church of Raithin (Rahan).

As part of the monastic reform of Ireland, in the middle of the twelfth century the monks at Rahan adopted the Rule of St Augustine. The beautiful Romanesque cruciform church that stands on the site today dates from that period. The church may have been built between 1160-80, a time when the monastery was ruled by the O'Kelly family.

Inside the church, the division between the chancel and the nave is defined by a beautiful, but very simple, chancel arch. Two stylised faces, with powerful regal expressions above long curling moustaches, adorn the corners of the capitals that face the altar. They look eastwards, possibly symbolising their worship of God.

The unusual ground floor plan of the church may reflect influences from as far away as Syria or Armenia. Small, round-headed doorways in the north and south walls of the chancel lead to two small chambers.[13] Although rare in the architecture of Western churches, this floor plan is common in the early churches of the Byzantine East.

In Syrian churches, the room to the north, called the Diaconian chamber, was used as a sacristy. The main function of the chamber to the south, the Prothesis, was to store relics. Sometimes referred to as the 'Chapel of the Martyrs,'[14] it often became a centre of popular devotion where the public could visit the relics of the monastery.

At the church in Rahan, a staircase inside the east wall leads above the chancel to what was once a small A-shaped chamber in the apex of the roof. This room would have been very similar to the house-shaped shrines of the founder saints of early Irish monasteries. It is possible that the saint's relics were stored in this loft space and brought down into the Prothesis for public worship. If this were the case, the chamber would have warranted a window as beautiful and elaborate as the one that survives in the east gable today.

Heads of the Round Window

Wonderful carvings of heads decorate the external stone surround of the round window. The use of the disembodied head as a decorative architectural feature is characteristic of Irish Romanesque architecture.[18]

Looking up from the ground below, one notices four human heads on the right side of the window: a bishop, two bearded monks and one clean shaven tonsured monk with protruding ears.

The left side is decorated with three heads of fantastic animals from the Otherworld. The masons who carved these animal heads may have been inspired by monastic tales in which holy saints battled against fantastic monsters, representing the struggle of Good versus Evil. One head may represent the horned ram often found accompanying the pagan god Cernunnos in Celtic art.[19] Another animal appears to be an ape or monkey. The bulbous eyes and spiral snout of the third animal could only have come from the vivid imagination of a medieval mind.

Chevrons, beading and foliage patterns decorate the rest of the window. One carving in the apex of a chevron at the top of the window arch may represent an exhibitionist figure.

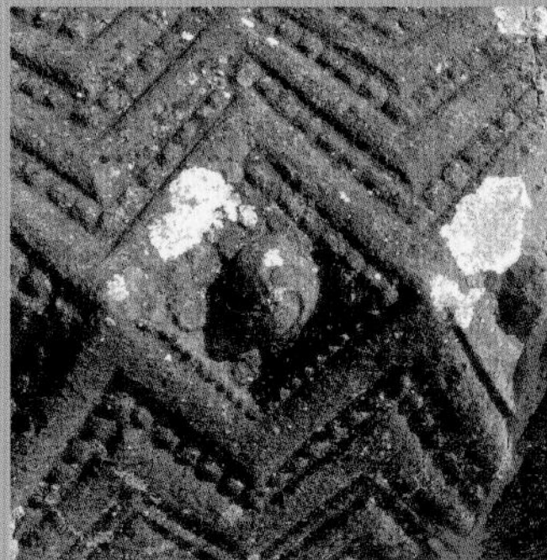

The inner face of the quatrefoil openings in the centre of the window are decorated with animal interlace in a style known as the Irish Urnes, which is a fusion of Irish and Viking art.

The decorative features of this window are so similar to the chancel arch in the Nuns' Chapel at Clonmacnoise that they may be the work of the same master mason. This window may have originally been located in the west gable of the church, and later moved to the east gable.[20] Some of the patterns on the window do not match up, a strong indication that it was taken apart and rebuilt. Fragments that may have belonged to the original window are incorporated into the graveyard wall.

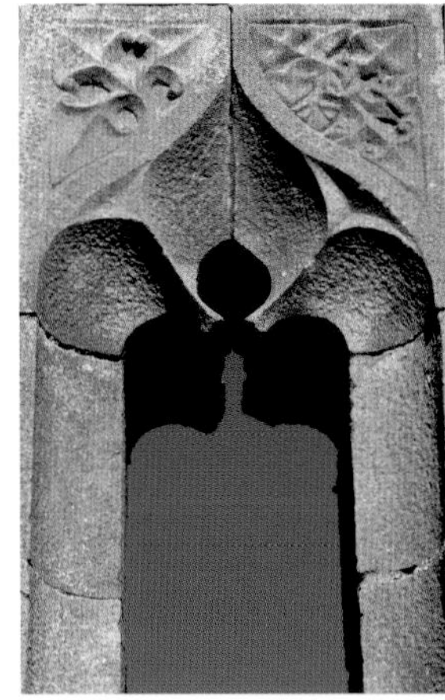

Traces of paint on the roll mouldings inside the east window suggest that it, along with the interior of the church, was originally painted in vibrant colours, in stark contrast to the cold, grey interior of the church today.

The church remained a place of worship until 1696, when Bishop Dopping ordered that its shingle roof be removed and reused to cover the church at Lynally. In 1732, the west end of the church was repaired, as stated on the date stone in its west gable. It has been used ever since as a place of worship by the Church of Ireland.

In the field to the east of the main church stands a small, lonely church. Its west gable possesses a fine Romanesque doorway. The hood moulding over the archway of the door terminates with carvings of two fantastic animal heads. The late medieval east window is decorated with a small bishop's head. A small, round-headed window on the south wall dates from the twelfth century, while other windows on the south and east walls date from the fifteenth or sixteenth centuries. Vine leaves carved in the spandrels of the later windows may symbolise the blood of Christ.

The modern cemetery contains the ruins of a small rectangular building identified as a church on the Ordnance Survey maps. A letter written from Charles O'Molloy in 1677 to Pope Innocent XI describes the presence of three churches at Rahan, 'one parochial, one of Christ and one of the Blessed Virgin, not destroyed but well desolated.'[15] In 1971, grave-diggers discovered a sheela-na-gig that may have fallen from the wall of this building. This sheela, which appears to have been made at the same time as the building, is now housed in the Museum of Athlone Castle.[16]

The history of Rahan began with the small monastery founded by St Carthage. Due to the personality and fame of this saint, Rahan quickly expanded into a large monastic community resembling something like a small town. After Carthage was expelled, the abbotship was taken up by the Uí Suanaigh and the O'Kellys, both of whom ruled the monastery until the early thirteenth century. The beautifully decorated Romanesque churches that one sees today are a fitting legacy to their time as abbots of the monastery.

The early thirteenth century saw the arrival of the Anglo-Normans, who for a short period ruled the monastery and probably turned it into a manorial church for a Norman lord. The Gaelic Revival of the fifteenth century saw the rise of the O'Molloys, who were the native Lords of Fir Chell. They assumed control of the church at Rahan, and until the sixteenth century, the clergy of Rahan were selected from this family.

After the Dissolution of the Monasteries and the plantation of the county, the church became a parish church for the new community. To this day it has continued to be a place of worship for the Church of Ireland.

MANCHAN'S GREY LANDS

Lemanaghan — Liath-Manchain — Grey lands of Manchan

If Manchan was to succeed in establishing his monastery amongst the Celtic people of this region, he needed to absorb and Christianise their most important spiritual places.

It is 645. On his way to the Battle of Carn Conaill (present-day Ballyconnell, County Cavan),[1] Diarmait, King of Ireland, stops at the monastery of Clonmacnoise to pay devotion to its founding saint, Ciarán. The monastery's abbot promises that he and his monks will pray to God and St Ciarán on Diarmait's behalf.

At the battle Diarmait defeats Guaire, the King of Connaught, and kills the two Cuans: Cuan the son of Enda, King of Munster, and Cuan, the son of Connell, Chief of Uí Fidgente.[2]

He returns to Clonmacnoise convinced that the prayers of the clergy have brought him victory. In gratitude, he grants the lands known as Tuaim-nEirc ('Ercs Mound') to the monastery of Clonmacnoise, to be held 'free from and without any charge in the world, as Altar-Sod to God and St Kieran, and a curse is placed on any future King of Meath, should any of his people take with violence, even so much as a drink of water there.'[3]

Soon afterwards a monk named Manchan leaves the great monastery of Clonmacnoise to establish a sister monastery at Tuaim-nEirc. These lands still bear his name: Liath-Manchain, 'the grey lands of Manchan.'

Division of Land

One day St Monaghan [Manchan] and St Ciarain [Ciarán] were talking of dividing the parish. They came to the conclusion that they would arise early the next morning and walk until they would meet each other. St Monaghan arose early and started on his journey expecting to meet St Ciarain, but at last he reached Clonmacnoise and found that St Ciarain was yet sleeping. Then St Ciarain said that he would throw his night-cap and where ever it would light that would be the dividing place. St Monaghan was delighted thinking that it would not go far. But when St Ciarain threw it a storm arose and the cap fell about three hundred yards from the cross-roads of Doon. This divided the two monasteries ever since then.[19]

Who was Manchan and where did he come from? The most promising theory is that he was born in Ulster, a grandson of Conall Gulban of Cenél Conaill (present-day County Donegal), the ancestor of the O'Donnell clan. His pedigree is given as 'Manchán of Liath, son of Indagh. Mella was the name of his mother, and his two sisters were Greallan and Greillseach.'[4]

In the *Annals of the Four Masters* he is known as Manchan of Maothla (present-day Mohill, County Leitrim). To this day there is a monastery in Mohill, which was reputedly founded by Manchan in the sixth or seventh century,[5] and in the village every year there is a fair known as the Fair of Manchan.[6]

Because of his deep knowledge of the scriptures and his 'habits of life and learning,' Manchan was often referred to as the 'Jerome of Ireland.' The *Martyrology of Donegal* identifies him as the accomplished poet who composed 'Manchan's Wish.'[7]

According to local tradition, Manchan was a tall, lame old man. Remarkably, in the nineteenth century when George Petrie opened the Shrine of St Manchan, which held the saint's remains, he was surprised at the dimensions of the leg bone, which could only have come from a very tall man. The shrine is now on display in the Catholic Church at Boher, where there is also a wonderful stained glass window by Harry Clarke depicting St Manchan, his cow and the shrine.

Manchan's Wish

I Wish O son of living God, eternal ancient King,
For a hidden hut in the wilderness that it might be my dwelling,

All grey shallow water beside it, a clear pool to wash away sins
through the grace of the Holy Spirit,

A beautiful wood close by, surrounding it on every side,
for the nurture of many voiced birds, for shelter to hide them,

A southern aspect for warmth, a little stream across its glebe,
choice land of abundant bounty which would be good for every plant,

A few young men of sense, we shall tell their number,
humble and obedient to pray the king:

Four threes, three fours (to suit every need), two sixes in the church,
both north and south:

Six couples in addition to myself ever praying to the King
who makes the sun shine;

A lovely church decked with linen, a dwelling for God from Heaven,
bright lights then, above the pure white scriptures,

One House to go for tending the body without meditation of evil

There is the husbandry which I would undertake and openly choose;
genuine fragrant leek, hens, speckled salmon, bees,-

Raiment and food enough for me from the King whose fame is fair,
to be seated for a time, and to pray to God in some place.[20]

The monastery

Manchan founded his monastery at Tuaim-nEirc, an island of dry land surrounded on all sides by the red bogs of the region. Initially Manchan may have chosen this site because of its isolation, but this seclusion was short-lived. An expanding network of wooden roads, or toghers, in the surrounding bogs soon ensured that the monastery was accessible to all.

Recent analysis of the wood used to build these roads shows that they were constructed between 600 and 1100. As well as connecting the island monastery to the rest of the county, the roads were used by pilgrims as they travelled to the sacred places of this region.

In 1997 a wooden crosier or pilgrim's staff, bearing an incised Greek cross, was found on a togher that has been dated to the late sixth or early seventh century.[8] It is tempting to see this as the walking staff of a monk or pilgrim who journeyed along that wooden road to the monastery of Lemanaghan.[9]

Another reason for selecting this location may have been its natural spring well, which would have provided the monks— and the community in the area before they arrived— with a source of clean drinking water.

It is possible that this well was once a focus of pagan rituals. As worshippers of nature, pre-Christian people may have used the well as a centre for ritual offerings throughout the year.

To succeed in establishing his monastery amongst the people of this region, Manchan had to 'convert' their most important spiritual places. By Christianising the well at Lemanaghan, Manchan would have enabled local people to accept the new religion without leaving behind their long established symbols of worship.[10]

Manchan perished in the epidemic known as the Yellow Plague of 664. Those who succeeded him took the title of 'Abbot of Liath Manchain.'[11]

Between the seventh and eleventh centuries the monastery at Lemanaghan was governed by abbots, some of whom were probably selected from the monastery of Clonmacnoise. Several cross slabs from this time may have marked the graves of these important men. These cross slabs are now kept in the schoolhouse.

The graveyard contains an upright slab decorated with spirals and a central maze pattern that may have been carved during the twelfth century. However, the function of this beautifully carved slab is a mystery.

St Manchan's Well

This story, written by Joseph Geraghty of Ballycumber when he was a pupil at Boher National School during the 1930s, tells of the origins and cures of St Manchan's Well.

There is a holy well in Lemanaghan. It is said one day St Manchan was very thirsty and he could get no water. He struck a rock with his stick and a spring well bubbled up. There are either three or four crosses in the bottom of it and it is believed that there is a spring in each cross. Nearly every disease is cured at it but the most miraculous ones are cancer and warts.

The person to be cured must go there on three successive Fridays and he must be there at three O'Clock sharp. Each Friday when he goes to the well he must take a bottle of water out of the well and he must bring the water to the Holy water font and pour it into it. He then blesses himself with it and says an Our Father and three Hail Mary's to St Manchan. He must come through the window in the end of the ruin on the third Friday and if his faith in the Saint is strong he will be cured. He must leave something in the font such as a penny or a button or a pin etc.

Once upon a time a man it is said got cured of warts and he left a penny. There is a local toss-pit nearby and one of the boys took the penny and in a few days his hands were covered with warts. He had to go back and leave a penny and do the same thing as the other man did.

During the twelfth century, the monastery at Lemanaghan experienced a Golden Age. This period saw the construction of the church, which had a beautiful Romanesque doorway. St Mella's Cell, a small stone oratory named after Manchan's mother, may also have been built around this time. This oratory stands in the centre of a stone walled enclosure, or cashel. It consists of a small room with a flat-headed doorway in the west gable. A window may have been in the east gable, providing light for this small chamber. This building and its enclosure probably provided a place where a monk could withdraw from the bustling monastery and be alone with God.

The stone flagged togher that leads from St Manchan's Church to St Mella's Cell may have linked up with the wooden roads that led to the outside world.

Local tradition says that the saint and his mother would meet every day at a large sandstone flag on this togher. Because Manchan had taken a vow never to speak to a woman, he and his mother would sit back to back, without communicating.

Several depressions in the flagstones are known as the 'hoof marks of St Manchan's Cow.' The boy who kept this cow is said to be the forefather of the Buckleys, a local family that played a central role in the history of the monastery.

SAINT ✱ MANCHAN

St Manchan's Cow

In the 1930s Kevin Buckley of Cooldorrogh, then a pupil at Boher National School, recorded the following story about Manchan and his cow.

St Monaghan [Manchan] was born in Mohill in County Leitrim and he founded a monastery there. It is not really known if he founded Leamonaghan but however he spent the greater part of his life there. St Monaghan had a cow and the cow supplied milk to all the people of Leamonaghan. One day while the St was out of the monastery the people of Kilmanaghan came and stole the cow. They brought the cow backwards and at every little well that was on the way the cow drank. As she came up from the wells she even left the track of her feet in the stone. The wells and the tracks of her feet in the stone are yet to be seen. When the saint came back he missed the cow and set out in search for her. The saint traced her the whole way and when he landed in Kilmanaghan he found that his cow was boiling in a pot. The hide of the cow was left behind the door and St Monaghan hit the hide a kick and up jumped the cow. She was every bit as good as she had been before only she had lost a bone and on this account she was a bit lame. When the cow came back of Leamonaghan she supplied milk to the people just as good as before. Ever since that time the people of Leamonaghan never sold milk and also they keep St Monaghan's day as a holiday of obligation.

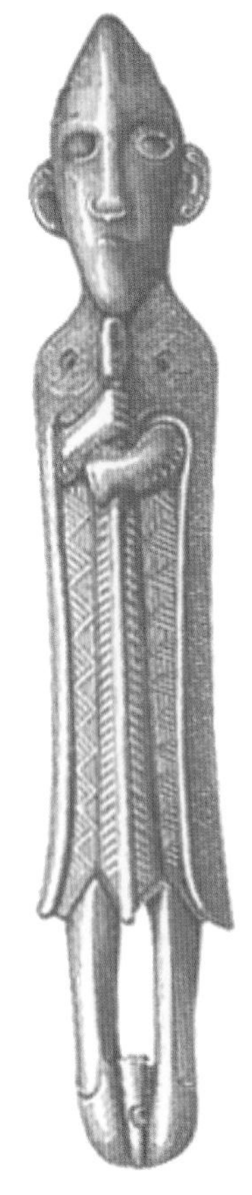

For much of the history of Lemanaghan, members of the Buckley family considered administration of the church to be their hereditary right. By the fifteenth century, the family supplied Lemanaghan with some of its parish priests. And in the early twentieth century, after the church at Lemanaghan was in ruins, the Buckley family continued to be the hereditary bearers of St Manchan's Shrine.[12]

In 1205, the *Annals* record the death of Gillebrenyn O'Bichoylle (O'Buachalla or Buckley), Abbot of Lemanaghan. Wars throughout the rest of the thirteenth century caused the monastery to go into a decline. By 1306, the papal taxation of the diocese reported that the church had been 'laid waste by the ravages of war' and was worth nothing.

However, as the Gaelic families regained their power in the fifteenth century, Lemanaghan experienced an upsurge in its fortunes. It was patronised by the Mac Coghlan family, who were the Lords of Delbna Bethra in ancient Meath. This family was known as the 'MawCoghlans of the Fair Castles of Garrycastle' because their territory consisted of most of the present barony of Garrycastle, including Lemanaghan, as well as the villages of Ferbane, Banagher and Cloghan. One of their 'seven fair castles,' now levelled, was located at Lemanaghan.

During this same period, the monastery at Clonmacnoise, which oversaw the monastery at Lemanaghan, began to dwindle in power.

In 1400 the vicarage of Lemanaghan was left vacant after the death of Cristinus Obuachala (Buckley). The position of priest appears to have been unlawfully taken up by Magonius Offlani, for in the same year the papacy ordered his removal from the vicarage of Lemanaghan. The Pope subsequently assigned this position to John Onniyl (O'Neill) of the Diocese of Ardagh, the fifteen-year-old son of a priest and an unmarried woman. However, he does not appear to have taken up this position, and ten years later the church was described as having gone for a long time without a vicar.

During this time the papacy became concerned about the local lords who, without papal sanction, were appointing secular clerks to serve as priests. Therefore in 1410, by order of the Pope, the right to appoint the vicar at Lemanaghan was transferred from Clonmacnoise to the Augustinian prior of the nearby monastery at Gallen.

Around this time, the church was extended to facilitate its role as the parish church to the people of Lemanaghan. Today, the graveyard contains the ruins of a square-shaped building known as the House of Manchan. During the 1400s, it may have been a residence for the parish priest.

In the late fifteenth century a conflict arose between the Roman church and the Buckleys, who considered the position of priest at Lemanaghan to be theirs by right of inheritance. In 1489, Philip Obuachalla (Buckley) was acting as the unofficial local priest of Lemanaghan. That same year, a priest named Robert Macadagyn (MacEgan) was granted perpetual vicarage of the church by papal orders.

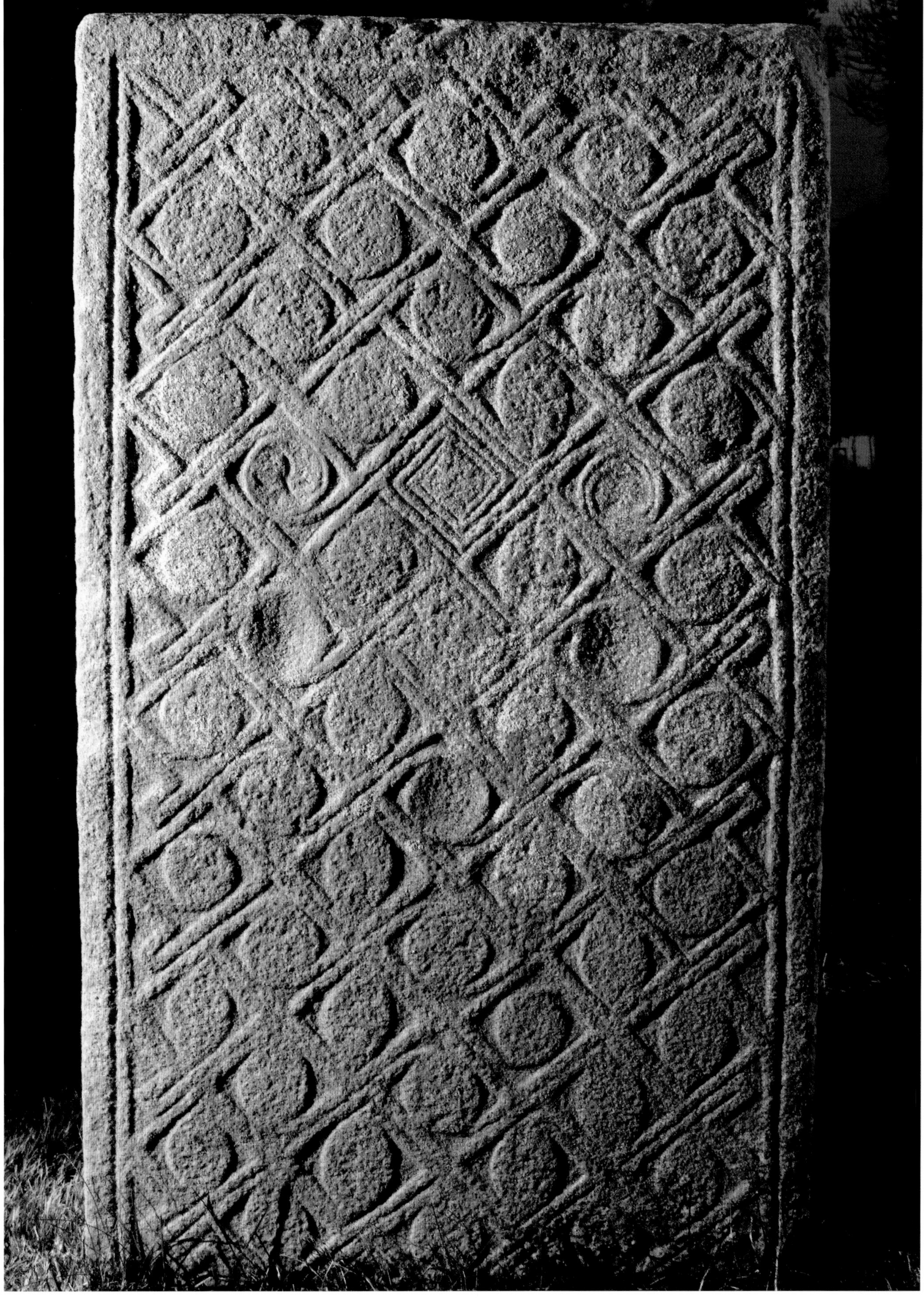

The papacy ordered that three canons of Clonmacnoise remove Philip Obuachalla from Lemanaghan, along with any other unlawful person or persons attached to the church. Although the Buckleys continued to be associated with the Shrine of St Manchan, their link with the administration of the church was severed forever.

During the sixteenth century, the Mac Coghlans assumed direct control of the church at Lemanaghan. In 1508 Maurice Macohclayn (Mac Coghlan), canon of the church of Clonmacnoise, was granted the vicarage and parish church of Liathmanchayn (Lemanaghan), though the union between the two churches was dissolved upon his death.

During the fifteenth and sixteenth centuries the clergy for the churches of Delbna Bethra were selected from the ranks of the Mac Coghlans. As a result, the church became embroiled in the local politics of this family. Disputes between different branches of the family sometimes created tension among the churches within their territory. Meanwhile, in the outside world, chieftains who were enemies of the Mac Coghlans began to target places such as Lemanaghan. As a result, in 1531, Murtough Mac Coughlan (Mac Coghlan), described as

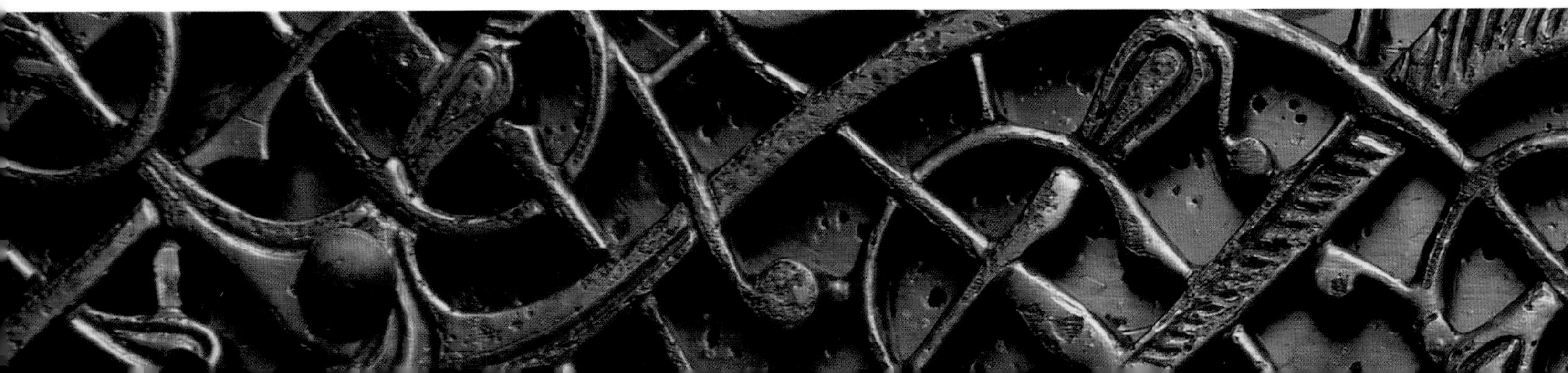

the 'Prior of Gallen and Vicar of Liath Manachain,' was 'treacherously slain' by Turlough Oge O'Melaghlin and Rory O'Melaghlin.

By 1615, the once thriving monastery had been reduced to a shadow of its former glory. It was described as: 'the old church situated in the middle of a bog, impassable in the time of winter.'[13]

Destruction of the church probably took place during the Rebellion of 1641. At the same time, the Shrine of St Manchan was taken into hiding. The castle passed into the hands of the Duke of Buckingham.

The end of the church finally came between 1682-85, when its Protestant vicar, George Lawder of Tissaran, began preaching once a fortnight in a private house.

Now in ruins, the church at Lemanaghan no longer serves the local community as a formal place of worship. Yet people still come to Lemanaghan throughout the year, particularly on the Feastday of St Manchan, 24 January. Today, St Manchan's Well and Holy Tree are frequented by people who simply want a quiet place to pray.

St Manchan's Shrine

St Manchan's Shrine was created during the twelfth century, which was the Golden Age of the monastery at Lemanaghan. This national treasure is one of the largest and best examples of a reliquary in Ireland. Made from yew, the wooden shrine replicates the steeply pitched roof of an early Christian oratory, similar to the one that would have covered St Mella's Cell. It stands 48 centimetres (19 inches) high and is 40 centimetres (16 inches) wide at its base. It measures 61 centimetres (24 inches) in length.

St Manchan's Shrine appears to have been made at Clonmacnoise around 1130. It was created in what is now known as the Connaught Style. The shrine may have been commissioned by Turlough O'Connor, High King of Ireland (1111-1151),[14] who commissioned a relic of similar style, known as the Cross of Cong, in 1123.

Archaeologist T.D. Kendrick described the shrine as 'a rich and dazzling Celtic bewilderment, a perpetual challenge to the eyes and a perpetual delight.'[15]

On each face of the shrine five circular bosses form a large cross. They are decorated with images of intertwined animals, along with inlays of red and yellow enamel. The crystals or gemstones that once topped the bosses are now missing.

The shrine consists of thirty-two panels of interlaced decoration and sixty small panels of geometric designs. Each of the ninety-two panels has its own original design.

The edges of the shrine are covered with exquisite pierced metalworking that features interlaced animals in a Hiberno-Viking style typical of the twelfth century. At the feet of the shrine there are four bronze rings measuring 6 centimetres (approximately 2¼ inches) in diameter. Timber poles threaded through these rings were used to carry the shrine.

The shrine of Manchan, of Maethail, was covered by Ruaidhri Ua Conchobhair [Rory O'Connor, King of Ireland], and an embroidering of gold was carried over it by him, in as good a style as a relic was ever covered.

In 1166 'The shrine of Manchan, of Maethail, was covered by Ruaidhri Ua Conchobhair [Rory O'Connor, King of Ireland], and an embroidering of gold was carried over it by him, in as good a style as a relic was ever covered.'[16] Although this account could refer to another shrine related to St Manchan, it seems very likely that it refers to the one described here.

In the last quarter of the twelfth century, fifty-two bronze figures were attached to the wooden shrine by bronze nails, the holes of which can still be seen today.[17] These figures were placed in the eight spaces formed by the arms of the crosses.

Today only eleven figures remain attached to the shrine and the fate of the other forty-one figures is unknown. The remaining figures, which may represent the abbots and monks of the monastery, are very similar to late twelfth-century crucifixion figures from Germany and Denmark.[18] Their prominent ears may be an indication that they are listening to the prayers of the faithful. The ribs of their bare chests are exposed in a manner similar to that of the crucified Christ.

Why then did early church leaders send this magnetic and successful monk into exile? There are conflicting explanations. Jealousy of Colum Cille's many foundations may have led churchmen to expel him at the Synod of Teltown, County Meath in 561. His loyal defender and former schoolmate Brendan of Birr called the excommunication 'unjust' and founded on 'some pardonable and very trifling reasons.'[7]

However, a darker legend may explain his exile. As a gifted scribe, Colum Cille was passionate about books. While he was staying at the monastery of Droma Find (in present-day Dromyn, County Louth), Colum Cille borrowed a manuscript of the Psalms from the monastery's founder, Finnian. Uncertain that Finnian would permit him to copy the exquisite manuscript, Colum Cille began to make his own copy in secret. One of the monks noticed what he was doing and reported back to Finnian, who was furious. He demanded that Colum Cille hand over the copy, as well as the original manuscript. Colum Cille refused.

The matter was taken before Diarmait mac Cerball, King of Tara. After hearing both sides, Diarmait issued a ruling that includes what may be one of the earliest references to the concept of copyright. He said:

> *To every cow its little cow, that is its calf, and to every book its little book [copy]; and because of that Colum Cille, the book you copied is Finnian's.*[8]

Very upset, Colum Cille returned to his native territory of Tír Conaill, where he told the kings of the Northern Uí Néill about the judgment. For the Uí Néill kings, the ruling was an insult, not only to Colum Cille, but also to them, as his kinsmen.

They took up arms. Colum Cille began a fast, hoping to persuade God to protect his kinsmen and make them victorious over Diarmait mac Cerball. The next day, the forces of the Northern Uí Néill and those of the King of Tara met at the Battle of Cúl Dreimne. The *Annals* record that around three thousand people were killed in the battle and that the king was defeated.

Grief-stricken about his responsibility for this battle, Colum Cille sent himself into exile as penance.

No one knows which explanation for Colum Cille's exile is true. What is certain is that, at the age of forty-two, Colum Cille and a group of twelve followers left his beloved Ireland. He entered exile on the desolate island of Iona in 563. There he established a monastic community and became its first abbot.

Thirty-four years later, on the 9 June 597, Colum Cille died at Iona. By the time of his death, he had fulfilled his mother's prophecy and set up monasteries all over Ireland, Scotland and Northern England. His successor Baithíne, who may also have been his foster-son, described Colum Cille's life's work:

> *He marked out, without loosening,*
> *three hundred fair churches, it is true;*
> *And three hundred gifted, lasting . . .*
> *bright, noble books he wrote . . .*[9]

The Moving Shrine

In the mid-1600s, the Shrine of St Manchan was moved for protection to a Penal Chapel with a thatched roof near Boher. This church, which served as school during daytime, stood on Michael Duffy's boreen about one hundred yards from his house. One night, the church burned down. However, the shrine was saved and given for safe-keeping to the Mooney family, who lived at a house called 'The Doon'[21] on the Boher-Clonmacnoise Road.

According to local folklore, so many people came to see the shrine that the Mooneys decided to hand it over to the parish priest of the Roman Catholic church at Boher. The priest gave the Buckleys, who claimed to be the hereditary bearers of the shrine, the task of carrying the shrine in a great procession from the Mooneys' house to the Catholic church.

St Manchan's Shrine was put on display at the Dublin Exhibition of 1853, where it was described and illustrated by Robert Travers, M.D.[22] It was displayed at a second exhibition in 1882,[23] and also appears to have been brought to London for one of the Great Exhibitions. During an exhibition in Paris, Napoleon III was so taken with the shrine that he sent a gold medal to Dr. Kilduff, Bishop of Ardagh.

Around this time, a potential buyer offered the people of Lemanaghan four hundred pounds sterling—a fortune at that time—to purchase the shrine.

They promptly refused.

According to local tradition, it was the parish priest of Ballinahown who encouraged the Mooney family to reclaim the shrine and bring it home. On its return, the people noticed that many of the figures that had been attached to the sides of the shrine were gone.[24]

In 1935, the Director of the National Museum of Ireland, Dr. Adolf Mahr, brought the shrine to the British Museum for cleaning and other conservation works. First, however, the shrine was opened and its contents, which consisted of a few blackened and crumbled bones, were removed for safe keeping. Today the shrine is on display in the Catholic Church at Boher.

His Boohil Boy

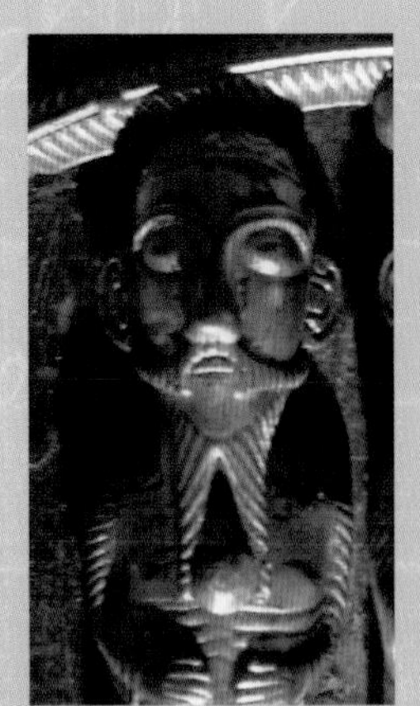

The Buckley family of Lemanaghan have a long history as the hereditary bearers of St Manchan's Shrine. Their family name comes from *buachail,* an Irish word meaning 'cow-keeper or herder.' Locally buachail is pronounced as 'bohooly' or 'boohil.'

Legend has it that the Buckleys were the herders of Manchan's cows before they became the hereditary bearers of his shrine. The following story was collected at Boher National School in the 1930s from Kevin Buckley of Cooldorragh, Ballinahowan, the last direct male descendant of this family. Kevin got the story from his father Michael Buckley.

St Monaghan had a servant boy named Boohil. On his way to Leamonaghan he went into Boohely's house and there was a number of little boys in there and he rested for a good while and he agreed to bring one of the little boys with him. The boy was satisfied and set off with the saint. The boy remained with the saint and went to every place with him.

When Saint Monaghan died the people of Leamonaghan wanted him to be buried there and the people of Kilmanaghan wanted him to be buried in Kilmanaghan. However both parties fought at Mac Guinness's gate in Clough, and after a long struggle a lady on a white horse rode up between them and told them to turn their back to the coffin. They did as they were told and when they turned back there were two coffins on the road. The fight was now over for each party could take a coffin. One coffin was buried in Leamonaghan.

A good while after, the saint appeared to his Boohil boy. The boy was so delighted to see him that he ran to shake hands with him but no sooner had he touched him when he fell into bones. The bones were taken up and put in the shrine which is still preserved in Boher Church which was built in 1860. It is believed to be on the grave in Leamonaghan that he appeared to the boy and it is believed that he is buried there.

In recent years a medieval grave slab, which was reputedly the grave slab of the Buckley family, was moved from Lemanaghan graveyard to the grounds of Boher church. Today it is located in the churchyard in front of the grotto, so that even in death the Boohil boy is keeping vigil over the Shrine of St Manchan.

The presence of the well and the holy tree

offer people a centre of ritual

that remains unbroken to this day.

Islands of Tranquillity

The saints who brought Christianity to County Offaly left behind a landscape rich in sacred places. Tribal warfare and the passage of time have taken their toll on these religious foundations. While some are still used as places of worship, many others have faded back into the soil from which they arose.

This gazetteer offers a glimpse into the stories that surround eleven of Offaly's sacred places. These sites have been chosen as a sample from a total of eighty-five religious sites in the county.

The following descriptions offer an insight into the development of Christian Offaly. Each listing begins with the English place-name of the site, followed by its Irish name and the English translation of that name, as recorded in the *Ordnance Survey Field Name Books,* written between 1837-8. A brief history— including significant folklore, legends, and descriptions of the art and architecture— follows.

Ballyboy — *Baile Átha Buí* — the Mouth of the Yellow Ford

This picturesque village lies on the banks of the Silver River at the foothills of the Slieve Bloom Mountains. According to local tradition, the ruins of a Church of Ireland building, constructed in 1815, are located on the site of a convent founded by St Brigit in the sixth century. A cross-inscribed slab in the graveyard supports the idea that Ballyboy was an early Christian foundation.

Ballyboy was originally part of the lands of the kingdom of the Fir Chell ('Men of the Churches'), an ancient territory that stretched from Kilcormac to Durrow in North Offaly. In 1268, the *Annals of the Four Masters* recorded the death of one of its rulers: 'Fercall O'Molloye, Prince of Fircell, was deceitfully and treacherously slain by the English of Athboye.'[1]

The village remained part of the parish of Fir Chell until 1640, when it was dissolved and five new parishes were created: Ballyboy, Lynally, Killoughy, Tinnycross (Drumcullen) and Eglish. After this date the chapel at Ballyboy became a church of the newly created parish. Records that date from 1693 state that all the chapels of Fir Chell, except Lynally and Ballyboy, had been in ruins since 1641.[2]

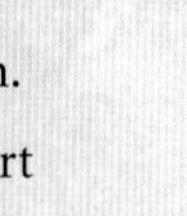

According to 'Bishop Dopping's Visitation Book,' which dates from 1682-5, the nave of the church at Ballyboy was repaired in 1682, while its chancel was left in ruins.[3] This selective maintenance of different parts of older churches was common after the Reformation.

A carved head on the wall of the old corn mill in the village may once have been part of the medieval church. The menacing features of this grooved face may have been intended to warn parishioners about the dire consequences of failing to adhere to Christian principles.

Clonsast — *Cluain Sosta* — Meadow of Tranquillity

The townland of Clonsast is the site of a monastery founded by St Broghan (also known as Brachan or Bearchan) in the late seventh century.[4] The monastery occupies an island of dry land surrounded by the Bog of Allen in the parish of Clonbullogue. It would have offered early monks an idyllic refuge in which to meditate on the Word of God.

The townland name, 'meadow of tranquillity,' captures the very essence of this monastic foundation. It is likely that St Broghan and his followers chose this isolated site because it was suitable for an eremitical-style monastery, in which hermitages were clustered around a church, rather than the busy community-based monasteries found elsewhere in the county.

The *Martyrology of Donegal* describes St Broghan as one of the four great prophets of Erin. It also says that he was a 'Fordáleithe . . . man of two parts,' who spent half of his life in Ireland and the other half in Alba (Scotland).[5] The little village of Kilbarchan in Renfrewshire, West Scotland, was probably named after the saint.

After his death around 650 St Broghan was interred, along with three other saints, on the island of Inishmore in the Aran Islands. A church built over the burials was called the Church of the Four Illustrious. St Broghan's Feastday is 4 December.

The monastery at Clonsast was accessed by an ancient togher, or wooden road, measuring three metres (nearly ten feet) in width. Known as St Broghan's Road, it traversed the Bog of Allen; pilgrims may have used this road on their journey from the outside world to the island monastery. In the 1940s, archaeologists excavating the road described it as 'composed of brushwood, sand and gravel,' and dated the track to between the eighth and tenth centuries.[6]

The scribe of the *Leabhar Breac* recorded that, until the sixteenth century, the *Book of Berchan* (also known as the *Book of Clonsast*)—which now, unfortunately, is lost—was housed in the monastery of Clonsast.[7]

Very little survives of the monastery, except for the partial remains of an early medieval church. In 1837, the church ruins at Clonsast were described as 'a vicarage in the barony of Coolestown, in the diocese of Kildare, without glebe or parsonage';[8] this is pretty much as one sees it today.

Two fields to the north of the church lies St Broghan's Well (Tobair-Brachain). A statue of the saint still guards the well. A nearby holy stone, known as St Broghan's Stone, is said to bear the impression of St Broghan's head. Years ago, people suffering from headaches would pour water from the holy well into the hollow in the stone, and then bathe their heads.[9]

The thorn bush close to the church may have been a rag bush or 'holy bush' that was frequented during the pattern to the church, well and stone.

In the past on St John's Day (24 June) a large pattern, which lasted for a week, was held in the field between the church and the holy well. The crowds that attended this pattern were so large that tents, put up by pilgrims on St John's Eve, remained there for the week.

The event included not only devotions, but also other social activities, including drinking.[10] This brought pilgrims into conflict with the local parish priest. Like many of the clergy of that time, he was influenced by Father Theobald Mathew's temperance campaign. The founder of the pioneer movement in Ireland, Father Mathew was known as the 'Apostle of Temperance.' Ultimately, the local clergy put a stop to the patterns at Clonsast, which ended, according to John O'Donovan, '. . . in consequence of the bad effect of whiskey.'[11]

Killaderry—*Cill Rátha Dairthí*—Church of the O'Durhys

Just outside the village of Daingean, the highest part of a medieval graveyard bears the faint outline of a levelled church. According to the *Ordnance Survey Field Name Books,* a local family, the O'Durhys, originally built the church as a chapel of ease. When the population of the area increased, this private chapel was converted into a parochial church.

In 1546, the *Annals of the Four Masters* described the destruction of this church: 'The English erected the Castle of Daingean, having torn down the Church of Cill-O'Duirthe to procure building materials from it. They also killed the Parson of Cruachan [i.e., the parish priest of the Parish of Croghan].'[12]

Today an elaborately-carved nineteenth-century gateway stands over the entrance to the graveyard. Above the archway there are a series of thirteen corbels, each carved with a face and a letter underneath. No one now knows the identities of these faces or the meaning of

the letters below them. Above this corbel table, there is a panel depicting scenes of the death and the resurrection of Christ.[13]

The grave of Father Andrew Mullen, a native of Daingean, has become a focus of modern pilgrimage for people from all over Ireland. Before his death in 1818 at the age of 27, he served as parish priest in Clonmore, County Carlow, where he dedicated his life to the poor and the sick. Eventually, he gained a reputation as a healer.

After his death, Father Mullen was buried beside the old church in Clonmore. Five weeks later, however, the people of Daingean exhumed his body and brought it to Offaly, where the priest was re-interred in Killaderry graveyard. Many consider his grave a sacred place where the sick may be cured and wishes fulfilled.

KILCOMIN — *Cill Chuimín* — St Cuimín's Church

The *Ordnance Survey Field Name Books* record that this place was known as Diseart Chuimin. 'Diseart' means hermitage, or isolated place, while Chuimin is another variation of the saint's name.

St Cuimín (Cummian) established a monastery here in the seventh century. During his lifetime, the Christian church engaged in its first great debate over when to celebrate Easter. Cuimín was a keen supporter of the Roman time for the Easter celebration, unlike Sarán Ua Critáin of Tisaran in the west of the county, who was a supporter of the date favoured by the Celtic church.

Cuimín may have been the author of the historical document on this Easter controversy known as the 'Letter of Cummian to Abbot Ségéne of Iona.'[14] Sources suggest that this Cummian (Cuimín) was the Abbot of Durrow, a position that he may have assumed after he founded the monastery at Kilcomin.

The *Annals of the Four Masters* state that Cuimín died on 12 November 661.

Today a field adjoining the graveyard at Kilcomin contains remnants of a circular field boundary that may be part of the enclosure that originally surrounded Cuimín's monastery. Within the graveyard there is a cross-inscribed early Christian grave slab. One can also see the ruins of a medieval church, the west end of which served as a priest's house. Three flagstones in the northern corner of the graveyard are known as St Cuimín's Seat.

According to legend, the saint was 'wont to frequent a well, which lies in Cnocan Ruadh, about twenty perches to the west of the churchyard.'[15] In his *History of Birr,* Cooke records that the ancient bell of St Cuimín was discovered in this well, and kept in the parish until the 1840s. The bell is now housed in the British Museum, but the well has disappeared.

Not far from Rutland House, and immediately to the right of a road that branches to Dunkerrin from Kilcomin, is a site that was considered sacred in the nineteenth century. Beneath three elms known locally as St Cuimín's Trees, lies a stone linked to the saint. Local tradition says that, as Cuimín prayed, his knees and head left indentations in this stone.[16]

According to the *Annals of the Four Masters,* in 1162, the relics of Cummine Fada (Cummine the Tall) were removed from the earth by the clergy of Brenainn (Clonfert) and then enclosed within a shrine. Cummine Fada was a son of Fiachna, Bishop of Clonfert, who was of the Eoghanacht tribe from County Kerry. No one really knows if he was the same saint who founded the monastery at Kilcomin, or if he was another saint, with a similar name, who came afterwards.

Whoever he was, Cummine's tutor, Colman Ua Clasaigh, composed a poem in his memory. It was recorded under the year 661 in the *Annals of the Four Masters:*

The Luimneach did not bear on its bosom,
of the race of Munster, into Leath Chuinn,
A corpse in a boat so precious as he,
as Cumine, son of Fiachna.

If any one went across the sea,
to sojourn at the seat of Gregory Rome,
If from Ireland, he requires no more
than the mention of Cumine Foda.

I sorrow after Cumine,
from the day that his shrine was covered;
My eyelids have been dropping tears; I have not laughed,
but mourned since the lamentation at his barque.

A Carmelite Frier

KILCORMAC—*Cill Chormaic*—the Church of Cormac

It is uncertain whether there was a Christian foundation at Kilcormac before 1430, when the O'Molloys invited the Carmelite Friars to establish a monastery there. Its founder, Aedh O'Molloy, died in 1454 and was buried in the friary church before the high altar. In the *Kilcormac Missal,* his name is entered in Latin as 'Odo Ymolmoy qui erat capitaneus suae nationis,' which means: 'Aedh O'Molloy, chief of his nation.'

The friary at Kilcormac had an important scriptorium. Two manuscripts were written there: a fifteenth-century missal (mass book) and breviary (prayer and hymn book for the worship of God by a monk). Both are now housed in Trinity College, Dublin.

The missal records many events in the history of the friary, including the murder of Aedh O'Molloy's sons by Charles O'Molloy. On 13 January 1536, two sons of Aedh O'Molloy, namely Aedh and Con, were taken by force from the abbey, and 'were slain near the gate of the monastery of Kilcormac.'[17]

The O'Molloys retained possession of the monastery until around 1560, when their lands were confiscated and granted to the English planters. By 1567, the land of Kilcormac belonged to Henry Cooley, including the 'rectory of Kylharmik.' This first reference to the rectory reveals its transition from a Carmelite Friary to a parish church.[18] A year later, on 24 November, the church annals record the death of one of the last white friars of Kilcormac, Brother Rory O'Morrisey.[19]

The Kilcormac Pietà

The present Catholic Church in Kilcormac stands on the site of the Carmelite friary. The church contains a Pietà that, according to local tradition, came from Spain and was donated to the parish by a rich lady in the sixteenth century.[20] A second tradition states that it came from Italy through one of the Magawley family who lived in Temora, Kilcormac.[21]

Local folklore records the following legend about how the Pietà survived the ravages of Cromwell's troops:

> *It was placed in the parish church, which at that time was in the village of Ballyboy, about one mile from Kilcormac. There it remained until 1650 when Oliver Cromwell's army was reported approaching from the direction of Cadamstown.*
>
> *Everyone gathered up their possessions and prepared to flee to the woods when two women thought of the Pieta. They rushed to the church, took the Pieta outside and buried it in a heap of rubbish. Later, under the cover of darkness, a number of men brought it out and re-buried it in a bog, where it was to lie for over sixty years.*
>
> *Had the Pieta not remained safely preserved in the bog for those years, it is unlikely that it would have survived to this day. During the years of persecution, the churches in Kilcormac and Ballyboy were reduced to ruins. To return to the Pieta, it is thought that sometime between 1700 and 1720, only one man remained alive who knew where it was buried, and, according to tradition, he was carried on his deathbed to point it out.*
>
> *The carving was carefully recovered and when it was examined it was found to be in perfect condition. It was then placed in the church that had recently been built in Kilcormac, the whole parish was overjoyed to have their valued Pieta among them again. It almost left the parish some years after that when a priest, who was moving to Borrisokane, took it with him! However the parishioners brought it back and it has remained in the parish church of Kilcormac to this day.*[22]

KINNITTY — *Cionn Eitigh* — the Head of Eiteach

The pretty village of Kinnitty stands at the foothills of the Slieve Bloom Mountains, in the Diocese of Killaloe. Legend says that this place got its name because the head of Eiteach, an ancient Irish princess, is buried nearby.

The present Church of Ireland building stands on the site of the monastery founded by St Finan Cam ('Finan the Crooked') in 557. Finan was from the tribe of Corca Dhuibhne (present-day Corcaguiny in northwest Kerry) and his feastday is 7 April. There once was a well within the village of Kinnitty, which local tradition identified as Finan's Well.[23]

In 884, the *Annals of the Four Masters* records the death of 'Colcu, son of Connacan, Abbot of Ceann Eitigh, doctor of eloquence, and the best historian that was in Ireland in his time.'

Inside the church, a large sandstone pillar is inscribed with a cross that contains spiralling serpent-like forms. The form, size and decoration of this slab suggest that it may originally have been a prehistoric standing stone, which was later Christianised through the incision of a Latin cross.

The graveyard contains the recently uncovered remains of a window surround from a thirteenth-century church, further proof that the existing church and graveyard were built on the site of the monastery. Behind the graveyard stands the pyramid-shaped mausoleum of the Bernard family of Castle Bernard, now Kinnitty Castle. The mausoleum was constructed in the nineteenth century.

The grounds of Kinnitty Castle contain a fine ninth-century high cross. Its ornate decoration includes three biblical scenes: the Presentation in the Temple, Adam and Eve and the Crucifixion. Intertwined birds and interlacing and geometric motifs cover the rest of the cross.[24]

Although it is called the Kinnitty High Cross, its inscription dedicates the cross to the King of Meath. If the monks at Kinnitty had ever commissioned a cross, it would have been dedicated to their king, the King of Munster, rather than to the King of Meath, who was his rival. Therefore, it is more than likely that this cross came from the church at Drumcullen.

Letter—*Leitir Lúna*—St Lughna's Hillside

In the foothills of the Slieve Bloom Mountains, near the village of Cadamstown, is the tranquil site of the monastery of Letter (also called Littir or Leitir). Although only a small portion of the church survives, the site retains a wonderful sense of calm, which almost transports one back to the time of the early Christian monks. There is a natural spring well, known as Tobar Lugna, beside the church. In the fields around the church, it is also possible to discern the faintest remains of a possible enclosure.

During the sixth century, Lugna founded this monastery beside an ancient road, locally known as the 'Old Munster Road.' This road runs across the mountain, past the village of Clonaslee, in County Laois, and then continues on down the mountain, passing by the monastery of Letter and into the village of Ballyboy. From there it joins up with the Slighe Mór, one of the five great roads that existed during the early years of Christianity in Ireland.

Today, all that survives of Lughna's monastery is the west wall of a medieval parish church, and the arch of a stone roof of a two-storey priest's house, which was built inside the west end of the church during the Middle Ages.

Throughout the fourteenth and fifteenth centuries, two families—the O'Hogans and the O'Scullys—engaged in an intense rivalry for control of the vicarage at Letter. In 1473, Conchobhar Ó hÓgáin (O'Hogan) was listed as the parish priest of Letter. He was accused by Tadhg Ó Scolaighe (O'Scully) of both neglecting and selling 'the precious moveable goods' of the church and 'converting them to evil uses.'[25] The same Conchobhar was accused of keeping a concubine in the 'priest's house' with whom he fathered a son called Pádraig.

In 1486, Pope Innocent VIII ordered the removal of Conchobhar from Letter, and requested that his illegitimate son Padraig, then a clerk at Killaloe, be promoted to holy orders and appointed as 'vicar of Leitir [Letter].'[26]

By the early seventeenth century, the church at Letter had been abandoned. In 1613, it was described as a ruinous church with both 'church (nave) and chancell downe.'[27]

On the external face of the west gable of the Catholic Church in Cadamstown, one can see an early Christian cross-inscribed grave slab, as well as the carved head of a decorated animal, which dates from the twelfth century. Another carving in this gable is that of a human face, which local people refer to as the face of St Lugna. All of these stones and many more were taken from the church at Letter as building material for the dwellings in Cadamstown.

Local people once held a pattern day at the holy well near the monastery on 27 April. Then, in 1850, the Manifold family of Letter House discouraged the people from holding the event.[28] Today a local man, Paddy Heaney, has restarted the pattern to the well, which will hopefully be maintained for many years to come.

MONASTERORIS—*Mainistir Fheorais*—the Monastery Mac Fheorais (the Monastery of the Sons of Pierce de Bermingham)

This monastery, which is located just outside of Edenderry on the banks of the River Boyne, takes its name from its founding Anglo-Norman family, the Berminghams, who, like many Anglo-Norman families, adopted Irish ways and customs and over time became 'more Irish than the Irish themselves.' Eventually the family formed an alliance with the O'Conor Falys in their opposition to the English.

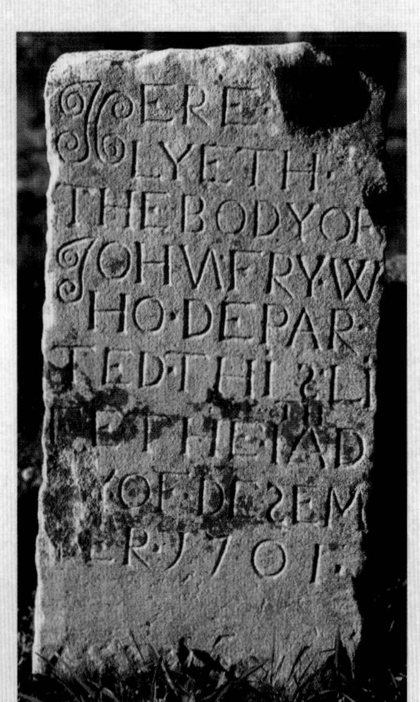

After the death of Pierce de Bermingham, the family adopted the Gaelic name *Fheorais*, which is the Irish name for 'Pierce.' Ever after, the family was known as *Mac Feorais Bermingham* – 'the sons of Pierce Bermingham.'[29]

One of Pierce Bermingham's sons, John de Bermingham, Earl of Louth, founded the Franciscan friary in 1325.[30]

During the Middle Ages, this monastery was also known as 'Castro Petre de Mortoto and Totmoy,' a reference to Pierce's castle, which was situated near or beside the Franciscan friary in the ancient Gaelic territory known as Tuath Muighe or Totmoy.[31] The medieval town of Totmoy consisted of two castles, twenty dwellings, a Franciscan friary with farm buildings, a pigeon house and a grange with a watermill.

In 1550, the site at Monasteroris was described by Walter Cowley as consisting of two castles, 'one newlie builded and thother all ruynose,' with a friary which was 'burnyd and rasid' and a mill and orchard.[32]

After the Dissolution of the Monasteries by Henry VIII in 1537, the land at Monasteroris was granted to various people. A grant in 1574 to Nicholas Harberte of Portlester describes the place as the 'old town of Monasteroris with its dissolved friary, two castles and twenty cottages.'[33]

In 1645, the Franciscans returned to Monasteroris and stayed in the area until the eighteenth century. The last friar of Monasteroris was Father Matthew Walsh, vicar of Daingean, who died in 1794.

The site today consists of a medieval nave and chancel parish church and a graveyard. A field to the north of the graveyard contains the remains of the pigeon house and a range of buildings that may originally have been the manor house of the de Berminghams before they donated it to the Franciscans, who may have used it as a monastic grange.

The graveyard contains some of the earliest carved headstones in the county, dating from the late seventeenth and early eighteenth centuries.

A large Celtic cross, erected in 1874, is dedicated to Father Mogue Kearns and Colonel Anthony Perry. In 1798, these two men were executed in Edenderry. According to local tradition, Colonel Perry, who was an English officer, gave his horse to the Catholic priest, who was being pursued by priest hunters. Both men were captured in the village of Clonbullogue, brought to trial, and sentenced to death. The cross's inscription says that the men died 'for their love of country.'

Rathlihen — *Ráth Lithean* — Fort of Lithean

This monastery was founded in the sixth century by Bishop Illand (also known as Ilathan and Iolladhan), in the territory of the Fir Chell in the province of Meath.

St Illand's Feastday is 10 June.[34] According to the *Monasticon Hibernicum,* in the eighteenth century the church on this site contained a statue of St Illand with his episcopal mitre and a crosier in his hand. However, the statue's head was broken off. This damage may date from the latter half of the seventeenth century when the established church destroyed many such religious statues because it considered them to be 'idols of the popish faith.'

Today one can see the remains of a medieval church, with a priest's residence at the west end of the building. To the east of the church there is a large earthen mound, or *motte,* which served as the foundation for an Anglo-Norman timber castle. This castle was constructed sometime between 1180-1220 and it is likely that during this same time period the monastery at Rathlihen evolved into a chapel of the parish of Fir Chell. During the fifteenth century the barrel-vaulted residence for a parish priest was built onto the church. Around this time Rathlithen became the chief residence of the O'Molloys.

Centuries later, in the 1860s, local people pulled down the walls of the church and used its stone to build a graveyard wall.[35]

Nearby on the Mountbolus to Ballyboy Road, a holy well, known as Lady Well, has long been a place of popular devotion. According to tradition, many requests have been granted there through the intercession of Mary, the Mother of God. In 1962, local people erected a stile and stations. They also built new walls, in which they inserted a plaque of the Madonna and stones from Bethlehem, Nazareth, Gethsemane, Croagh Patrick and Lough Derg. The traditional prayers offered at the well are the nine Hail Marys and the Hail Holy Queen. In the past, the Pattern Day at Lady Well was observed on the first Sunday in September.

TIHILLY — *Teach Theille* — House of Tellius

It is unclear when a religious community was first established on this site. What is known is that in the seventh century Cera, the daughter of Dubhe from Muskerry, in present-day County Cork, established a nunnery here. Soon afterwards, however, the nuns moved to Kilkeary near Nenagh, in what is now County Tipperary.

Around 636, a monastery at Tihilly was led by an abbot named Tellius (also known as Telle or St Telli). In the *Martyrology of Donegal,* he is described as son of Seigin, of Tigh-Telle, in Westmeath, who was of the race of the Colla-Da. According to O'Clery's *Irish Calendar,* the Feastday of St Tellius is 25 June.

The monastery lies within the parish of Durrow, in the Diocese of Meath. According to the *Book of Lismore,* St Tellius's monastery was situated on lands belonging to the monastery of Durrow, of which it was a daughter house.[36]

The monastery was marked Templekieran Abbey on the first edition of the Ordnance Survey map in 1838. Today its remains include a ruined medieval parish church with a ninth-century high cross, an early Christian cross-inscribed grave slab and a filled-in holy well. A partial inscription on the grave slab reads 'OR DO OGAIN' ('Pray for Ogain'), which may refer to a monk or abbot of Tihilly. A second early Christian grave slab described in 1896 has since been lost.

Two biblical scenes decorate the high cross at Tihilly: Adam and Eve in the Garden of Eden and the Crucifixion of Christ with the Two Roman Soldiers. Panels on the shaft of the cross contain geometrical and animal motifs.[37]

Close to the old monastery are the remains of Coleraine Flour Mill. According to local tradition, when this mill was built, old tombstones from the church were laid as the floor of the kiln that was used to dry the grain. However, when the miller went to fire this kiln, the fire would not light. The local people persuaded the miller to take up the floor and return the grave slabs to the monastery. Once the tombstones had been returned to their rightful place, the kiln began to work.[38]

By the nineteenth century, the holy well had been filled in and the high cross was being used as a scratching post for cattle.

WHEERY — *Foíre* — Woods/Woodland

Wheery is situated in the parish of Killagally. The place-name of this parish comes from the Irish Cill a Ghallaigh, meaning 'the Church of the Stranger, or Gaul.'[39] Interestingly enough, the monastery at Wheery was founded in the late fifth or early sixth century by such a 'stranger': St Rioc, the son of Conan Meriadog, King of Brittany.

Today, visitors to the site can see the ditch of an early Christian enclosure, along with the low grass-covered walls of a medieval church.

This church is listed in the ecclesiastical taxation of 1306. In 1398, a vicar was appointed to the parochial church of Wheery in the Diocese of Clonmacnoise.

The *Ordnance Survey Field Name Books* record that in 1837 a ruin called the 'Old Church of Wheery' seems to have been the original parish church. In 1849, during the drainage of the River Brosna near the monastery, an old hand bell was discovered.[40] It is known locally as St Rioc's bell. According to local tradition, during times of religious persecution in the seventeenth century, the local people hid the bell in the bed of the river at a spot called Poll a Chloig. This location was forgotten until the bell was re-discovered in 1849.

When it was unearthed, the bell was contained within a shrine, which was sold to an iron and rag store in Athlone, County Westmeath. The shrine was described by the finder as consisting of 'white metal, enriched by ornament, and set with amber coloured beads.'[41]

By the time the local parish priest arrived at the store to retrieve it, the shrine had been sold. He was unable to trace its whereabouts. However, to this day the bell is kept in the parochial house in the town of Ferbane. Once a year, it is brought back to the church for the celebration of an annual mass.

NOTES

INTRODUCTION : OFFALY

A FLOWERING GARDEN OF MONASTERIES

1 Simington, R.C. (1961) *The Civil Survey 1654-56*, Vol. X, Miscellanea, p. 27.

2 Ibid.

3 Byrne, F. J. (1973) *Irish Kings and High-Kings*, p. 170.

4 Richardson, H. (1987) 'Observations on Christian Art in Early Ireland, Georgia and Armenia,' in M. Ryan (ed.), *Ireland and Insular Art AD 500-1200*, p. 129.

5 Simms, K. (1978) 'Guesting and Feasting in Gaelic Ireland,' *Journal of the Royal Society of Antiquaries of Ireland*, Vol. 108, p. 93.

CHAPTER 1: CROGHAN HILL

THE HOLY MOUNTAIN

1 Comerford, Rev. M. (1883) *Collections Relating to the Diocese of Kildare and Leighlin.*

2 O'Flanagan, Rev. M. (compiler) (1933) 'Letters Containing Information Relative to the Antiquities of the King's County Collected during the Progress of the Ordnance Survey in 1839,' p. 39.

3 Information from Croghan National School website, www.croghannationalschool.com [Accessed 15 April 2005].

4 Coyne, F. & Collins, T. (2005) 'Mount Brandon, Co. Kerry – Dingle's holy mountain,' Heritage Guide No. 29, *Archaeology Ireland*, Spring 2005.

5 O'Flanagan (1933), p 40.

6 Ibid p 41.

7 Ibid p 37.

8 Connolly, S. & Picard, J. M. (1987) 'Cogitosus Life of Saint Brigit,' *Journal of the Royal Society of Antiquaries of Ireland*, Vol. 117, p. 14.

9 Morris, R. (1989) *Churches in the Landscape*, p. 70.

10 Spenser, E. (1596) *A Veue of the present state of Irelande*, Part Two, from Grosart (1894), University of Oregon (Internet)©The University of Oregon, January, 1997, http:darkwing.uoregon.edu/~rbear/veue2.html [Accessed 10 February 2005].

11 Ibid.

12 MacNiocaill, G. (1972) *Ireland before the Vikings*, p. 17.

13 Fitzpatrick, E. (1998) 'The Early Church in Offaly,' in Nolan, W. & O'Neill, T.P., (eds), *Offaly History and Society*, p. 95.

14 Smyth, A. (1982) *Celtic Leinster*, p. 70.

15 Bhreathnach, E. (1995) *Tara: A Select Bibliography*, Discovery Programme Reports 3, p. 69.

16 Connolly, S. & Picard, J. M. (1987) 'Cogitosus Life of Saint Brigit,' p. 11.

17 Anon (1916) 'Croghan (alias Young Colleystown), King's County,' *Journal of the Kildare Archaeological Society*, Vol. 8, pp. 384-5.

18 *Ordnance Survey Field Name Books 1837-38*, Part 1, p. 185.

19 Local folklore, Croghan National School website, www.croghannationalschool.com [Accessed 15 April 2005].

20 Raftery, B. (1994) *Pagan Celtic Britain: the Enigma of the Irish Iron Age*, p. 83.

21 Ibid. p. 64.

CHAPTER 2: SEIRKIERAN

BURYING PLACE OF THE KINGS OF OSSORY

1 Gwynn, A. & Hadcock, G. (1988) *Medieval Religious Houses in Ireland*, p. 194.

2 Archdall, M. (1786) *Monasticon Hibernicum*, p. 404.

3 Plummer, C. (ed.) (1922) *Lives of Irish Saints*, Vol. 2, p. 99.

4 Bitel, L. (1990) *Isle of the Saints: Monastic Settlement and Christian Community in Early Ireland*, p. 55.

5 Sperber, I. (1998) 'The Life of St Ciarán of Saigir,' in Nolan, W. & O'Neill, T.P. (eds.), *Offaly History and Society*, p. 137.

6 Folklore recorded by James Shanahan, Killanure, Clareen National School, from the Schools Manuscript Collection, Department of Irish Folklore, UCD.

7 Plummer (1922), p. 99.

8 O'Sullivan, Dr. M. (1996) *An Illustrated Guide to Seir Kieran County Offaly*, p. 22.

9 Smyth, A. P. (1982) *Celtic Leinster*, p. 97.

10 Bitel (1990), p. 217.

11 Stokes, W. (1905) *Félire Óenguso Céili Dé*, pp. 204-5.

12 Bitel (1990), p. 93.

13 Plummer (1922), p. 107.

14 O'Sullivan, Dr. M. (1996) *An Illustrated Guide to Seir Kieran County Offaly*, p. 6.

15 Smyth (1982), p. 97.

16 Gwynn, A. & Hadcock, G. (1988) *Medieval Religious Houses in Ireland*, p. 194.

17 Ibid. p. 155.

18 Ibid. p. 195.

19 Archdall (1786), p. 406.

20 Ibid.

21 Folklore recorded by James Shanahan, Killanure, Clareen National School, from the Schools Manuscript Collection, Department of Irish Folklore, UCD.

22 Keating, G. (1908) *The History of Ireland Foras Feasa ar Érinn*, Vol. 2, pp. 217-221.

23 Stokes, M. (1878) *Christian Inscriptions in the Irish Language, chiefly collected and drawn by George Petrie*, Vol. 2, p. 49.

24 Byrne, F. J. (2001) *Irish Kings and High Kings*, p. 266.

25 Ibid. p. 162.

26 O'Sullivan (1996), p. 21.

27 Folklore recorded by Margaret O'Neill, Clareen National School, from the Schools Manuscript Collection, Department of Irish Folklore, UCD.

CHAPTER 3: GALLEN

THE CHURCH OF THE WELSHMEN

1 Murphy, D. (ed.) (1993) *Annals of Clonmacnoise*, p. 131.

2 Ibid. pp. 8-9.

3 Macalister, R.A.S. (1908) 'Some Notes on the Sculptured Slabs at Gallen Priory,' *Journal of the Royal Society of Antiquaries of Ireland*, Vol. 18, pp. 323-27.

4 Gwynn, A. & Hadcock, G. (1988) *Medieval Religious Houses in Ireland*, p. 154.

5 Fitzpatrick, E. & O'Brien, C. (1998) *The Medieval Churches of County Offaly*, p. 105.

6 O'Flanagan, Rev. M. (compiler) (1933) 'Letters Containing Information Relative to the Antiquities of the King's County Collected during the Progress of the Ordnance Survey in 1839.'

7 Nicholls, K. (ed.) (1994) *The Fiants of the Tudor Sovereigns*, Vol. 2, No. 1680.

8 Griffith, M. C. (ed.) (1966) *Calendar of Patent Rolls of Ireland*, James I, p. 232.

9 Stokes, M. (ed.) (1878) *Christian Inscriptions in the Irish Language, chiefly collected and drawn by George Petrie* (Two Volumes).

10 Lionard, P. (1961) 'Early Irish Grave-slabs,' *Proceedings of the Royal Irish Academy*, Vol. 61, p. 146.

11 Harbison, P. (1992) *Pilgrimage in Ireland*, p. 202.

12 Pena, I. (1997) *Early Christian Art of Byzantine Syria*, p. 233.

13 Ibid. p. 172.

14 Smyth, A. P. (1982) *Celtic Leinster*, p. 84.

15 Ibid. p.117.

16 Herity, M. (1993) 'The Forms of the Tomb-Shrine of the Founder Saint in Ireland,' in Spearman, R.M. & Higgitt, J. (eds.), *The Age of Migrating Ideas*, p. 191-2.

17 Ibid. p. 191.

18 Ibid. pp. 190-1.

19 Ibid. p. 189.

20 Ibid. p. 194.

21 Edwards, N. (1990) *The Archaeology of Early Medieval Ireland*, p. 164.

22 Pena, I. (1997) *Early Christian Art of Byzantine Syria*, p. 232.

23 Murphy, G. (1956) *Early Irish Lyrics: Eighth to Twelfth Century*, p. 35.

CHAPTER 4: KILLEIGH

THE CHURCH ON THE LONG RIDGE

1 Comerford, Rev. M. (1883) *Collections Relating to the Dioceses of Kildare and Leighlin*, Vol. 2, p. 184.

2 Ibid. p. 186.

3 Ibid. p. 185.

4 Ibid. p. 186.

5 Ibid. p 188.

6 Watt, J. (1972) *The Church in Medieval Ireland*, p. 6-7.

7 Ibid. p. 12-13.

8 Friar, S. (1998) *A Companion to the English Parish Church*, p. 29.

9 Watt (1972), p. 17.

10 Ibid. p. 17

11 Comerford (1883), p. 189.

12 Friar (1998), p. 290.

13 Cotter, F. J. (1994) *The Friars Minor in Ireland from Their Arrival to 1400*, p. 75.

14 Ibid. p. 51.

15 Conlan, P. (1978) *Franciscan Ireland*, p. 19.

16 Fitzpatrick, E. & O'Brien, C. (1998) *The Medieval Churches of County Offaly*, p. 98.

17 Comerford (1883), p. 189.

18 Ibid. p. 190.

19 Ibid.

20 Ibid.

21 Fitzpatrick & O'Brien (1988), p. 86.

22 Comerford (1883), p. 192.

23 Venarde, B. L. (1997) *Women's Monasticism and Medieval Society Nunneries in France and England, 890-1215*, p. 12.

24 Gwynn, A. & Hadcock, G. (1988) *Medieval Religious Houses in Ireland*, p. 321.

25 Curtis, E. (1929) 'The Survey of Offaly in 1550,' *Hermathena*, Vol. 20, p. 346.

26 Green, D. & Kelly, F. (eds.) (2003) *Irish Bardic Poetry: Texts and Translations, Together with an Introductory Lecture by Osborn Bergin*, p. 154.

27 Fitzpatrick, E. (1992-3) 'Mairgreag an-Einigh O Cearbhaill "The Best of the Women of the Gaedhil,"' *Journal of the Co. Kildare Archaeological Society*, Vol. XVIII, p. 28.

28 Comerford (1883), p. 193.

29 Ibid. p. 194.

30 Fitzpatrick (1992-3), 'Mairgreag an-Einigh O Cearbhaill,' p. 32.

31 Comerford (1883), p. 193.

32 Freeman, A. M. (ed.) (1983) *The Annals of Connacht (A.D. 1224-1544)*, p. 493.

33 Green & Kelly (2003), p. 285.

CHAPTER 5: BIRR

THE CHURCH OF THE ILLUMINATOR

1 Ní Dhonnchadha, M. (2001) 'Birr and the Law of Innocents,' in O'Loughlin, T. (ed.) *Adomnán at Birr AD 697: Essays in Commemoration of the Law of the Innocents*, p. 13.

2 Ibid. p. 20.

3 Hemphill, S. (1911) 'The Gospels of Mac Regol of Birr: A Study in Celtic Illumination,' *Proceedings of the Royal Irish Academy*, Vol. 29, p. 3.

4 Ibid. p. 5.

5 Rynne, E. (1969) 'The Art of Early Irish Illumination,' *The Capuchin Annual*, Vol. 36, p. 214.

6 Ibid. p. 215.

7 Henry, F. (1947) *Irish Art in the Early Christian Period*, p. 124.

8 Hemphill (1911), p. 3.

9 Fitzpatrick, E. (1998) 'The Early Church in Offaly,' in Nolan, W. & O'Neill, T.P. (eds.), *Offaly History and Society*, p. 115.

10 *Annals of the Four Masters*, O'Donovan (ed.) (1865), p. 1409.

11 Ní Dhonnchadha (2001), p. 146.

12 Chadwick, N. (1968) *Studies in the Early British Church*, p 146.

13 Ní Dhonnchadha (2001), pp. 61-2.

14 Sharpe, R. (1995) *Adomnán of Iona, Life of St. Columba*, pp. 352-3.

15 Reeves, W. (1874) *Life of Saint Columba, Founder of Hy. Written by Adamnan, Ninth Abbot of that Monastery.*

16 Sharpe (1995), p. 214.

17 Henry (1947), p. 135.

18 Pirotte, E. (2002) 'Ornament and Script in Early Medieval Insular and Continental Manuscripts Reasons, Functions, Efficiency,' in Hourihane, C. (ed.) *From Ireland Coming*, p. 278.

19 Bundy, M. (2001) 'Deciphering the Art of Interlace,' in Hourihane, C. (ed.) *From Ireland Coming*, p. 96.

20 Pirotte (2002), p. 278.

21 Ibid.

22 Ibid.

CHAPTER 6: CLONMACNOISE

CIARÁN'S SHINING CITY

1 Kehnel, A. (1997) *Clonmacnois – the Church and Lands of St Ciarán*, p. 1.

2 Ibid. pp. 246-7.

3 Monahan, Rev. J. D. (1886) *Records Relating to the Dioceses of Ardagh and Clonmacnoise*, p. 43.

4 Murphy, D. (2003) 'Excavation of an Early Monastic Enclosure at Clonmacnoise,' in King, H. A. (ed.) *Clonmacnoise Studies*, Volume 2: Seminar Papers 1998, p. 23.

5 Joyce, P. W. (1869) *Irish Local Names Explained.*

6 Manning, C. (1994) *Clonmacnoise*, p. 9.

7 Reeves, W. (ed.) (1874) *Life of Saint Columba, Founder of Hy. Written by Adamnan, Ninth Abbot of that Monastery.*

8 Murphy (2003), pp. 1-2.

9 Ibid. p. 19.

10 Boland, D. (1996) 'Clonmacnoise Bridge,' in Bennett, I. (ed.) *Excavations 1995: Summary Accounts of Archaeological Excavations in Ireland*, pp. 75-6.

11 O'Sullivan, A. & Boland, D. (1998) 'Clonmacnoise: Early Medieval Bridge,' in Bennett, I. (ed.) *Excavations 1997: Summary Accounts of Archaeological Excavations in Ireland*, pp. 148-9.

12 Murphy (2003), p. 19.

13 Carroll, M. P. (1999) *Irish Pilgrimage, Holy Wells and Popular Catholic Devotion*, p. 111.

14 Henderson, G. (1987) *From Durrow to Kells: the Insular Gospel-books 650-800*, p. 184.

15 Cox, L.F. (1969) 'Iseal Chiarain the low place of St Ciaran, where was it situated?' *Journal of the Old Athlone Society*, Vol. 1, p. 6.

16 Kehnel, A. (1997) *Clonmacnois – the Church and Lands of St. Ciarán*, pp. 264-5.

17 Ibid. p. 189.

18 Fitzpatrick, E. & O'Brien, C. (1998) *The Medieval Churches of County Offaly*, pp. 146-7.

19 Manning, C. (1994) *Clonmacnoise*, p. 16.

20 Carroll (1999), p. 42.

21 Connolly, S. J. (1982) *Priests and People in Pre-Famine Ireland 1780-1845*, p. 111.

22 Ibid. pp. 140-1.

23 Ibid. p. 137.

24 Otway, C. (1839) *A Tour in Connaught*, p. 73.

25 Ibid. pp. 76-7.

26 Monahan, Rev. J. D. (1886) *Records Relating to the Dioceses of Ardagh and Clonmacnoise*, p. 52.

27 Ibid. p. 79.

28 Ellison, C. C. (1975), 'Bishop Dopping's Visitation Book 1682-1685,' *Ríocht na Midhe*, Vol. 6 (1), p. 12.

29 Fitzpatrick, E. & O'Brien, C. (1998) *The Medieval Churches of County Offaly*, pp. 146-7.

30 Kehnel (1997), pp. 31-39.

31 Ibid. p. 242.

32 Otway (1839), p. 72.

33 Rynne, E. (1987) 'A Pagan Celtic background for Sheela-na-Gigs?' in Rynne, E. (ed.) *Figures from the Past: Studies on Figurative Art in Christian Ireland in Honour of Helen M. Roe*, p. 190.

34 Ibid.

35 Kehnel (1997), p. 171.

36 Logan, P. (1980) *The Holy Wells of Ireland*, p. 23.

37 Carroll (1999), p. 74.

38 Logan (1980), pp. 23-24.

39 'The Dead of Clonmacnoise,' attributed to Angus O'Gillan (fourteenth century), T.W. Rolleston (translator) (1857-1920).

CHAPTER 7: BANAGHER
THE CHURCH OF THE ABBESS RYNAGH

1 Story taken from the Banagher parish website at www.strynaghschurch.net/rynagh.html, [Accessed on 3 February 2005].

2 Trodd, V. (1985) *Banagher on the Shannon*, p. 5.

3 From the website of the Ulster Place-Name Society at www.ulsterplacenames.org/early_churches_in_place_names.htm, [Accessed 7 February 2005].

4 *Journal of the Association for the Preservation of the Memorials of the Dead*, Ireland, Vol. 2, No. 1 (1892), pp. 158-9.

5 O'Flanagan, Rev. M. (compiler) (1933) 'Letters Containing Information Relative to the Antiquities of the King's County Collected during the Progress of the Ordnance Survey in 1839,' Vol. 1, p. 85.

6 Hogan, M. (1980) *The Early History of the Town of Birr or Parsonstown by Thomas Lalor Cooke with a new introduction by Margaret Hogan*, p. 328.

7 Ibid. p. 317.

8 For a full description of this cross see Cooke, T.L. (1852-3) 'The Ancient Cross of Banagher, Kings County,' *Journal of the Royal Society of Antiquaries of Ireland*, Vol. 2, pp. 277-80.

9 Ibid. p. 280.

10 Monahan, Rev. J.D.D. (1886) *Records Relating to the Diocese of Ardagh*, p. 369.

11 Henry, F. (1940) *Irish Art in the Early Christian Period*, p. 106.

CHAPTER 8: DURROW
THE CHURCH ON THE PLAIN OF OAKS

1 Lacey, B. (1997) *Colum Cille and the Columban Tradition*, p. 30.

2 Stokes, W. (1877) *Three Middle-Irish Homilies on the Lives of Saints Patrick, Brigit, and Coulmba*, p. 102-3.

3 Ibid. p. 99.

4 Ibid. p.101.

5 Lacey, B. (1998) *The Life of Colum Cille by Manus O'Donnell*, p. 33.

6 Ibid. p. 33.

7 Reeves, W. (1874) *Life of St. Columba, Founder of Hy. Written by Adamnan, Ninth Abbot of that Monastery.*

8 Lacey (1998), p. 98.

9 Stokes (1877), p.113.

10 Murphy, G. (1956) *Early Irish Lyrics: Eighth to Twelfth Century*, p. 69.

11 Lacey (1998), p. 148.

12 Stanley, T. (1870-1) 'Proceedings,' *Journal of the Royal Society of Antiquaries of Ireland*, Vol. 2, p. 28.

13 Stokes (1877), p. 111.

14 Henderson, G. (1987) *From Durrow to Kells: the Insular Gospel-books 650-800*, p. 184.

15 Lionard, P. (1961) 'Early Irish Grave-slabs,' *Proceedings of the Royal Irish Academy*, Vol. 61, No. 5, p. 127.

16 Gwynn, A. & Hadcock, G. (1988) *Medieval Religious Houses in Ireland*, p. 174.

17 Ibid.

18 Murphy, D. (1993) *The Annals of Clonmacnoise*, p. 227.

19 Gwynn & Hadcock (1988), p. 175.

20 Ellison, C.C. (1975) 'Bishop Dopping's Visitation Book 1682-85,' *Ríocht na Mídhe*, Vol. 6 (1), p. 5.

21 Ibid.

22 Murphy, G. (1956) *Early Irish Lyrics: Eighth to Twelfth Century*, p. 71.

23 Ó Murchadha, D. & Ó Murchú, G. (1988) 'Fragmentary inscriptions from the West Cross at Durrow, the South Cross at Clonmacnoise, and the Cross of Kinnitty,' *Journal of the Royal Society of Antiquaries of Ireland*, Vol. 118, pp. 53-66.

24 Lacey (1997), *Colum Cille and the Columban Tradition*, p. 78.

25 Gwynn & Hadcock (1998), p. 174.

26 Roth, U. (1987) 'Early Insular Manuscripts: Ornament and Archaeology, with Special Reference to the Dating of the Book of Durrow' in M. Ryan (ed.) *Ireland and Insular Art AD 500-1200*, p. 28.

27 Henderson, G. (1987) *From Durrow to Kells: The Insular Gospel-Books 650-800*, pp. 54-5.

28 Meehan, B. (1996) *The Book of Durrow*, p. 9.

29 O'Neill, T. (1997) 'Columba the Scribe,' Bourke, C. (ed.) *Studies in the Cult of Saint Columba,* p. 76.

30 Meehan (1996), p. 9.

31 Ibid.

32 Henderson (1987), p. 19.

33 Henry, F. (1947) *Irish Art in the Early Christian Period*, p. 62.

34 Ibid. pp. 65-6.

35 Murphy, D. (1896) *Annals of Clonmacnoise*, p. 96.

36 Herity, M. & Breen, A. (2002) *The Cathach of Colum Cille: An Introduction*, p. 3.

CHAPTER 9: DRUMCULLEN

THE CHURCH ON THE HOLLY RIDGE

1 *Life of St. Mochuda of Lismore* (edited from a manuscript in the Library of Royal Irish Academy), translated from the Irish with introduction by Rev. P. Power, University College, Cork, released 2004-02-01 at www.gutenberg.org/etext/10937 [Accessed 4 December 2004].

2 Hogan, M. (ed.) (1990) *The Early History of the Town of Birr or Parsonstown by Thomas Lalor Cooke*, p. 155.

3 Fitzpatrick, E. (1998) 'The Early Church in Offaly,' in Nolan, W. & O'Neill, T.P. (eds.) *Offaly History and Society*, p. 118.

4 Fitzpatrick, E. & O'Brien, C. (1998) *The Medieval Churches of County Offaly*, pp. 121-2.

5 Nicholls, K. (1994) *The Irish Fiants of the Tudor Sovereigns*, Vol. 1, p. 104.

6 Fitzpatrick & O'Brien (1988), p. 123.

7 Ibid. p. 115.

8 Coote, C. (1801) *Statistical Survey of the King's County*, p. 100.

9 Fitzpatrick & O'Brien (1988), p. 66.

10 Healy, Rev. J (1908) *History of the Diocese of Meath*, (Two Volumes).

11 Purser, O. (1918) 'Fragment of a Celtic Cross Found at Drumcullen, Kings County,' *Journal of the Royal Society of Antiquaries of Ireland*, Vol. 148, p. 77.

12 Morris, R. (1989) *Churches in the Landscape*, p. 70.

13 Heaney, P. (2002) *At the Foot of the Slieve Bloom: History and Folklore of Cadamstown*, p. 204.

14 Purser (1918), pp. 74-77.

15 Lyons, S. (2003) *The Forgotten Navigator – Saint Barron*, p. 125.

16 Healy (1908).

17 Plummer, C. (1922) *Lives of Irish Saints*, Vol. 2, pp. 48-51.

18 De Paor, L. (1929) 'The High Crosses of Tech Theille (Tihilly), Kinnitty and Related Sculpture,' in Rynne, E. (ed.) *Figures from the Past: Studies on Figurative Art in Christian Ireland in Honour of Helen. M. Roe*, p. 140.

CHAPTER 10: LYNALLY

THE CHURCH OF SWANS

1 O'Flanagan, Rev. M. (compiler) (1933) 'Letters Containing Information Relative to the Antiquities of the King's County Collected during the Progress of the Ordnance Survey in 1839,' p. 33.

2 Clancy, T. O. & Markus, G. (1995) *Iona: the Earliest Poetry of a Celtic Monastery*, p. 195.

3 In Scotland, the churches dedicated to St. Colman are at Kilcalmonell in Knapdale, Argyll; Colmanell in Ayrshire, and Buittle, Galloway.

4 Bitel, L. (1990) *Isle of the Saints: Monastic Settlement and Christian Community in Early Ireland*, p. 55.

5 Plummer, C. (ed.) (1922) *Lives of Irish Saints*, Vol. 2, p. 162.

6 Hughes, K. (1966) *The Church in Early Irish Society*, pp. 8-9.

7 Plummer (1922), p. 163.

8 Ibid. p. 173.

9 Ellison, C.C. (1975) 'Bishop Dopping's Visitation Book 1682-85,' *Ríocht na Mídhe,* Vol. 6 (1), p. 7.

10 Ibid.

11 Fitzpatrick, E. & O'Brien, C. (1998) *The Medieval Churches of County Offaly*, pp. 144-5.

12 Ellison (1975), pp. 3-13.

13 Plummer (1922), p. 166.

14 Ellison (1975), p. 7.

15 Plummer (1922), p. 164.

16 Ibid. pp. 170-1.

CHAPTER 11: RAHAN

THE CHURCH ON THE LAND OF FERNS

1 *Life of St. Mochuda of Lismore* (edited from a manuscript in the Library of Royal Irish Academy), translated from the Irish with introduction by Rev. P. Power, University College, Cork, released 2004-02-01 at www.gutenberg.org/etext/10937 [Accessed 4 December 2004].

2 Plummer, C. (ed.) (1922) *Lives of Irish Saints*, Vol. 2, p. 282.

3 *Life of St. Mochuda of Lismore*.

4 Ibid.

5 Stanley, T. (1870-1) 'Proceedings,' *Journal of the Royal Society of Antiquaries of Ireland,* Vol. 2, pp. 27-9.

6 Stout, M. (1998) 'Early Christian Settlement, Society and Economy in Offaly,' in Nolan, W. & O'Neill, T. P. (eds.) *Offaly History and Society*, p. 64.

7 Plummer (1922), p. 297.

8 Ibid. pp. 303-4.

9 *Life of St. Mochuda of Lismore*.

10 Lacey, B. (1997) *Colum Cille and the Columban Tradition*, pp. 42-3.

11 *Life of St. Mochuda of Lismore*.

12 Ibid.

13 Leask, H. (1966) *Irish Churches and Monastic Buildings*, Vol. 1, p. 90.

14 Pena, I. (1997) *Early Christian Art of Byzantine Syria*, p. 236.

15 Shaw, Rev. A. L. (1967) *The History of Ballyboy, Kilcormac and Killoughey*, p. 25.

16 Newman Johnson, D. (1971) 'Sheela-na-gig at Rahan, Co. Offaly,' *Journal of the Royal Society of Antiquaries of Ireland*, Vol. 101, pp 169-70.

17 Carthage, F. (1937) *The Story of Saint Carthage*, pp. 56-7.

18 Garton, T. (2001) 'Masks and Monsters: some recurring themes in Irish Romanesque sculpture,' in Hourihane, C. (ed.) *From Ireland Coming*, p. 127.

19 McNab, S. (2001) 'The Human Figure in Early Irish Art,' in Hourihane, C. (ed.) *From Ireland Coming*, p. 173.

20 Harbison, P. (1970) *Guide to the National Monuments of Ireland*, p. 207.

CHAPTER 12: LEMANAGHAN

MANCHAN'S GREY LANDS

1 Murphy, D. (ed.) (1993) *Annals of Clonmacnoise*, p. 103.

2 Ibid. p. 104.

3 Monahan, Rev. J. D. (1886) *Records Relating to the Dioceses of Ardagh and Clonmacnoise*, p. 351.

4 Graves, Rev. J. (1874-5) 'The Church and Shrine of St, Manchán,' *Journal of the Royal Society of Antiquaries of Ireland,* Vol. 13, pp. 134-50.

5 Moore, M. (2003) *Archaeological Inventory of County Leitrim*, p. 183.

6 O Liathain, S. (1903) 'Gearr-Chuntas ar Mhanachan Naomhtha' ('A Short Account of Saint Manachan'), *Ard na h-Eireann.*

7 Murphy, G. (1956) *Early Irish Lyrics: Eighth to Twelfth Century*, pp. 29-31.

8 O Carroll, E. (2001) *The Archaeology of Leamonaghan–the Story of an Irish Bog.*

9 Murray, Griffin, *Archaeology Ireland*, Spring 2004.

10 When Petrie visited Lemanaghan in 1838 he described three holy wells that offered cures for the blind, the lame and other chronic diseases.

11 In 851 the *Annals of the Four Masters* record the death of 'Flann, son of Reachtabhra, Abbot of Liath Manchain.'

12 Graves, Rev. J. (1874-5) 'The Church and Shrine of St. Manchán,' *Journal of the Royal Society of Antiquaries of Ireland,* Vol. 13, p. 142.

13 Ibid. p. 137.

14 Kendrick, T. D. & Senior, E. (1936) 'St Manchan's Shrine,' *Archaeologia,* Vol. 86, p. 110.

15 Ibid. p. 112.

16 Graves (1874-5), p. 135.

17 Kendrick & Senior (1936), pp. 113-14.

18 Ibid.

19 Irish Schools Manuscript Collection, Boher N. S., Department of Irish Folklore, UCD.

20 Murphy, G. (1956), *Early Irish Lyrics: Eighth to Twelfth Century*, pp. 29-31.

21 'The Doon' is the local name for Doon House, residence of the Mooney family on the Boher-Clonmacnoise Road.

22 Kendrick & Senior (1936), p. 105.

23 Ibid. p. 106

24 Story recorded by Kevin Buckley using information received from his father Michael Buckley of Cooldorough (Cooldorragh), Ballinahown, Co. Offaly, Irish Schools Manuscript Collection, Boher N.S., Department of Irish Folklore, UCD.

CHAPTER 13: ISLANDS OF TRANQUILLITY

1 O'Flanagan, Rev. M. (compiler) (1933) 'Letters Containing Information Relative to the Antiquities of the King's County Collected during the Progress of the Ordnance Survey in 1839,' Vol. 2, p. 40.

2 Ellison, C.C. (1975) 'Bishop Dopping's Visitation Book 1682-85,' *Ríocht na Mídhe,* Vol. 6 (1), pp. 5-6.

3 Fitzpatrick, E. & O'Brien, C. (1998) *The Medieval Churches of County Offaly*, p. 115.

4 Gwynn, A. & Hadcock, G. (1988) *Medieval Religious Houses in Ireland*, p. 377.

5 Comerford, Rev. M. (1883) *Collections Relating to the Diocese of Kildare and Leighlin*, p. 125.

6 Fitzpatrick, E. & O'Brien, C. (1998) *The Medieval Churches of County Offaly*, p. 18.

7 Ibid. p. 18.

8 O' Donovan, J. et. al (1837) *Ordnance Survey Field Name Books*, Pt. 1, p. 155

9 Comerford (1883), p. 124.

10 Ibid. p. 125.

11 O'Flanagan (1933), Vol. 1, p. 20.

12 Ibid. p. 468.

13 Comerford (1883), p. 300.

14 Smyth, A. P. (1982) *Celtic Leinster*, p. 93.

15 O' Donovan, J. et. al (1837) *Ordnance Survey Field Name Books*, Pt. 2, p. 468.

16 Cooke, T. L. (1875) *The Early History of the Town of Birr or Parsonstown*, pp. 211-13.

17 O'Dwyer, Rev. P. (1968) 'The Carmelite Order in Pre-Reformation Ireland,' *Irish Ecclesiastical Record,* Vol. 110, p. 362.

18 Nicholls, K. (ed.) (1994) *The Irish Fiants of the Tudor Sovereigns*, Vol. 2, p. 134.

19 O'Dwyer (1968), p. 362.

20 Shaw, Rev. A. L. (1967) *The History of Ballyboy, Kilcormac and Killoughey*, p. 71.

21 MacLeod, C. (1947) 'Some late medieval wood sculptures in Ireland,' *Journal of the Royal Society of Antiquaries of Ireland*, Vol. 77, p. 62.

22 Folklore recorded at Ballyboy National School in 1939, from the Schools Manuscript Collection, Department of Irish Folklore, UCD.

23 O' Donovan, J. et. al (1837) *Ordnance Survey Field Name Books*, Pt 2, p. 527.

24 Harbison, P. (1970) *Guide to the National Monuments of Ireland*, p. 201.

25 Fitzpatrick & O'Brien (1988), p. 137.

26 Fitzpatrick, E. & Heaney, P. & Rosse, A. (1995) *The Wet Hillside of Saint Lugna*, pp. 12-13.

27 Ibid. p. 17.

28 Ibid. p. 5.

29 An entry in the *Annals of the Four Masters* from the year 1261 describes them as 'Mac Feorais Bermingham.'

30 Gwynn, A. & Hadcock, G. (1988) *Medieval Religious Houses in Ireland*, p. 255.

31 Fitzpatrick & O'Brien (1988), p. 107.

32 Ibid. pp. 108-9.

33 Ibid. p. 109.

34 Shaw (1967), p. 71.

35 Ibid. p. 71

36 Fitzpatrick & O'Brien (1988), p. 18.

37 De Paor, L. (1987) 'The High Cross of Tech Theille (Tihilly), Kinnitty, and related sculpture,' in Rynne, E. (ed.) *Figures from the Past: Studies on Figurative Art in Christian Ireland in Honour of Helen M. Roe*, pp. 131-58.

38 De Courcy Williams, S. (1897) 'The old graveyards in Durrow Parish,' *Journal of the Royal Society of Antiquaries of Ireland*, Vol. 27, pp. 128-49.

39 O' Donovan, J. et. al (1837) *Ordnance Survey Field Name Books*, Pt. 2, 766

40 Anon. (1868-9) 'Proceedings,' *Journal of the Royal Society of Antiquaries of Ireland*, Vol. 10, 1868-9, p. 347.

41 Ibid.

LIST OF IMAGES

Photographs by James Fraher

INTRODUCTION: OFFALY
A FLOWERING GARDEN OF MONASTERIES

CHAPTER 1: CROGHAN HILL
THE HOLY MOUNTAIN

CHAPTER 2: SEIRKIERAN
BURYING PLACE OF THE KINGS OF OSSORY

Chapter 3: Gallen
The Church of the Welshmen

Chapter 4: Killeigh
The Church on the Long Ridge

CHAPTER 5: BIRR
THE CHURCH OF THE ILLUMINATOR

CHAPTER 6: CLONMACNOISE

CIARÁN'S SHINING CITY

Chapter 7: Banagher

The Church of the Abbess Rynagh

Chapter 8: Durrow

The Church on the Plain of Oaks

CHAPTER 9: DRUMCULLEN

THE CHURCH ON THE HOLLY RIDGE

CHAPTER 10: LYNALLY

THE CHURCH OF SWANS

Chapter 11: Rahan

The Church on the Land of Ferns

160
Top left – Face of St Carthage from the stained glass window in the Church of Ireland building.
Bottom centre – The small church at Rahan with its fine Romanesque west doorway.

161
All three of these carved faces are found on the capitals of the pillars that support the twelfth-century chancel arch in the Church of Ireland building at Rahan.
Double page background – The Rahan area in the 1838 edition of the Ordnance Survey map.

162
Top Left – Stained glass window of St Carthage in the Church of Ireland building.
Bottom centre – Archway of Romanesque doorway in west wall of small church.

163
Top right – Profile of carved faces on capital of twelfth-century chancel arch in the Church of Ireland building.
Bottom right – Nineteenth-century antiquarian drawing of a doorway in the west wall of small church at Rahan from Petrie, G., (1845) *The Ecclesiastical Architecture of Ireland*, p. 244.

164
Double page – Carved moustachioed face on capital of twelfth-century chancel arch in the Church of Ireland building.

166
Top left – Aerial photograph of the monastic enclosure defining the precinct of Rahan monastery; church and graveyard in centre of enclosure, copyright reserved Cambridge University Collection of Air Photographs.
Bottom centre – Monastic lands of Rahan, showing small church to left and large Church of Ireland building to right.*

167
Top Centre – Rahan monastery and its large monastic enclosure, as shown in the 1838 edition of the Ordnance Survey map.
Bottom left – Side of twelfth-century circular window in the east gable of the Church of Ireland building.*
Top right – Decorative panel containing a chequerboard pattern, chevron and beading from the twelfth-century circular window.*
Bottom right – Scandinavian style animal interlace on inner face of quatrefoil opening from the twelfth-century circular window.*

168
Top left – A horse-like animal with one bird on its back and another pecking at its hind foot, from spandrel of late medieval ogee-headed window located on the south wall of the small church at Rahan.
Bottom – Scandinavian style animal interlace from inner face of quatrefoil opening of twelfth-century circular window in the east gable of the Church of Ireland building.*

169
Top right – Vine-leaf decorated spandrel of late medieval ogee-headed window from east gable of the small church.*
Bottom centre – Decorated bulbous base of twelfth-century chancel arch in Church of Ireland building.

170
Top centre – Window in east wall of the Church of Ireland building.
Bottom left – Chevrons, beading and small carved faces on stone surround of twelfth-century circular window in the east gable of the Church of Ireland building.*

171
Top right – Nineteenth-century antiquarian drawing of carved faces on chancel arch of Church of Ireland building from Petrie, G., (1845) *The Ecclesiastical Architecture of Ireland*, p. 240.
Bottom right – Late medieval ogee-headed window in east gable of small church; note carved bishop's head to right.*

172
Top Right – Bishop's head located on the arris (edge) of the stone surround of the twelfth-century circular window in the east gable of the Church of Ireland building.*
Centre left – Nineteenth-century antiquarian drawing of twelfth-century circular window in the east gable of the Church of Ireland building from Petrie, G., (1845) *The Ecclesiastical Architecture of Ireland*, p. 241.
Bottom right – Floral motif contained within lozenge space created by opposing chevrons on the arris (edge) of the stone surround of the twelfth-century circular window in the east gable of the Church of Ireland building.*

173
All five of the images on this page were carved in lozenge spaces created by opposing chevrons on the arris (edge) of the stone surround of the twelfth-century circular window in the east gable of the Church of Ireland building.*
Top left – Monk's head.*
Top right – Head of animal from the Otherworld.*
Centre – A pair of monks' heads with triangular-shaped beards.*
Bottom left – Monk's face.*
Bottom right – Head of animal from the Otherworld.*

174
Top left – Late medieval ogee-headed window in east gable of small church.*
Bottom centre – East gable of Church of Ireland building; note Romanesque circular window in apex of gable.*
Graveyard and south wall of Church of Ireland building at Rahan.*

** By permission of Kevin O'Dwyer, © Kevin O'Dwyer 2006*

Chapter 12: Lemanaghan

Manchan's Grey Lands

176
Top left – Early Christian cross-inscribed slab from Lemanaghan.
Bottom centre – Lemanaghan church and graveyard.

177
Top right – Nineteenth-century drawing of ecclesiastical figure that may have come from St Manchan's Shrine (*Dublin Penny Journal*, vol. 1, 1832, p. 97).
Bottom centre – Decorative metalworking detail from St Manchan's Shrine.
Double page background – Seventeenth-century map of Lemanaghan and its environs.

178
Top background – Original handwriting from the Schools Manuscript Collection.
Bottom left – St Manchan, as depicted in a stained glass window by Harry Clarke Studios from Boher Catholic Church, Ballycumber.
Bottom right – St Manchan's Shrine, now housed in Boher Catholic Church, Ballycumber.

179
Background – Clouds over Lemanaghan.

180
Top centre – Togher (flagstone roadway) leading to St Mella's Cell from the church at Lemanaghan.
Bottom left – Line drawing of early Christian cross-inscribed slab decorated with cross-of-arcs.

181
Top centre – Lemanaghan Castle and St Managhan's (St Manchan's) Church and Holy Well, as depicted in the 1838 edition of the Ordnance Survey map.
Middle right – Steps leading down into St Managhan's (St Manchan's) Holy Well.

CHAPTER 13: ISLANDS OF TRANQUILLITY

INDEX OF PERSONS AND PLACES

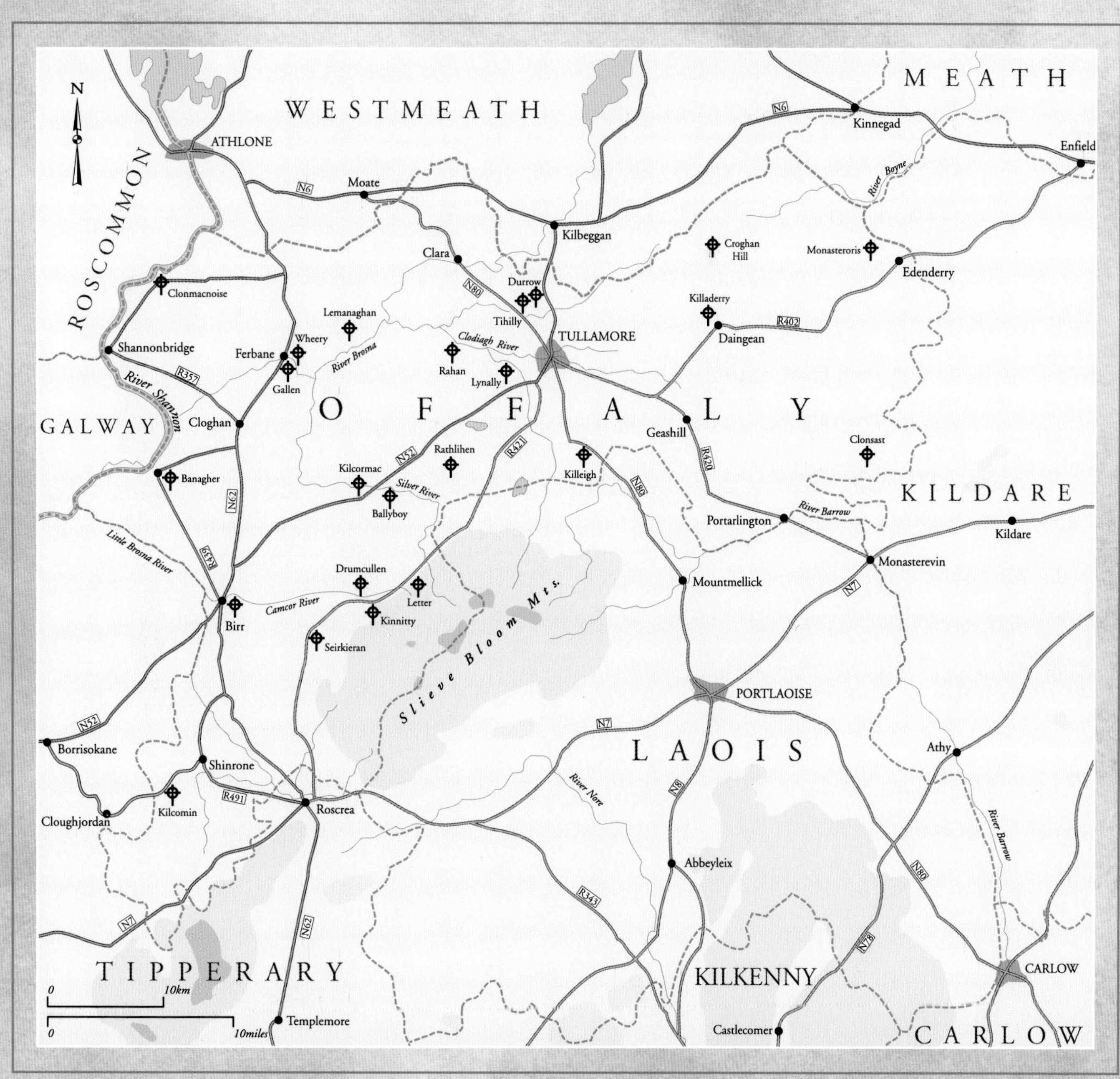

Location map of churches mentioned in text

Pilgrim's Poem

Time for me to prepare to pass from the shelter of a habitation,

To journey as a pilgrim over the surface of the noble, lively sea.

Time to depart from the snares of the flesh, with all its guilt,

Time now to ruminate how I may find the great son of Mary.

Time to seek virtue, to trample upon the will with sorrow,

Time to reject vices, and to renounce the Demon.

Time to reproach the body, for of its crime it is putrid,

Time to rest after we have reached the place wherein we may shed our tears.

Time to talk of the last day, to separate from familiar faces,

Time to dread the terrors of the tumults of the day of judgment.

Time to defy the clayey body, to reduce it to religious rule,

Time to barter the transitory things for the country of the King of heaven.

Time to defy the ease of the little earthly world of a hundred pleasures,

Time to work at prayer, in adoration of the high King of angels.

But only a part of one year is wanting of my three score,

To remain under holy rule in one place it is time.

Those of my own age are not living, who were given to ardent devotion,

To desist from the course of great folly, in one place it is time.

— Celedabhaill, son of Scannal, AD 926
on the occasion of his pilgrimage to Rome